Trial and Triumph

Trial and Triumph

Presidential Power in the Second Term

ALFRED J. ZACHER

PRESIDENTIAL PRESS

FORT WAYNE, INDIANA

353
ZAC

If you have any questions or comments concerning this book, please contact the publisher:
Presidential Press
444 East Main St., Suite 203
Fort Wayne, Indiana 46802-1910

Publisher's Cataloging-in-Publication Data
Zacher, Alfred J.
Trial and triumph: presidential power in the second term/ Alfred J. Zacher. —
Fort Wayne, Ind. : Presidential Press, c1996.
     p.   ill.   cm.
Includes bibliographical references and index.
     ISBN 0-9651087-0-8
1. Presidents—Rating of—United States. 2.Presidents—United States
—Public Opinion. 3.Presidents—United States—History 4. United
States—Politics and government.   I. Title.
JK511.Z3 1996
353.0313—dc20   95-73089

Project Coordination by   JENKINS GROUP INC.

Printed in the United States of America

10 9 8 7 6 5 4 3 2 1

To Hannah:
for her support and patience.

★ CONTENTS ★

★ PREFACE ★

I became interested in the presidential second term when I read Henry Adams' *The History of the United States During the Administrations of Thomas Jefferson*, in which Adams described Jefferson's troubled second term. The plights of both Johnson and Nixon were still vivid memories, and I recalled clearly how his court-packing effort plagued Franklin Roosevelt in his second term. I questioned whether there was something about this time in office which deserved examination, so I began my study.

My approach was to investigate in considerable detail each of seventeen Presidents elected to a second term, regardless of how they acceded to their first term.

My research led to a chapter on each President and a search for a conclusion. The book now contains an introduction that outlines ten measures a President must fulfill for success and a chapter on each of the two term Presidents. A Conclusion attempts to draw all of this together, reviewing how Presidents grasp hold of the office to achieve their objectives, and why some failed. Finally, I have inserted a rating of each of the two term presidents, using the ten measures for success for the reader to rank the Presidents as well.

I owe a special thanks to all of those who have aided and encouraged me in this endeavor. David Allen and Betty Stein gave me insightful suggestions and insisted that I pursue publication when I was most discouraged. Norma Slatin provided remarkably extensive editing that was invaluable. Dr. Elliot Bartky, my tutor, provided essential technical criticism and biographical and creative perspectives into each of the Presidents. Alex Moore gave advice well beyond his job description of Production Editor at Jenkins group. And my appreciation to Mark Dressler for his superior efforts in coordinating the publication of this book. Tom Beadie, Ted Schuchat, Dorothy Gitlin and Sarah Gabard were stalwart readers of each chapter, providing important criticism. Marcia Adams offered meaningful suggestions on publishing in addition to her ever present moral support. Dianne Giannakeff helped in editing and added much needed training in syntax and punctuation. George Mather and Mike Westfall were responsible for the completion of the book, by asking me to present a paper on the second term to the Fort Wayne Historical Society. That assignment led me to formalize the insights I derived from the study of the two term Presidents. And a thank you as well to Ward Crago for his comments and suggestions and to David Morley for his suggestions that assisted the formation of my Conclusion. I, of course, take full responsibility for any errors that may exist in this manuscript.

Introduction
Succeeding in a Second Term

Any list of America's greatest Presidents is dominated by those who have been elected to a second term. As Michael Beschloss stated: "One of the best things a sitting President can do to burnish his reputation among future generations is to get reelected." It is the second term that not only tests the mettle of the President, but also offers a lens that focuses on the enduring essence of the presidency itself.

Paradoxically, the elements essential for successful presidential leadership have not changed over time, despite the growth of government, the fear of an "Imperial Presidency," the break up of party influences and the power of television, allowing a comparative evaluation of Presidents from the days of George Washington to the present. Although the final judgment of a presidency is a melding of his two terms in office, the second term provides the best measure of the Chief Executive, for it is then that a President has experience in office and can most comfortably wear the mantle of authority granted by

the electorate. It is then that the President is under the greatest scrutiny and stress that draw forth his true character and temperament.

Eighteen Presidents have been elected to a second term, a threshold for greatness, yet for many of these, frustration, failure and even
disaster followed their reelection. For others, success meant overcoming seemingly insurmountable obstacles, while for still others apparent success was followed by failure in the judgment of history. The
second term has been a time of great stress or travail for such Presidents as Jefferson, Monroe, Grant, Cleveland, Wilson, Franklin
Roosevelt, Johnson and Nixon. But for others, such as Washington,
Jackson, Theodore Roosevelt and even Reagan, their second terms
were times of success, even triumph. What caused this great variation?
Why have some Presidents succeeded where others faltered?

It is in the second term that the elements of presidential leadership are crystallized, when innovation can be implemented and authority expanded. By the second term, Theodore Roosevelt found
more meaningful ways to communicate with a public now familiar
with his rhetoric. For Monroe and Wilson, Congress found the means
to frustrate the agenda of the Chief Executive. In some respects
Jefferson became a lame duck with diminished political power in his
second term. In several instances, unexpected crises arose, denying
the President the benefit of the authority granted a newly reelected
President, particularly when there was a landslide victory. Both Cleveland and Johnson faced this challenge. Franklin Roosevelt's re-election victory led to a spirit of invincibility, clouding his judgment.
Historically, the second term became a time of trial or triumph.

Vision, leadership, courage in the face of adversity, honesty and
political skill embodied in the character and temperament of a President interplay to affect his leadership through the four long years of a
second term.

The ability of a President to survive and sometimes triumph

through what can be the fire of the second term tells much about the American people and their idea of what a President ought to accomplish. The public will approve and even applaud innovation by a President; but this must conform to the following deep-seated convictions which appear not to have changed significantly from the founding of the nation, namely those implicit in the Declaration of Independence, the Constitution, the Bill of Rights, and the writings of the founders:

First, the American people want to feel secure from attack, external or internal, real or imagined.

Second, Americans strive for economic security and individual freedom. This becomes the first priority for Americans if there is no foreign threat. This, of course, was and is the foundation for freedom and democracy.

Third, America is historically conservative. Only economic upheaval, foreign threat and social stress will cause the nation to veer from that path. Although the body politic holds primarily conservative, isolationist views, this is weighed against an internationalist and liberal perspective. Franklin Roosevelt modified the path of domestic policy sustained by crisis. He could not, however, alter the nation's isolationist stance until events strengthened his hand. Further, change, once implemented, frequently becomes the norm.

Fourth, the nation believes, *conditionally,* in fair play. The treatment of Native Americans and African Americans provides evidence that civil rights, civil liberties, or economic innovation becomes a cause for this nation only when strong leadership is joined with a sizable discontented minority demanding change.

Fifth, law and order, with moralistic and religious overtones to preserve freedom and democracy, are part of the American psyche. The President has traditionally been considered the high priest of morality and justice. This is one reason that Nixon was deposed so quickly after Watergate. It is why Grant lost favor with his party as evidence of graft in his administration was revealed. Conversely, it is one reason Jefferson was loved, despite his failings.

These five characteristics of Americans are particularly relevant to the second term, because a President must tend to achieve or take into account fulfillment of many of these goals to be reelected and then to achieve success in a more challenging second term. The leadership role of a President must relate to these consistently held values of the American people.

The lessons of history may not induce the nation to select the best candidate for the presidency, but the public may better judge the candidate's potential in office from the message given by history. To succeed, Presidents must fulfill the challenge of a significant number of the following ten measures which express the goals of Americans:

1. The President must provide defense against foreign or domestic threat.

2. The President must retain or expand economic, political and/ or social opportunity.

3. The President must display innovative, visionary leadership that incorporates the basic political character of Americans.

4. The President must exercise influence over and effectively communicate with the nation. He must be able to communicate persuasively. Such "communication" is almost beyond definition. Popular adulation for Jackson rivaled that enjoyed by Franklin Roosevelt or Ronald Reagan. Television mastery is now required, as was influence with the press in bygone eras, but the results remain the same. Jefferson encouraged his friends to communicate his messages for him; Lincoln used speeches, de-

bates and letters to convey his message. The President must communicate; and, whatever the means, he must do so persuasively.

5. The President must effectively lead Congress. Since the nation began, there has been a perennial conflict between the executive and legislative branches of government. Most Presidents will extend their exclusive bands of authority to the utmost. Jackson was the first President to clearly establish the executive branch as being "first among equals." Congress, on the other hand, generally seeks to limit the President's freedom of action. It maintained a dominant role for over twenty years, beginning with the latter days of Jefferson's administration. Congress does not readily give up its effort to be the dominant branch; and, if it succeeds in a first term, this is one basis for a President's failure to win reelection. By the second term, Congress has made its judgment of the President, often irrespective of party affiliation or party control. It then makes the most of its insights to hamper the President in his intuitive, sometimes extra legal, use of his power and authority potentially turning him into a lame duck. By the second term, Congress will have established the ground rules for its match with the President. The outcome is a measure of the effectiveness of the Chief Executive.

6. The President must have the courage to lead in the face of adversity and diminished popularity. He must establish priorities. This, of course, assumes that the goals and priorities of such leadership are in the best long-term interest of the nation, a criterion that may be lacking when such courage is manifested.

Throughout history, Presidents have faced the challenging task of leading the nation into unpopular directions. Truman presented the Marshall Plan to a Congress that wished to turn only to domestic concerns after the war. Lincoln faced riots and general unrest in response to the draft and a war that seemed to drag on endlessly, as battle after battle was lost and the number of dead and wounded mounted.

7. The President must avoid a spirit of invincibility, of hubris, which might cause a President to lose touch with political reality. The President elected to a second term, particularly if by a landslide, will be tempted by the exhilaration of victory to feel an inordinate sense of power, of excessive self-confidence. The temptation is then to maneuver Congress and the nation to implement plans and programs which the nation or Congress is not ready to adopt or which are ill-advised and inappropriate.

8. The President must provide effective and consistent leadership throughout his eight years. He must show ability to govern. He must sustain his leadership despite all the stresses of office and changing events, no matter how catastrophic. The character and temperament of a President may function effectively only within a limited set of circumstances, and a tenure of eight years expands the possibility that events may arise to bring out the worst of these qualities. In eight years, the diversity of events and crises takes the full measure of the man.

9. The President must have self-confidence. No quality in a President exceeds that of self-confidence and of knowing himself. Some degree of realistic self-preservation is needed; for if the President does not survive, the nation is diminished. The President must be comfortable enough with himself to select capable advisors and to listen to their advice. He must pay attention to the world outside a cloistered White House. The President must be flexible; he must learn to change with times and events and

to comprehend the nature of the obstacle at hand. He must inspire confidence.

10. The President should leave a legacy for the nation. The majority of the American people must have believed in his integrity and have sustained a substantial level of pride in the President throughout his eight years in office, despite specific shortcomings. He must have strengthened the nation, on balance, by his actions.

The measures for a successful President listed in this introduction may be utilized to allow a voter to compare candidates and to evaluate how their character and temperament will function in the office of the Presidency. Further, these measures may give some clue about how Clinton might fare in a second term were he reelected.

In many respects Bill Clinton's performance as President is baffling. He is intelligent, educated, can be a capable communicator and is an experienced public administrator. Clinton has failed in the tests of a President on several very essential measures. First and foremost, he failed to understand the conservative tendency in America. This failure of insight was implicit, early on, in his championship of gay rights in the military. Far more indicative, however, was the particular form of health care proposals advanced by the administration. These were perceived as too complex and frightening, involving extensive incursion by the federal government, and possibly greater change than was required. This endeavor, that so consumed the nation prior to the 1994 election, became the focal point of voter decision.

Clinton blamed the defeat of the Democrats in the 1994 midterm election on his tax increase and his failure to sell America the program he proposed. In the first two years of his administration Clinton actually was quite successful in communicating with and influencing Congress and the nation. Appropriately or not, the administration sold their deficit reduction plan eloquently, and its passsage was followed by lower interest rates and a rapid expansion of the economy which included millions of new jobs. A sense of insecurity with the employment picture all but evaporated. He won approval for the North American Free Trade Agreement and the G.A.T.T. trade treaties.

The failure of Clinton to grasp the animus of America was a primary progenitor of political defeat in the mid-1994 election, but there was another test he failed to meet, namely the confidence in the President as a moral leader of the nation. The accusation of his extramarital escapades, the Whitewater scandal, and the plight of so many of his appointees, cabinet or otherwise, cast a pall over the character of the President.

Clinton is questioned for his compromises and his political pragmatism, but these might be readily accepted in a President whose vision had been communicated to the people, whose proposals appeared to match the apparent needs of the electorate, and who conveyed moral suasion.

Bill Clinton has moved toward the center, politically. But for him to be reelected there must be no new revelations on Whitewater, and the economy cannot falter. He must communicate a vision with programs that reflect the mood of a majority of Americans. Most importantly, however, to succeed in a second term he must effectively lead Congress to implement his agenda. To do so, he must not only have the cooperation of the Republican members of Congress, whether or not they be in the majority, but also he will need the full support from his own party. Unfortunately, history does not bode well for Clinton in this regard. Congress has not been a compliant body for Presidents in their second term. Eisenhower and both Theodore and Franklin Roosevelt found their own parties most uncooperative at times. Wilson and Reagan were thwarted by Congress. And Lincoln found his own party hostile to both his reelection and his Reconstruction plans.

Congress, with those rare exceptions during times of foreign threat and economic crisis, have been spoilers for Presidents during their second term. Clinton can be expected to fare no better, with Congress making every effort to turn him into a lame duck.

First, of course he must be reelected. Clinton's first term will be taken into account, but so will the opponent he faces. The voters will judge between the candidates as best they can. Contemplating the lessons in history may help.

The following are chapters on seventeen Presidents elected to second terms. Lincoln is included because he fulfilled his vision for the nation and for himself as President in his brief second term. McKinley is excluded, as his second term was cut short before any achievement was possible. A President elected to a second term is included, whether his first term was by election or succession. Readers may judge for themselves how effectively each President used the mantle of authority given him by his reelection and the impact of character and temperament on his success, utilizing these ten elements of leadership. Further, the reader is encouraged to observe the ebb and flow of Congressional power and the level of responsibility given the federal government over time.

A chart is placed at the end of each chapter so that the reader may grade the Presidents on a scale of one to ten for each category of achievement, with ten being the highest rating. At the end of the book the reader is encouraged to summarize these conclusions.

George Washington

$$\underline{2}$$

George Washington

Character, temperament, political acumen and great insight into the meaning of democracy and freedom and of liberty were somehow distilled in George Washington. They came together in such unique proportion that the United States would be assured of its ascendency among nations and of the elevation of its creative form of government to become the standard for others to follow. The fulfillment of the office of the presidency cannot be other than a reflection of the character of the man holding the office and of the times in which he serves. In no instance is this more clearly revealed than it is with George Washington in his second term.

The British, the French and their emissaries bore down on George Washington during his second administration. During the Revolution the British had been his enemy and had considered him a traitor, whereas the French had rescued the rebel who was the Commander-in-Chief of the Revolutionary forces. They sent funds and men to assist the American Revolution, sufficient in the minds of some to have brought down the French Empire. The French General Rochambeau planned the Battle of York and he, in fact, was probably the strategist of that great success. The French fought side by side

11

with the American forces, and Lafayette was like a son to Washington. But all of this faded into memory as Washington's second term began. The adversity encountered by Washington after his second inaugural came no less from the British, from the French, from the rapidly developing Democrat-Republican party, from a revolt of distillers in Western Pennsylvania and from those who opposed his Jay Treaty with England.

Washington, that imposing patrician of six feet three inches, had hands which Lafayette said were the largest he had seen. His complexion was fair, but florid; his weight was above 220 pounds. Washington was a man who endeavored to conceal his sensitivity to public criticism and to control his tendency to be enraged by attacks against him. He projected dignity and self-confidence, but he held himself aloof in a way which impressed all who came into his presence.

His self-confidence, his dignity, his love of country, his great honesty, his pride, his aloof bearing characterized Washington. He perceived that the county would grow and flourish if protected from all but commercial foreign involvement, and this determined the spirit of his terms in office, particularly his second. He had visited New England and knew the British and the French. He had exulted in the farming of his estate, but he had observed New England manufacturing and trading as well. He had witnessed the financial sagacity exhibited in Philadelphia. And it was this perspective and these experiences which came to bear on his second term.

Washington understood both the nation's potential and its weaknesses in relation to the major powers. He understood his own nature and understood that he would be called upon to carry the nation through its incubation. His very bearing, his determination, his mediation, his guidance, the allegiance he could elicit from all competing forces would be the threads he would use to weave a fabric binding the people together. He and the nation must rise above the fray. It must be a great nation, and he must be a great leader for that to occur.

* * * * *

I.

George and Martha Washington thrived at Mount Vernon, absorbing the pleasures of plantation life to which Washington returned after retiring as Commander-in-Chief of the Revolutionary forces in 1783. He reluctantly left Mount Vernon to act as presiding officer of the Constitutional Convention which convened in Philadelphia in 1787, bringing much needed prestige to that gathering.

When the first electoral college met in the nation's capital, New York City, in 1789, it unanimously elected George Washington as President. Washington was loath to accept the Presidency, but the country thought only of him for the highest office in the land.

The Washington presidency in its initial term was a time for formalization and implementation of the institutions created by the Constitutional Convention and the Constitution. Governing over a nation of four million people in thirteen states, George Washington perceived clearly that each step he took represented the establishment of a precedent with an awesome influence upon the future of the nation. He perceived the importance of the separation of authority of the legislative, judicial and executive branches of the government, and he believed it to be his duty to help establish that independence within reasonable bounds.

Washington steered his administration through several initiatives during his first term. These included Alexander Hamilton's plan to pay the war-time debts of all of the states and of the Congress under the Articles of Confederation.

Congress moved the Federal capital to Philadelphia during this time and later passed a bill establishing a new national capital to be located in a federal district on the Potomac. Washington tolerated the feud between Alexander Hamilton, his Secretary of Treasury, and Thomas Jefferson, his Secretary of State, over the constitutionality of a national bank. After much dispute, Congress approved the bank, and Washington willingly signed the law. This was the first battle of what was to become a developing conflict between Hamilton's Federalist party and Jefferson's Democrat-Republican party.

The feud between the two men was steeped in philosophical, political, economic, and personal differences that ran deep. Hamilton saw the future of the country in a very different light than did Jefferson. Hamilton promoted the strong cultivation of manufacturing through government action. The plan set forth in his "Report on Manufacturing" would have promoted the manufacture of products in the North utilizing Southern crops to unify and strengthen the nation. He saw an ever stronger and expanding government involving itself in finance, through the bank and in support of manufacturing. Jefferson feared this larger government would lead to a form of monarchy. He and James Madison believed that democracy could only survive and thrive if government was in the hands of the producers of goods, the farmer who tilled his field, the craftsman who worked with his hands. They feared that the manufacturing employee evolving under Hamilton's plan would not be part of the democratic process but would be subjugated by his employer; and that the nation would, in fact, head toward power in the hands of wealthy manufacturers, becoming a kind of monarchy. Jefferson would fight to preserve democracy for the unfettered, freedom-thinking individual—in fact, the farmer of his day. Hamilton would build a financially and industrially strong economic base for the nation run by an intellectual and business elite.

Although Washington had decided to retire after his first term, he was persuaded by the arguments of Madison, Hamilton, and most particularly by Jefferson, to accept a second term. Washington came to understand that the nation might split asunder were he to leave office. The conflict between the Hamiltonians and Jeffersonians, coupled with a growing regionalism, required the steady hand that only Washington could provide. He was a man willing to risk his popularity—and that he surely had—to hold the nation together while it gathered its governmental strength. As with his first nomination, he was unopposed and was elected unanimously by the electors to a second term. John Adams was again elected to be his Vice President. The first term had been a time for organization and implementation for the Chief Executive and the new nation, a time to find its way and test its institutions. The second term would be filled with greater controversy.

* * * * *

II.

The second term began in 1793 with hostility toward Washington's administration from throngs of pro-French citizens who felt a kinship to their now full-blown revolution and saw Washington as a man drawn toward monarchy. It was glib to point to his aloofness, to his elegant dinner parties and to his solitary rides in a carriage as a basis for the charges. But more was at stake in the pro-French criticism. In the minds of many Americans, the French Revolution fulfilled Jefferson's definition of democracy as a direct government of all of the people. Consequently, the pro-French in America typically favored Jeffersonian policies and opposed Hamilton's Federalist views which were perceived as aiding the rich and as being synonymous with British rule and the power of a monarchy. Unfortunately, Washington was tarred with the brush of Hamiltonian "monarchy," and the personal attacks deeply affected the sensitive President.

In his second Inaugural Address, Washington confronted the task of fulfilling his duty in office in the face of such criticism. He spoke of the right and obligation of citizens to upbraid him and if necessary to meet upon him constitutional punishment if he did not fulfill his administrative duties satisfactorily. In a rather perfunctory statement, he reiterated that he would attempt to fulfill the high honor and confidence bestowed upon him by the country. Washington stated firmly and succinctly that he and the nation would adhere to the highest and most rigid standards of constitutional and democratic governance. It was an uninspiring address, one that could hardly fill the listener to action in support of the newly reelected President. That was not its purpose. Washington, stalwart and self-confident, was simply addressing squarely and quietly the task he set for himself and the nation—to get on with the implementation of government that had so recently begun.

* * * * *

III.

1793 witnessed the intensification of European conflicts. The revolutionary upheaval in France erupted in a war between France and Austria, Prussia and Great Britain. Although other European nations joined the hostilities, Great Britain and France became the primary combatants. The war between France and Britain consumed those two European powers and much of the continent. Washington was determined to remain apart from the belligerents, hoping that the infant country would grow, mature and flourish in a protected and unmolested environment. He, as well as Jefferson, believed that trade with foreign nations was possible without political or military consequences. Much as a parent prefers a somewhat controlled and sequestered environment for the development of a child, Washington felt that excessive military and political contact with other nations would harm the young American state.

The European wars would not stay their place, however. America's growing merchant fleet traded prolifically with Britain. The British, who ruled the seas, followed policies which would eventually bring the infant republic squarely into the fray between the Continental powers. The British Navy lacked seamen. Their rough treatment of naval crews caused widespread desertions to American ships, prompting the British to stop many American vessels to recoup or indenture any sailors who had jumped ship to the more appealing U.S. vessel.

But who was to distinguish the British sailor from the American? The resulting indenture of American merchant men resulted in a fire storm of protests. To further complicate matters, both the British and the French confiscated any property on an American vessel which they determined to be the property of their enemy. Early in the conflict, this was a frequent British practice and the sizeable American merchant marine, without naval protection, was swamped by seamen boarding from British warships who promptly relieved the American ships of their valued cargos as well as their seamen.

The French had their own scenario to play out for the American merchant marine. Foreign countries asserted the right to lease the merchant ships of the United States, outfitting them with military capability for their own purposes. The plunder taken from the ships of an opposing country could then be sold in the outfitting country for a handsome profit. The French, having a small navy, depended on this privateering of U.S. vessels to plunder British merchant ships sailing the Atlantic, confiscating and profiting in the process, intensifying the British-French conflict and America's involvement in that feud.

The public was overwhelmingly pro-French. No matter how much bloodshed the guillotines brought, American citizens felt a kinship with the revolutionary French whose nation had once assisted their own revolution. No matter that it was the French king who aided the American Revolution. No matter the violent and restrictive leadership at the French helm; in American eyes, a monarchy had been deposed, intensifying American support for the rule of government by the people.

The potential for a war with Britain heightened daily as the French expanded their surrogate navy provided by U.S. merchant ships. Washington and his cabinet feared that the British would not distinguish between an American vessel "privateered" by the French and one which was an American ship.

As tension increased, the vast popular support for the French cause weighed in the balance. Against this was the potential for war with Great Britain over attacks on British ships by American privateers and the indenturing of American seamen and plundering of American vessels by the British. Washington finally moved to action, declaring a policy of inaction known as the Neutrality Proclamation, which affirmed that no measures would be taken which would give assistance to either warring party. Washington was entering upon unchartered waters for the office he held, proceeding judiciously yet with deliberation.

Washington would have preferred that his Proclamation be approved by the Senate prior to its being issued. It was the first such proposal contemplated by the new nation. Further, Washington saw some personal political benefits from having a friendly Senate approve a plan that the pro-French might not like. The Constitution did not specifically grant the President the right to enforce neutrality except under his authority to conduct foreign policy. Only Congress could declare war. But could the President declare peace, which the Proclamation was designed to accomplish? Further, the Proclamation might be interpreted as aiding the British more than the French, for the nation would no longer provide the much needed privateers for the French to ward off attacks from the well outfitted British Navy. There was ample room for Constitutional as well as political controversy. But the Senate was not in session. Washington had no choice. Abandoning his strict constitutional interpretation concerning the separation of powers, he issued a proclamation asserting that all Americans were to "pursue a conduct friendly and impartial toward the belligerent powers." Citizens were cautioned that they would be prosecuted if their acts contributed to hostilities on the high seas.

On the surface, the Neutrality Proclamation would most immediately affect the privateering which served the French. The Republicans, led by Jefferson, Madison and James Monroe, were outraged. They saw the proclamation as a pro-British plot perpetrated by an administration favoring monarchy and influenced most clearly by Hamilton. His Secretary of State, Thomas Jefferson, who had voted for the neutrality position, attacked Washington and the policy openly and through his correspondence with Madison and Monroe. He encouraged these allies to oppose the Neutrality Proclamation, which he had supported out of an underlying belief in neutrality and his feeling of loyalty to Washington. Jefferson opposed the Proclamation, however, as a Hamiltonian move which enhanced the power of the executive and denied Congress its authority, while it abrogated a treaty of friendship with France.

The Democrat-Republican press delivered scurrilous attacks on Washington, asserting that the Administration had been forced by the pro-British segment of the populace to propose the Neutrality Proclamation. Washington felt besieged and was angered by these attacks on him from this group which had previously shown such affection for him. (There had been a brief episode during the Revolution when an effort was made to replace him as Commander-in-Chief, but the public overwhelmingly came to his defense.) Now, his popular support appeared to be overshadowed by his vocal and hostile opponents.

The issuance of the Proclamation effected a great schism within his cabinet and within the nation, which Washington had desperately sought to avoid. Just as Washington wished to steer a neutral path between the two warring nations in Europe, so did he wish to avoid factionalism at home. The Democrat-Republicans saw Washington and his Administration as anti-French, pro-British and, therefore, pro-monarch. "Pro-monarch" in the minds of the Democrat-Republicans signified that the United States was destined to move toward Hamilton's elitist society and his program for the country.

It is reasonable to state that a paranoia blanketed the Democrat-Republicans' thinking and their insight into the nature and character of Washington. While it was true that Hamilton and most Federalists admired and wished to emulate England and its form of government, including its financial institutions, this was hardly synonymous with wishing to crown George Washington king. Although the Jeffersonians were alarmed by what they believed to be the Hamiltonian threat of an elitist central government, there was little to support the view that Washington had been persuaded by Federalists as much as the Federalists would have liked or to the degree that the Democrat-Republicans believed. Washington was of one view: the young republic must mature without undue influence from demagogues of any persuasion. Citizens must be permitted to make up their minds without undue influence from any minority strongly holding a particular view. In Washington's mind, to flourish, the young nation needed to be free from major commitments to parties, causes or foreign pressures, all of which he believed to be equally dangerous.

One of the more notorious events which took place during the controversy over the Neutrality Proclamation was the arrival of Genet. The recently appointed Ambassador from the newly formed Republic of France was the very symbol of the French Revolution. The American public voiced uncritical support for France and its envoy. Genet took the utmost advantage of his country's popularity to promote privateering of U.S. merchant ships in behalf of France. Even Jefferson admitted that this flew in the face of the Neutrality Proclamation. Genet asserted he would go over the head of the President and appeal directly to the people. Not satisfied with promoting privateering, he also developed a plan to raise an army of American citizens to seize Louisiana from Spain, thereby creating an independent nation and French Protectorate on the North American continent.

Washington unalterably opposed Genet's intrigues and ordered them squelched, not only because they violated his presidential authority but also because they were totally inconsistent with his views on neutrality. In addition, Genet's plans were altogether counter to Washington's considered views on the West and the frontier. He saw the undeveloped wilderness as a source of future growth which would enable consolidation of the Union. Any further entrenchment of a European power on the continent was anathema to Washington's vision for the future of the country.

Ultimately Genet carried his audacity too far. When the public was fully informed of Genet's belief that he could overrule the President on matters of privateering and arming Americans, the public reversed itself and supported Washington, despite its strongly pro-French bias. Genet was relieved of his post as Ambassador and the controversy subsided, but not before Washington once again had been subjected to an intensive series of personal attacks in the press. One cartoonist depicted Washington being guillotined for his aristocratic demeanor, which the pro-French public perceived as a crime against democratic government.

Pressures built within Washington's cabinet. Hamilton, a devoted follower of Britain, its customs and its government, hated and feared Jefferson and his Democrat-Republican party. He believed that the Jeffersonian conviction that power must be decentralized and his own fears about the growth of the power and strength of big-city financial and business interests might split the nation apart, North against South, farmers against businessmen. Jefferson, for his part, hated and distrusted Hamilton whom he saw as one who would crown Washington king, abolishing the Constitution in the name of industrial, financial and mercantile expansion. Much could be said about the nature of the conflict which raged between Hamilton and Jefferson as it related to the personalities of both men.

Hamilton saw government in terms of action, particularly as it related to commerce, industry, trade and finance. It was a vigorous, overt, assertive world he saw. He trusted men of power who practiced his beliefs.

Jefferson, as his presidency would reflect, viewed the world through a different glass. Although sometimes covert, he was a thoughtful, reflective, contemplative individual who trusted the common man to preserve the Constitution and individual freedoms. Jefferson was concerned that Hamilton's men of power would tyrannize the ordinary citizen. Hamilton feared that excessive individualism would lead the nation toward economic mediocrity and possible anarchy.

It was Washington's deeply felt opinion, based on his experience as a farmer at Mount Vernon and through his observation while traveling through and staying in New England, New York and Philadelphia, that the young country needed the farmer, the small rural community and the agrarian state. But he understood that the country also needed its financiers, merchants and industrialists. He believed that the country should not be dependent on British-manufactured goods but should develop an industry of its own. To emphasize and express this point of view, he wore a suit made in New England to his first Inaugural. Above all, he wanted his cabinet to reflect these two views fully. He drank deeply from the cup of both Hamilton and Jefferson, drawing his own conclusion with each topic at hand, but also depending on the contribution of their ideas. He sought, through the force of his charisma, character and his own convictions to lead the cabinet and the nation through a political dispute that might rip the fabric of cohesion.

Jefferson felt compromised, however. He would not continue his presence in the cabinet, believing his position could find no expression, and that he and his views would be subverted by staying within the cabinet. As a member of Washington's cabinet, he felt that loyalty bound him to support the Neutrality Proclamation, though he distrusted it as being pro-British. By leaving the cabinet, he took no further chance of supporting any measure which was not fully to his liking. Jefferson, in fact, had become an unrelenting advocate of the Democrat-Republican agrarian position. His mind would admit no platform for which the scales might be balanced between one point of view and another. He found Washington to be weak by seeking balance and compromise. Jefferson could no longer abide an administration which evaluated all options but which appeared to side all too frequently with Hamilton. He broke loose from the cabinet, from Washington and from what he felt was a monarchial-loving administration. The break between these old friends, fellow Virginians and revolutionaries was complete and final. Washington experienced the departure as a tragic and catastrophic loss.

While the wars continued in Europe and the conflicts within his cabinet became acute, a potentially dangerous set of events was being set in motion for Washington in the western sections of the nation.

* * * * *

IV.

Hamilton and the Federalists, with Washington's concurrence, were diligent in their pursuit of a stronger federal government with an executive holding enhanced power and authority. Hamilton had consistently fostered programs in various formats which brought the national government into commerce, manufacturing and finance, expanding the role and scope of federal power. As an expression of this, Hamilton encouraged the passage of a tax on whiskey production, underscoring the power of the government to tax, to influence commerce and to exercise its authority in the implementation of its laws. Washington, Hamilton and Congress acted, and the whiskey producers responded.

While the tax on whiskey was assessed on all distillers alike, frontiersmen resented it most. Although all distillers were taxed, the small mountainside still was the major source of an impending fight. A tax on whiskey had been established as early as 1790, but it was not until 1794 that a crisis developed in western Pennsylvania over the tax. The settlers of that rugged western region, individualists somewhat brazen in their temperament, were unprepared for interference from a distance federal government. Washington, in overseeing the law that set the tax, attempted a compromise that would have achieved a solution within the law, but the frontiersmen were not placated. There was strong encouragement of the rebel position by the Democratic Societies - a swiftly developing group of clubs dedicated to the principles of Jefferson and Madison. The Societies saw the tax as a clear example of Hamiltonian interference with individual freedom. And Washington's support of the tax solidified their hostility toward Hamilton and the President. There soon evolved a battle of the small independent farmer and distiller against the encroachment of government through its taxing authority. The small distillers refused to pay the whiskey tax and threatened to secede from the Union.

The Whiskey Rebellion was not to be the traumatic set of events that it might have been for Washington. After every attempt at compromise failed, he was determined to defeat the movement which proclaimed that the tax would not be enforced. Washington clearly saw that the impending danger might set a precedent in this matter. Any minority group, section or state that opposed a federal law might refuse to obey the law and secede. Washington acted. He called up the militia of several states, with the volunteers exceeding the need. The rebellion and the threat of secession were put down, while the authority of the federal government to enforce its laws was established.

* * * * *

V.

Washington's final battle as President emanated from his desire to maintain peace for the United States in its relationships with Britain and France so as to allow the infant nation to grow and flourish. The United States became a significant sideline player in the battle between these warring nations. The same events which led to the Neutrality Proclamation were rife as no American seaman, merchant ship or cargo was safe on the high seas. The British failed to release land they occupied in the western territories, and they were suspected of being the motivating force behind Indian raids and massacres.

Washington was determined to maintain peace, and to some it seemed to be at all costs. But for Washington, the successful avoidance of war outweighed the significance of any compromise by a young country without navy or army to defend itself or to enforce its terms. He pursued his policy of avoidance of war unflinchingly and with steadfast courage.

Early in the spring of 1794, Washington selected John Jay, Chief Justice of the Supreme Court, to act as his envoy to Great Britain, entrusting him with full power to negotiate a treaty resolving the disputes between the United States and Great Britain. After protracted delays for what seemed endless months, the treaty was delivered to Washington in March of 1795.

The treaty was a mixed bag of achievement and failure. The British had committed to withdraw their western troops, and arrangements were also made for the payment of pre-revolutionary debts which Americans owed British merchants. Unfortunately, Jay failed to negotiate the outlawing of Britain's practice of searching American shipping for goods that might be bound for France and removing such cargo. Although the cargo was ultimately paid for by the British at full value, lengthy delays in such payments and the interference with free commerce made the intrusion a highly inflammatory one for the American ship owners, which the treaty should have resolved. Adding further insult, the treaty failed to make any reference to the continuing British policy of indenturing American seamen from ships they boarded.

One section of the treaty alarmed both the President and the Senate. It concerned a restriction on American shipping to and from the West Indies which prohibited Americans from trading in any West Indian products. The purpose of this prohibition was to prevent the French from benefiting from the delivery by American merchant ships of West Indies goods in short supply in France. Since France desperately needed the assistance of the ever-growing American fleet to supplement its own infant merchant establishment, the British were not disposed to permit that practice to continue.

The treaty cut off French supplies, but it also impaired the commercial exploitation of trade with either France or Britain by American commercial interests. Unfortunately, the products grown in the West Indies included cotton, a rapidly growing cash crop in the United States. The restrictions which Jay unwittingly approved were meant to affect the cotton grown in the islands. However, treaty language actually denied America a world market for cotton, its new source of wealth.

The Constitution gave the Senate power over treaties, and Washington, ever the trustee of constitutional authority, called upon the Senate to implement its authority of "advice and consent" over the Jay Treaty. Washington sought the full involvement of the Senate not only to evaluate but also to revise, amend and, of equal moment, to help sell the treaty to the American public.

The Treaty caused an uproar across the country for which Washington was totally unprepared. The Democrat-Republicans, the pro-French generally, and now even the Federalist New England merchants and traders suddenly moved upon the Senate in protest. Washington's pride and self-image were at stake. He felt his leadership slipping away.

Protest groups were formed. Numerous articles were published in the Democrat-Republican press, alleging that the Treaty had turned on America's closest friend during the Revolution, the country that followed the American Revolution with one of its own, albeit now somewhat undone. All of this pro-French sentiment was coupled with an unbridled distaste for the British and their warlike acts. Once again Washington found the sentiment rising against him. His compatriots were no longer in his cabinet nor were they available for counsel. (John Adams was Vice President, but his jealousy made him of little value to Washington.) Perceiving his isolation and the public uprising against the "pro-British" treaty, Washington strategically leaned heavily upon the Senate to crystallize public support for the treaty and to help in its final draft.

The Senate finally ratified the Jay Treaty, except for the odious section on West Indies Trade. Although it was far from being a satisfactory agreement, Washington sought its ratification to avoid a devastating war with Britain by assuring that nation of America's neutrality in their war with France. Washington had once again brought his political acumen and commanding personality to the fore. He had caused the Congress and the nation to set politics aside and to seek peace. He had risked his prestige and rapport with the populace to lead the country away from the potential of armed conflict which would surely overwhelm the nation.

* * * * *

VI.

The Democrat-Republicans thought Washington weak, indecisive and vain. They saw him as a general of modest strategic ability at best. They protested that Washington was anti-French, pro-British and a monarchist. This criticism which may have been a political maneuver against the powerful "Federalist" President had little outward effect on Washington who would clearly demonstrate his strength of character and his political astuteness in his final months as President.

The first of these opportunities was Washington's Seventh Annual Address given in the Senate on December 8, 1795. The nation's fight over the Jay Treaty was at its height, and he was being attacked viciously. Everyone was prepared for an address carrying a virulent attack on his enemies, coupled with a resounding defense of the Jay Treaty. Instead, Washington dwelt singularly on the gratitude which should be felt by one and all "to the Author of all good for the numerous and extraordinary blessings we enjoy." He itemized these as

General Wayne's military victories and negotiated peace with Indian tribes in Ohio. Piracy in the Mediterranean, where the Barbary pirates had raided U.S. merchant ships, had been eliminated, at least temporarily. He made brief mention of the Jay Treaty, which had been approved and amended by the Senate, stating that the West Indies Trade amendment would soon be approved by Great Britain. The resolution of conflicts with the Indians, in the Mediterranean and with Britain provided Washington with an opportunity "for consoling and gratifying reflections—and a time of diminishing external discord which have heretofore menaced our tranquility." The country was not enduring the travail of war as were those on the Continent, he argued. The problems of trade were far outweighed by the benefits of neutrality, and the country was growing and prospering, exhibiting a national happiness never before equalled. He reminded his audience that the Whiskey Rebellion was behind them and that the western territory was now flourishing. He went on to encourage a humanitarian policy toward the Indians and concluded by urging temperate discussion of matters before Congress, proclaiming its necessity for the "peace, happiness and welfare of the country."

Washington had defused and disarmed the opposition. He was an executive who took upon himself the task of leading the country and Congress in the direction he had selected. The address was a brilliant, thoughtful and persuasive effort. The tenor of public opinion, which was slowly moving his way, was being expressed in newspapers throughout the country.

The second remarkable challenge for Washington in his final year became apparent when the House of Representatives insisted that the Jay Treaty be submitted to the House for approval as well as to the Senate. They protested that they were the legislative body elected by a popular vote; the Senate was still selected by state legislators. They based their position on the constitutional provision that the House has authority to pass on appropriations. The treaty could not be law, as Congress saw it, without approval by the House and the subsequent appropriation of needed funds.

To initiate its authority in the matter, the House demanded that certain papers and memoranda associated with the evolution of the Treaty document be delivered to them for examination. Washington remained adamant. The House of Representatives would not interfere with the power of the President to make treaties with the "advice and consent" only of the Senate. The effect of this demand would be to permit the House full authority to supervise the President's activity in all matters, thus encroaching upon the powers of the executive branch. Washington would not succumb; it was the House against the President, and Washington stood his ground. Congress fully expected compromise on the part of the President, but found none. Their position was clearly in jeopardy. When a torrent of public protests appeared in defense of the Treaty, the House retreated and approved the appropriation needed to implement the Treaty by a vote of fifty-one to forty-nine. Washington had prevailed.

The conflicts with England had barely been alleviated when the French reaction to the Jay Treaty took over center stage in American foreign policy. The French profoundly resented the Jay Treaty. They looked upon America as a traitor to their cause in their fight with England, resulting in a contentious final six months in office for Washington. The French refused to accept America's appointed Ambassador, they attacked Washington personally, they stopped and boarded American vessels loaded with goods bound for England and confiscated the cargo without any intent of repayment. Washington made peace with England only to find that France had surfaced as a war-minded adversary.

It was a conflict that would not be resolved during Washington's administration. It was also one which he could not comprehend. Nor could he comprehend why Jefferson and the Democrat-Republicans could not be persuaded of the significance of France's hostility. The pressures first from Great Britain, then France, caused Washington to alter his views on neutrality and isolationism. He recommended that the country establish a navy to protect the merchant fleet and deter foreign aggression.

Americans who were blindly pro-French used the Jay Treaty as the signal to reinstitute their virulent attacks on Washington. Forged letters surfaced, as they had during the Revolution, which purported evidence of Washington's desire to abandon the Revolution. He was accused of overdrawing his Presidential salary, all of which drove Washington to private emotional diatribes against the newspaper attacks against him. Although it was a tempestuous end to Washington's long public career, he shouldered his responsibility to resolve the public threat and to absorb, with courage, the personal attacks against him.

* * * * *

VII.

Washington's faith in the new republic and in its survival was well-expressed in his Farewell Address, which was published in September of 1796. The address first stated that he would not seek a third term as President, which set a precedent followed until Franklin Roosevelt in 1940, almost 150 years later and at the onset of fighting a world war, ran for his third term. Succession to the office of the presidency by election was rare in the annals of history, where in fact one usually found that leaders had been despots who either died in office or were deposed. The experiment of Constitutional government was thriving.

Washington noted this in his Farewell Address by congratulating the citizenry on the success of its democratic institutions. He highlighted neutrality and the importance of avoiding involvement with European conflicts. He spoke forcefully on the preservation of the union as the source and bulwark of prosperity and self-protection. Washington reiterated his great concern about political parties and the possibility of demagoguery which might result. He feared the pitting of one group against the other, with the surviving group becoming despotic, as was occurring in France. This was Washington's greatest concern for the future of the country and also the source of his greatest feelings of failure. He sensed, as Lincoln did in his second Inaugural, that the country's greatest threat came from within, particularly from the pernicious influence of political parties and from regional conflicts. He spelled out this concern in the Farewell Address, but to no avail. While Washington had faith in the ability of the people to reach sound decisions, he did not believe they would function democratically through a party system where individual judgment would be controlled by manipulative, self-serving party leaders. It is interesting to note that although he and Jefferson shared a common faith in the reasonableness of man, Jefferson approved the political party in a free society as the means whereby individuals might best express political thoughts.

Washington's address set the tone for neutrality in American foreign policy which was to last for a century, and he inspired nationalism over regionalism, a subject which would all too soon tear the country apart.

The speech, appreciated as it was for its content, was received with mixed emotions. Although there was great regret at the departure of their revered leader, there was recognition that a peaceful transfer of power was at hand.

The public set aside its bickering with George Washington as he left office. All eyes were on him during the inauguration of John Adams, and the crowd gave Washington a tumultuous send-off when he departed. It had always been a small but vocal minority of the public who opposed Washington. For the vast majority, however, he was their beloved President, Commander-In-Chief, hero.

George Washington was a remarkable and, yet, a relatively uncomplicated man. He was confident, determined and quite comfortable with himself. During his second term he displayed patience and unusual endurance, facing issues without precedent. He perceived the momentous times in which he served the nation without adopting the trappings of a political philosopher. He was the great facilitator and implementor of the ideas of a free government, of individual freedom and of a Constitution that balanced forces. He certainly encouraged the roots of the Revolution, but he left to others to plant those roots, to perfect the Declaration of Independence and write the Constitution. But he was the one who saw to the early tillage and harvesting, which was leading the war and serving as the first President. Washington gave unique dignity and prestige to both the office of the presidency and to the nation that no other could have provided. He secured the authority of the presidency from undue interference from either Senate or House. He firmly established the authority of the Federal government to enforce its laws in the face of the "Whiskey Rebellion." He fended off attacks from the Jeffersonians and the pro-French. He brought dignity and prestige to the office of the presidency which would set the pattern for all who followed. He sought a cloistered environment for the country through neutrality, allowing the nation to find its own way without interference from foreign powers. He was persuaded of the evils of political influence over the free-thinking individual. He asserted all of his prestige to permit the maturation of the electorate and of the government before these would come under the influence of political parties.

In his remarkable second term, George Washington brought forth political wisdom from that individualistic crowd that made up the early American Republic, and by the force of his judgment, honesty and character set the nation on its democratic course.

Reader's Score of George Washington

Defense: _____

Economic: _____

Vision: _____

Communication: _____

Lead Congress: _____

Lead without Popularity: _____

Invincibility: _____

Consistency: _____

Self-Confidence: _____

Strengthen Nation: _____

TOTAL POINTS: _____

Thomas Jefferson

3

Thomas Jefferson

Thomas Jefferson, more than any other single individual, was the political philosopher whose concept of democracy and liberty drove the American colonies to independence. He was a man both resolute and practical. He was a thinker, a tactician, a planner, and, on occasion, a schemer. A man of contrasts, he was intensely passionate in his convictions, yet he absorbed reality as it swirled around him to formulate patterns of action. But above all, he trusted reason—the thoughtful, reflective, undisturbed utilization of the mind—to resolve all issues, to resolve all conflicts. He dedicated his reason most passionately to implement freedom and democracy for the colonies.

Jefferson had experienced great success throughout his early career as a lawyer and as a delegate to the various Virginia legislative bodies, always demonstrating inspiring writing talents. From his pen flowed the foundation for independence from Great Britain and, later, for the Declaration of Independence itself. His courage in standing firm against the tyranny of the King and his deputies was the model for others to follow.

For all his success as a lawyer and delegate, he was reluctant to confront his adversaries directly, preferring reason to debate and litigation, pursuing confrontation through means that tended to shield him from altercation. Jefferson suffered from a weak voice and an unappealing speaking manner, and this defect, which others struggle to overcome, blended well with his temperament allowing him to remain somewhat separated and apart from the fray into which he nonetheless entered in his own unique and dedicated way.

Jefferson was deeply committed to the study of not only general and political philosophy, but also music, architecture and literature, although farming remained his greatest passion. He was a world authority in many of these fields. But it was as a politician that Jefferson spent much of his adult life and where one gleans the greatest measure of his character and temperament.

Jefferson had been in France during much of the time the country struggled under the Articles of Confederation. He had not witnessed first-hand what some called "an excess of individualistic democracy." In contrast, James Madison, his longtime political ally, had seen the frailty of a government which had no strong administrator at the helm to rein in the disorganized and undisciplined masses. Many believed anarchy would be the country's destiny, and the Constitutional Convention was convened as a reaction to this concern. Some leaders of the young republic lacked faith in the ability of ordinary men to manage the affairs of government. There was the belief that natural forces within each person—greed, desire for power, jealousy—had to be harnessed and balanced for the good of the whole.

Jefferson supported the Constitution, particularly after the addition of the first ten amendments enhanced the protection of liberty. He held throughout his public life that the individual could and should be entrusted with a maximum of self-rule and a minimum of government control. Jefferson's view extended to the office of the presidency which he down-played in every manner possible. He permitted no public fanfare for the office. Despite the fact that he was frequently a strong leader, he generally approached issues with Congress and the electorate as an individual, not as President. Hamilton and the Federalists viewed this as leading to the destruction of government and, eventually, to the end of freedom. Hamilton believed the government should grow in size and authority and be run primarily by an educated elite class. This broad conflict not only lay the foundation for Jefferson's long battle with Hamilton, the Federalists, and Washington, but also affected his management of government during his second term, when he rarely found it appropriate to have government forcefully confront issues.

This political philosophy caused Jefferson to see democracy and individual liberty as synonymous. He perceived a free republican form of government dependent upon the agrarian community, and no other, as the bulwark of the survival of American democracy. The agrarian way of life epitomized Jefferson's politics, but it also reflected his temperament and character. The rural life was non-confrontational. Farmers plied their skills independently, free of subservience to an employer, yet part of an economic and political system which they controlled through representative government.

Jefferson was convinced that the wealthy business men and financiers would tyrannize their employees and would repress the individual and destroy democracy. He was reluctant to reconcile his own view with the Hamiltonian and Federalist doctrine that government must grow and encourage business, finance and commerce. He was deeply suspicious that underlying Federalism was a wish to restore some form of monarchy and despotic rule. And this perspective broadly impacted his administration of the presidency.

* * * * *

Jefferson served as the young nation's representative in Paris, as Secretary of State during much of George Washington's administration and as Vice-President under John Adams. He was elected President in 1800 after the popular Jefferson defeated an equally popular Aaron Burr in a run off vote by the House of Representatives. Jefferson's first term as President was a most satisfying one. Taxes were cut; he sent ships to the Mediterranean, settling for some time a festering dispute with the Barbary Pirates. The military was reduced; he sent Lewis and Clark on their exploration of the West; and, above all he moved with dispatch and skill to purchase Louisiana from the French.

The Louisiana Purchase is so momentous in the history of the United States, and its manner of purchase so apparently un-Jeffersonian, that its ironic aspects must be recounted. France had only recently been ceded the territory from Spain causing some alarm in the Administration and Congress concerning the free flow of commerce through Mississippi and Florida. The American delegation in France opened a dialogue with French ministers to protect America's rights and to seek land in Florida. Napoleon, fearing British forays into Louisiana and preferring to move upon the continent of Europe rather than pursue the colonization of distant shores, offered to sell the entire Louisiana territory to the United States for fifteen million dollars. The irony is that the dreaded conflict between Britain and France, which was to plague Jefferson and the nation during his second term, was the principal cause of Napoleon's decision to sell Louisiana.

James Monroe, one of the delegates to France, is credited with having acted decisively, far in excess of his authority, in accepting Napoleon's proposal.

Jefferson, always the proponent of limited government, who could not abide the thought of an authoritarian chief executive for America, acceded to the plan, although he questioned whether he had constitutional authority to do so. He purchased the territory without Congressional approval, willingly treading upon constitutional boundaries, yet believing first, that the people of the nation supported the purchase and, further, that it was within the power of the people to undo his act if they saw fit to do so. He was a people's President, and it was a people's Constitution. Jefferson was decisive and pragmatic in the purchase. His action reflected his historical perspective for the nation, his practicality and his ability to be objective, to be the empiricist. But even more to the point, he had expanded the territory in which the agrarian life might be pursued. It was a brilliant political move to assure the conflict-free world he sought. Fortunately for the non-confrontational Jefferson, he faced only minimal conflict with Federalist opponents, allowing him to crown his first term with a triumph of managerial and political achievement.

★ ★ ★ ★ ★

Jefferson's second term began on a sour note. Although the popular President had won the election of 1804 with an overwhelming 90% of the electoral votes, he did not summon a quorum for his Inaugural Address, which he delivered in a quiet monotone to a joint session of the houses of Congress. It was an inauspicious event, without pomp, befitting Jefferson's modesty both as a person and as President. Jefferson somewhat naively let no time elapse before he conveyed to intimates that he would follow George Washington's example in not seeking a third term. He believed that the office of the presidency should not remain too long with one individual. Jefferson had developed the Democrat-Republican party to pursue his political philosophy with the assistance of his close friend James Madison, maintaining his leadership of the party from the days of Washington's first term. However, seeds of discontent within the party leadership appeared for the first time when it became apparent that four years hence there would be a race for the White House. John Randolph, the powerful Congressman from Virginia, would seize every opportunity to expand his own authority within the party and to establish his candidacy for President in 1808 by attacking Jefferson's policies, both domestic and foreign.

Unfortunately for Jefferson, foreign affairs which preoccupied the President during most of his second term would involve matters over which Jefferson could apply little control, despite his vast experience and training in the field. It was the management of these affairs and their impact on the country and Jefferson's response to them which bear the primary scrutiny of his second term.

★ ★ ★ ★ ★

Jefferson had firmly believed that Western Florida, which belonged to Spain, would become a part of the country along with the Louisiana Purchase. However, the Spanish were irate with what they felt to be the heavy-handed transfer of the Louisiana Territory to the new nation by their protector, France. So infuriated were they, that Spain refused to honor agreements to pay reparations due the United States for prior war damages. Spain not only refused to consider ceding Western Florida to the United States but also disputed the Louisiana cession and claimed that its territorial borders extended westward almost to the Mississippi.

The acquisition of Western Florida became an obsession with Jefferson. He sensed that France could provide means whereby Florida would be acquired, and, early in his second term, he set about to use the good offices of the French government to obtain West Florida. He devised a scheme whereby the United States would bribe France to persuade Spain to cede Florida to the U.S. He maneuvered with Congress for an appropriation of some five million dollars to fulfill his plan, concealing for some months the purpose of these funds and hinting only that it would effect foreign affairs. Although a select few in Congress knew the details of the plan, the House, with authority to initiate appropriations, was kept in the dark for some time. This was fertile ground for the first salvo to be fired by John Randolph in his ongoing battle with the Chief Executive. It became a vicious struggle, due not only to the secrecy of the effort but also to Randolph's strategy to oppose Jefferson in all matters. Randolph, who sought to control the Democrat-Republican party and become its candidate for the presidency, used every platform to achieve that goal. Jefferson finally persuaded Congress to approve an appropriation of $2 million to pay to France to acquire Spanish-owned west Florida.

Despite his keen appreciation of the importance of Florida for America's future, Jefferson's handling of the west Florida matter was flawed from the start. Above all, it reflected his temperament which led him to avoid confrontation to achieve his objective. First, he could not negotiate with a hostile Spain, so he sought refuge with France, trusting that France could be bribed to entice Spain to cede territory to the United States. It was a naive venture, a charge which would be made repeatedly during Jefferson's second term. Further, Jefferson was insensitive of Congress in being both secretive and devious over the appropriation of funds. Nevertheless, west Florida was not acquired during Jefferson's second term, as France's influence over Spain waned. The money which Congress appropriated was spent for naught. The matter frustrated Jefferson deeply and festered as one of many items in an unfulfilled agenda during his final years in office.

The ceding of Florida can be seen in a somewhat broader context, however. Jefferson as scientist and explorer, a man renowned for his political and geographic insight, could visualize a great expanding nation spreading from ocean to ocean. As with the Louisiana Purchase, Jefferson sought to expand the agrarian, democratic way of life into Florida. One can only wonder at his reluctance to utilize his great political influence to maneuver Congress more directly and openly in support of his Florida plan. Avoiding a showdown, he staunchly refused to call upon his power of persuasion.

The Florida affair was in many ways a clear expression of Jefferson's pattern of leadership. He believed in action which was compatible with his pragmatic political philosophy and his temperament, frequently utilizing his party to achieve his goals for the country. He did not confront, believing the presidency must not become too powerful; the common man, not the elite, must rule, and reason must prevail. Jefferson believed that he was elected to be the guardian of the people, not to aggrandize the office of the presidency. He resisted any move which might enhance the power of that institution although he personally, without emphasizing the office, would gently maneuver Congress and the public through his political party. His faith in the inherent intelligence and good sense of the common man, coupled with his aversion to confrontation, frequently caused him to appear weak and disingenuous.

Jefferson readily utilized his personal power as President to complete the Louisiana Purchase, as he would again in establishing an embargo against Great Britain and France. Yet he sought to have his party, which he controlled, influence legislation without personal confrontation. He wanted, and generally maintained, popular approval. He would not risk this prized perquisite to obtain a vote from Congress or the allegiance of the masses for a cause which was unpopular. Once he was assured of voter support without his taking a public stand, he would proceed; until then, twists and turns were to be expected. Reason was Jefferson's great weapon, for it avoided conflict; but it had to wait upon consensus. He would not risk his popularity. Although this is not rare among politicians, Jefferson may have been more reluctant than some to spend his political clout to influence a Congress which was difficult to control. It was this nature of the man which set the tone of Jefferson's second administration.

★ ★ ★ ★ ★

The second term had barely commenced when a domestic crisis erupted. Word spread of a plot by Aaron Burr, who had nearly wrested the presidency from Jefferson in the contested race of 1800 and had served as Jefferson's Vice President during Jefferson's first term. Early evidence of the plot came from anonymous memos and from reports from territorial officials. All sources pointed to a treasonous plan by a power-hungry Burr, now an outcast from his own party. He had gathered an independent army to occupy Louisiana, to separate all lands west of the Alleghenies into an independent nation, and, finally, to attack Mexico to bring that weak nation under his leadership.

Jefferson unfortunately delayed his response for as long as he dared. After considerable procrastination, he finally acted by issuing a proclamation to all territorial governors and military commanders with specific orders to confiscate all military materials in the hands of known rebels and to arrest Burr. Burr turned himself in, escaped, was captured, and was finally indicted on charges of treason and high misdemeanors. General James Wilkinson, Commanding General of all United States armed forces and governor of the Louisiana Territory, was not only heavily implicated in the Burr plot but was also alleged to be in the employ of the Spanish government. Following Jefferson's proclamation on Burr, the General maneuvered swiftly and cunningly. He turned against Burr and immediately became the government's chief witness against the former Vice President.

Although it was handled with diligence from a military standpoint, the Burr conspiracy caused considerable public concern, and a shadow was cast across Jefferson's administration in its handling of significant aspects of the affair. First, Jefferson, believing his testimony was essential for conviction, gave broad defense of and support for Wilkinson throughout the episode, much to the dismay even of Jefferson's friends. He was unwilling to acknowledge any taint of wrongdoing by his General, despite the most damaging evidence. Further, soon after

Burr's arrest, Jefferson made a public statement to a congressman that Burr was undoubtedly guilty of treason. So brash a statement by the Chief Executive was condemned by Jefferson's enemies and by Burr's friends and defenders and was, indeed, frowned upon by Jefferson's supporters. Jefferson appeared to take a significant and active role in the prosecution, much to the chagrin of Burr's attorneys and the Federalist Chief Justice John Marshall, who presided over the trial. Burr became the martyred hero of Federalists and those opposed to Jefferson, including the small band of Democrat-Republicans led by John Randolph.

Jefferson was subpoenaed to provide evidence, which he did, and to testify, which he refused to do. He thus established a precedent for the separation of powers between the judicial and executive branches. (The precedent continues as a point of contention to this day, with the Court ordering Richard Nixon to deliver tapes of his office conversations.)

Burr was acquitted of all charges and released after a trial which Jefferson felt was a victory for the Federalists and their friends. He perceived the acquittal as a personal defeat. He had again been thwarted in achieving a second-term objective: seeing that justice was done to a person he believed to be a traitor to the United States. While Jefferson could apply no influence to overturn the acquittal, he did protest against the power of the judiciary to subvert what he believed to be the judgment of the nation against Burr. Actions of the executive branch are subject to the vote of the people. The judiciary had no similar check from the people. Some 150 years later, Franklin Roosevelt experienced the same anger over an unresponsive judiciary. Had not other more pressing events intervened, Jefferson might have sought legislative and constitutional changes to correct judicial conduct that ignored evidence which he believed proved Burr's guilt. His anti-judicial stand was a continuation of his ongoing protest against the rule of a Federalist-privileged class in the management of the judiciary.

The trial of Aaron Burr diminished the stature of Thomas Jefferson. Although he was incensed that Burr would presume to reverse the expansion of the United States, he found the actions of Burr to be so beyond the bounds of reason that he responded slowly at first to the need to act decisively. He did, at last, set the military to the task of defusing the Burr conspiracy. But his public statements concerning Burr's guilt reflected a man confusing his roles as both individual and President in the presence of crisis. Defending Wilkinson appears to have been an act of desperation on the part of Jefferson to grasp at evidence that would convict this malcontent, this interloper into the grand flow of American development. He believed firmly that the American people supported him in the actions he had taken. Nonetheless, the Burr affair did not reflect well on Jefferson in his second term.

★ ★ ★ ★ ★

The Burr affair, however, faded out of perspective with the advent of a series of telling crises during Jefferson's second term.

The war between England and France grew more intense as Jefferson's second term advanced. Attacks against U.S. ships and seamen endured by George Washington continued, but at a rate and severity well in excess of that experienced by Washington. The British had defeated the French navy at Trafalgar and thus became absolute rulers of the seas. Napoleon had beaten the Austrians, and the Russians were in retreat, assuring Napoleon control over the continent. As the battle between the French and the British raged, the British determined to place a stranglehold on the flow of goods reaching France by sea. The young American nation became both a key player in and victim of the panoply of European conflict.

As they had during Washington's administration and before the days of the Jay Treaty, the British once again attacked American merchant vessels, removing cargo destined for France, continuing to halt and board both naval and merchant vessels to remove sailors they believed to be British seamen.

Despite the intensity of the battle between the two European combatants, Jefferson was determined to find a non-confrontational, neutral course. He tried to play the two nations off against each other. He thought of alliances first with Britain and then with France, then returned to his original position of complete neutrality. When he finally decided that a truce with Britain was necessary, he arranged for James Monroe to negotiate a treaty, assuring that American sovereignty would be respected on the high seas. Jefferson believed that trade and commerce, isolated from political and military entanglements, would be possible for nations. It was not to be. Nor would he achieve a world free of confrontation for America and himself.

The weak defenses of the young country was at least one factor in the plight of its merchant and naval vessels. Jefferson had asked Congress for increased funds to build gunboats very shortly after the $2 million appropriation had been made to obtain West Florida from Spain. No action on the gunboats was taken, and one wonders whether Jefferson's and Congress's failure to arm the country with a more substantial navy may have played into the hands of the aggressive British force. The signals sent by the nation reflected a failure of will to the powerful British.

As Jefferson sought peace through negotiation, confrontation intensified for the United States. The American frigate *Chesapeake* set sail for the Mediterranean in June of 1807 to protect American shipping against attacks by the Barbary Pirates. This action was taken despite a treaty with Tripoli initiated in his first term to defuse this situation. The ship had one British sailor and three American seamen on board who had deserted from a British warship to join the American crew. The three Americans had actually been volunteers in the British navy, but that was a small technicality in the chain of events which followed. The *Chesapeake* had hardly left its American port when it was fired upon by the *Leopard*, a British ship of fifty guns. The captain of the *Leopard* halted the *Chesapeake* and demanded the right to search the American vessel for British deserters. The American captain refused. Following a garbled exchange between the two captains, the British fired upon the totally unprepared U.S. ship, killing three American seamen, seriously wounding eight, and slightly wounding ten, including the captain. After ten minutes of return fire, the *Chesapeake* lowered its colors and turned its ship over to the British boarding party which promptly removed the four seamen who had served on a British ship.

The residents at the port of Hampton Roads, Virginia, where the *Chesapeake* docked the next day, became a mob and set about wreaking havoc against the British supplies stored there. The entire nation soon became incensed over the violation of its neutrality and its sovereignty.

More than a year before the *Chesapeake* attack, the British ship *Leander* had fired upon a U.S. merchant ship while attempting to board it, killing a U.S. seaman. After several days' delay, Jefferson issued a proclamation ordering British vessels out of all U.S. harbors. The British envoy formally apologized for the incident, and Jefferson permitted the crisis to pass. He had hoped that the British would improve their relations with the United States. Here again, Jefferson sought to avoid direct confrontation and overt hostility.

Shortly before the *Leander* affair in the spring of 1806, Congress had passed a Non-Importation Bill, limiting the importation of some British goods into the nation to focus attention of the British on the American position regarding its rights on the high seas. But the implementation of the Non-Importation Act was delayed to permit diplomatic efforts to continue, another possible signal to the British that the young American nation was vacillating.

With Congressional approval, Jefferson sent William Pinckney to join Monroe in England to negotiate a treaty with the British which might bring a restoration of civility toward American use of the high seas following the *Chesapeake* attack. The directive was to have Britain cease the impressment of sailors on all U.S. vessels. Although the British readily agreed to cease boarding naval vessels, they refused to avoid impressment of merchant seamen. Negotiations were a futile venture, for the British were locked in combat with Napoleon, and would not be diverted from that endeavor to acknowledge the sovereignty of America on the high seas.

The *Chesapeake* affair only emphasized the plight of the nation in a warring world. Jefferson issued another proclamation ordering British ships out of American ports. He also dispatched a ship to England carrying a message demanding reparations and a commitment to cease further impressment of sailors aboard U.S. ships. Congress and the nation were incensed over the state of affairs with Britain, but stern action was avoided as Jefferson manifested the diminishing leadership role which was to characterize his management of national policy until the final days of the fateful second term. Once again, he preferred to defuse the impact of the *Chesapeake* affair rather than appear to risk war with Britain.

A group of British merchant and working class families who suffered economic hardship from lost American trade due to the Non-Importation Bill pressured their government to come to terms with American claims against Britain. The British finally responded to the *Chesapeake* attack by sending a special envoy to Washington. But they would not agree to reduce significantly their impressment policy nor to abandon their removal of cargo from American merchant vessels bound for France. The Monroe-Pinckney treaty attempt failed at about the same time that negotiations over the *Chesapeake* came aground.

Jefferson had enjoyed success in his first term, showing leadership to diminish the incursions by the Barbary Pirates and to purchase Louisiana, each without approval from Congress. He had opened the exploration of the West. It was a time when he could lead without confrontation. By contrast, his second term was filled with conflict that challenged his very nature.

* * * * *

Jefferson struggled to defuse a world that would not respond to his reason. He believed he could not wage war with the British, nor did he wish to do so. He had few options. The Non-Importation Act was implemented in December of 1807 as a solution. In that same month Jefferson recommended to Congress that an embargo be established outlawing all American trade with England. It was a frenzied response to a new British order which drastically increased impressment against all U.S. ships, as the British pursued their authority on the high seas. In the face of this evolving conflict, Congress adopted the Embargo, which appeared to be the most peaceful option open to the administration. In addition, Jefferson recalled the nation's small navy, built shore fortification, and expanded the army to defend the country in case of war. Jefferson asked Congress to authorize 188 gunboats, which it approved in December of 1807.

The Embargo Act was the backbone of Jefferson's policy to combat Britain, avoiding any threat of war. Although it is not clear that any form of war-like threat would have had any influence upon the policies of Britain, it is clear that British leadership believed that the new nation would not go to war under any circumstances. This conviction, coupled with Britain's fight-to-the-death conflict with Napoleon, minimized the effect of Jefferson's plans. Although there is every reason to believe Jefferson understood this, he implemented his embargo with considerable determination.

The embargo placed a strangle-hold neither on the British economy nor its war-making capabilities, but it did devastate the merchant population of New England which looked to shipping and manufacturing as its life blood. It also stifled the export market for plantations in the

South, including Jefferson's Virginia. Enforcement became almost impossible, as blockade-running became rampant. Jefferson, in enforcing an unpopular law upon the nation, violated his most basic principles of a limited, non-coercive government to achieve some semblance of compliance. The embargo, which was an economic disaster for much of the nation, was also a political disaster for Jefferson. As he departed the presidency in March of 1809, it was repealed for all nations other than Britain and France. Jefferson believed that the country would understand that the embargo would improve their economic lot in the long run. He believed that the nation would follow his leadership, that Britain would restore trade in an effort to avoid confrontation. The people either did not understand his reasoning or they saw the folly of the embargo, for they did not follow Jefferson's leadership.

In his final months as President, Jefferson appeared to abdicate his office for all functions except enforcement of the embargo, which he pursued with great intensity. He would not counsel Congress or the nation on the goals of the embargo. Nor would he assist Congress in its deliberations as to the alternatives to the embargo, war or submission. Congress was leaderless; the nation was in a state of confusion. At a time when guidance was most needed, the chief magistrate provided no assistance.

* * * * *

It was the common view that Jefferson never had a personal quarrel with anyone. His was a peaceful nature; he sought to avoid conflict and to resolve differences through reason. It has been said that Jefferson was painfully and unrealistically optimistic. Farsighted in his view of the nation, he feared monarchy and was the world's foremost advocate of freedom for the individual. He trusted the common man. He saw the agrarian life as the very embodiment of freedom and prosperity. All these came together to permit Jefferson to fight first for the freedom and independence of the nation and later develop a political coalition that survived 24 years of uninterrupted control over the presidency, forming a party which survives to this day. His farsightedness and the expansion of the agrarian society would lead him to his greatest triumph, the Louisiana Purchase. But his character and temperament, set against almost insurmountable obstacles in foreign affairs, would also be the underpinning of his greatest frustrations, those stemming from his handling of foreign affairs during his second administration. It was a time when his personal need to avoid confrontation may well have aggravated the already tenuous relations with England and France.

The attempt to acquire Florida clearly reflected his vision for the country; but his avoidance of direct confrontation caused him to be secretive with Congress and the country about appropriating funds for that effort. Of far greater moment, Jefferson could never bring himself to confront directly and forcefully the British infringement upon American sovereignty and neutrality on the high seas.

Jefferson's strong belief in limited government influenced his decision to seek funds for gunboats to defend the ports and harbors of the country. Gunboats were no match for British warships and were, in the minds of some, worthless. But they were cheap, allowing Jefferson to preserve his constituency by not increasing taxes for military preparedness or an unpopular war. War was not something he wished to sell to the nation.

It is not clear whether the British might have responded to a firmer policy by the United States. It is clear, however, that Jefferson failed to lead Congress and the nation in any clear-cut program that might influence British leadership. Jefferson, always the optimist, hoped that the embargo would be a persuasive tool, short of war. But Jefferson's policy toward Britain made the failure of the embargo a foregone conclusion. The British looked upon the policy of the American administration as indecisive. It remained for his successor and heir, James Madison, to set a different tenor in foreign affairs.

Jefferson's critics looked upon his second administration as being filled with inconsistencies. This is not the case, however, if one takes into account his character and temperament and his political philosophy and the times in which he served. A young, relatively weak country faced the mightiest naval force in history. Jefferson's nature was to reason, but he could apply such reason only if consensus were his and only if the opposing party, namely Britain, would respond to reason. Under these circumstances he believed that his policy was the only alternative open to him.

He pursued the embargo, despite its certain failure, with the same commitment he had applied to his early fight for independence and to the Louisiana Purchase. But he would not adequately utilize the power of the presidency to implement the embargo. He would not confront Congress nor the populace with the merits he saw in the embargo. Jefferson almost seemed to have taken refuge in reason to retain a certain emotional equilibrium. But events in his second term would not respond to rationality.

Nonetheless, Jefferson's apparent weaknesses in the face of events in his final years as President should not be seen as diminishing the great shadow he cast over the nation and the world by clearly codifying and symbolizing America's democracy. Jefferson, who had kept the nation out of war, experienced continued popularity among the great throng of American citizenry upon his departure from the White House. He could easily have won a third term had he chosen to run again, despite the unrest caused by the embargo.

Despite his failures in his second term, Jefferson vindicated his faith in self-government by firmly setting the democratic and classless tone of this country. The question of whether Jefferson was temperamentally suited to be President arose from a letter he wrote: "Nature intended me for tranquil pursuits of science, by rendering them my supreme delight. But the enormities of the times in which I have lived have forced me to take a part in resisting them, and to commit myself on the boisterous ocean of political passions."

Jefferson achieved a measure of success in his first term, some of which must be attributed to events which responded to his rational nature and to good fortune. Many Presidents have faced particularly trying episodes in history for which their natures were ill-suited; the times seemed out of joint for them. This was particularly true of Jefferson's second term.

Reader's Score of Thomas Jefferson

Defense: _____	Lead without Popularity: _____
Economic: _____	Invincibility: _____
Vision: _____	Consistency: _____
Communication: _____	Self-Confidence: _____
Lead Congress: _____	Strengthen Nation: _____
	TOTAL POINTS: _____

James Madison

James Madison

Jefferson crept away from his second term, leaving a vacuum in executive authority which Congress readily filled with its own power. The James Madison who took office in March of 1809 displayed only slightly more courage in administrative leadership than had his predecessor in his final days. Ineptitude, dullness, spiritless bungling described the quality of leadership which Madison exhibited until the last two years of his second term. This was in dramatic contrast with the inspired, innovative, quietly courageous leadership which James Madison had displayed as an advisor and participant in government from the days of the Revolution to his presidency.

As a legislator in Virginia, he had the insight to observe that the weak administration of the government under the Articles of Confederation had an unfavorable effect on economic growth. He promoted a meeting of neighboring states to discuss the problems with their joint use of the Potomac. This meeting led Madison to schedule a conference in Philadelphia a year later with a far broader agenda. The Constitution which was produced by that convention was not written by Madison, but he was responsible for the preparation of the document, incorporating the important compromises that were achieved.

He assisted the compromises and wrote the most detailed account of the proceedings. He was among the greatest scholars and intellects at the convention, with considerable knowledge of constitutional theory and history. He was an intellectual influence on the convention, promoting individual liberty and the balancing of powers. He was a man of persuasion, energy, perseverance, perception and drive. He observed opposition to the Constitution arising among the state legislators and the population in general and promptly proceeded to promote ratification of the Constitution through his cogent treatises which later became an integral part of the *Federalist*. Although at first he opposed it, he later became a leader in the ratification of the Bill of Rights, with his particular emphasis on freedom of religion. Madison was a deliberate man who always saw to the completion of a task, even if it required some compromise and modification in his policies. In contrast to Jefferson, he never feared taking a public stand.

Madison had encouraged the Bill of Rights as a bulwark against a majority that might run headlong into an undemocratic rampage. The Articles of Confederation had led to near anarchy of mismanagement, and, although Madison feared a despotic executive in the office of the presidency, he perceived the potential danger of a majority running amuck. In the Fourteenth *Federalist* paper, Madison had expressed even greater concern about a runaway legislature which might overwhelm a weak executive and subvert the valid objectives of the people. He found comfort in the Bill of Rights and supported a strict and conservative interpretation of the Constitution to prevent such excesses. Interestingly, Madison had to be persuaded of the need for the Bill of Rights. He believed that the checks and balances and separation of power would protect freedom better than the Bill of Rights. He was concerned that if certain rights were delineated, the failure to list a specific right might eliminate it. But ever the flexible thinker, Madison came to support the first ten amendments.

When Madison became President in March of 1809, he had been in government services during most of his adult life. He had been legislator, congressman, possibly the greatest Speaker of the House in the nation's history and Secretary of State under Jefferson. As Secretary of State, he had consistently sought peaceful solutions to conflicts with France and Britain. He had strongly encouraged the embargo against Britain as an alternative to war and also as a means to give the young nation breathing room to grow and flourish unencumbered by war.

In this and in most respects he reflected Jefferson's views concerning war, which they both found repugnant. He shared with Jefferson a similar bent in personality in that he tended to avoid discord and direct confrontation and to prefer resolution through reason. Despite their similarities, it was most frequently Madison, not Jefferson, who wrote the great public attacks on the Federalists during the administrations of Washington, Adams and Jefferson. He was the great advocate of Democrat-Republican programs.

Madison was a small man with a wizened face who appeared frail and sick much of the time. He was a quiet, dignified and pleasant man who loved conversation. He was a great story teller and had a keen sense of humor, and he was known for his cautious judgment and common sense. According to Henry Clay, Madison was not the genius that Jefferson was, "Madison being cool, practical, dispassionate and safe." He was intellectual, energetic, a man who did not shun public action. He was not without courage, and he was certainly a public servant who would complete the task assigned him. Yet he was not an introspective man as was Jefferson. He did not foresee the consequences of acts nor of those of Congress in some context that might alter the future. He was a devoted follower of a strict interpretation of the Constitution. All of this frequently made him a man buffeted by events rather than one who caused or influenced them.

★ ★ ★ ★ ★

II.

Madison was elected to his first term in 1808 by a comfortable margin in the electoral vote of 122 to 47 over his Federalist opponent Charles Pickney. But he began his first term in office facing a Congress that had flexed its muscle against Jefferson by obstructing some of his appointments late in his second term. Members of the Senate and House were developing a regional, non-party allegiance and were out to show their mettle. Now they would demonstrate their authority to James Madison.

In the eyes of many, Madison had suffered great humiliation on countless occasions in dealing with Congress during his first term. His first and greatest defeat had been the rejection of his appointment of Albert Gallatin as Secretary of State. Gallatin, who had been born in Geneva, had been Secretary of Treasury during all of Jefferson's Presidency and had served with utmost skill and diligence in that capacity. He most certainly was among Jefferson's most valued counselors and advisers, second only to Madison, in all matters of governmental affairs, with particular skill in dealing with France and England. Many Republican Senators did not like Gallatin; they thought of him as a foreigner who was mean-spirited, greedy and uncompromising. Although they rejected his appointment, Gallatin stayed on to serve Madison well by continuing in his capacity as Treasury Secretary.

The Senate also rejected a Supreme Court appointment of Madison's, and they defeated a plan for a bank of the United States. As conflict with England and France heightened, Madison had asked for approval of a 10,000-man army; but Congress demanded that the army be increased to 25,000, further embarrassing the Chief Executive. On the other hand, Congress failed to provide taxes to pay for increased preparedness as an additional display of disdain for the soft-spoken President. Congress was determined to let everyone know where the the power lay.

Although Madison smarted under the reversals he experienced at the hands of a powerful and activist Congress, there is evidence that he accepted Congressional power more readily than would most Presidents. First, because he wanted unity and peace in government and harmony in his relations with Congress; and, second, because he accepted the will of a Congress which, in his judgment, was simply following the architecture of government derived from the Constitution which he helped write. He interpreted that document in a most literal fashion and suffered the consequences. He had become the very example of an executive suffering the tyranny of a powerful Congress. His now conformist, compliant personality overcame the action-oriented founding father he had been.

Despite his weak stance with Congress, Madison attempted to grapple more firmly and creatively with ever more challenging and complex events surrounding American shipping to France and Great Britain. U.S. vessels suffered their greatest losses as both the British and French now plundered men and cargo. Madison was not a man of strategy or cunning. He did not readily see the broad picture. The British and the French had subverted his many attempts to settle their differences. During his first term they each had tricked him into believing that a rapprochement was possible, only to find that their chicanery and his own misjudgment had frustrated his plans. The British were stirring up Indian uprisings in the West, they asserted power over the Mississippi, and they subverted U.S. trade with other nations. Britain, not France, became the greater threat. Neither embargoes nor trade blockades and restrictions would lessen the great humiliation Americans were suffering at the hands of these foreign powers. War appeared the last and only option open to a weak and vacillating and quite naive President who faced an uncompromising enemy and a Congress determined to go to war. In June of 1812, Madison sent a message of war to Congress.

It was not "Mr. Madison's war" as his Federalist, New England enemies would claim. Congress was more leader than follower in the declaration of the War of 1812, as it was with much of the legislation during Madison's terms in office. Although it was a Congress bent on combat that finally declared war, Madison believed that war was the only alternative. His aim, to quote historian Robert Rutland, was "to prove that the United States was a sovereign nation, deserving the respect of the world community." Yet, as one who adhered to a strict interpretation of the Constitution, Madison was ideologically throttled with the war, regardless of its consequences.

A group of strong leaders in Congress, led by Henry Clay and known as the "War Hawks," had pressed for war against England for some time. There were those who believed the "War Hawks" had a hidden agenda for that war, namely, to open the country to greater expansion to the West and South and most definitely North to include Canada. Florida, the Western Territories and even Canada might be the spoils of a successful war. A minority view holds that Madison was forced into war by the Senate Hawks, with his nomination as President for a second term in the balance. One might give little credence to this Federalist view, however, inasmuch as no one appeared on the scene as a reasonably strong alternate candidate. Madison, an experienced diplomat and America's best expert on Britain and France, understood the British threat; but it was the "War Hawks" who believed that the British had denied the United States any alternative to war. To these members of Congress, the choice was between retaining national self-respect and sovereignty or going to war. And so the war began.

★ ★ ★ ★ ★

III.

Madison won the November 1812 election to his second term by an electoral vote of 128 to 29 over his opponent, DeWitt Clinton, despite a crushing defeat of the army at Detroit. That attack had been part of an effort to take the Northwest area and Canada, a primary objective of the war. The commander of the army had shown unusual incompetence, a problem which plagued the weak President and nation through much of the war. Moreover, Madison saw war as a gentlemen's game in which violence would play only a small part. His civility and his thoughtful manner prevailed in much of the management of the war.

The war against Great Britain was fought across the Canadian border, where the early defeat in Detroit had occurred in the Great Lakes and in Western New York state and the Lake Champlain region, an access point to Montreal. Madison had wanted the emphasis of the war to be waged in the area of the Great Lakes and Montreal; but leaders in Kentucky and Ohio had persuaded the President that their Northwest region had to be secured from the Indians and the British, despite the difficulties of fighting in that wilderness.

Meanwhile, Napoleon retreated from Moscow in 1813, permitting the British to release a sizeable flotilla to set sail for the coast of the United States, where it successfully blockaded the harbors and systematically bombarded coastal towns. As the conflict wore on, Czar Alexander of Russia offered to mediate a peace and Madison accepted, appointing John Quincy Adams to head the peace negotiations. Both the war and the negotiations continued, with one having no effect upon the other.

The year 1813 surprisingly produced some marked success for the Americans. U.S. forces near Detroit regrouped and marched to York (now Toronto) and burned the city. More capable generals joined the military, including Winfield Scott (who was later to command the troops for Lincoln at the start of the Civil War) and Andrew Jackson, Madison's own choice to lead the troops in the South. Oliver Hazard Perry defeated and captured the British fleet on Lake Erie, cutting off the supply route to British forces and their Indian allies in the Northwest, thus assuring the impending fall of Detroit to American forces. He reported his victory with the famous phrase: "We have met the enemy and they are ours."

By the fall of 1813, the war turned sour, however. The British defeated the U.S. forces headed toward Montreal and destroyed Buffalo. Congress refused to pass a conscription law, refused to expand the size of the navy and rejected new taxes. The British, after a delay, determined that they would not permit the Russian Czar to act as intermediary, demanding that the Americans negotiate directly with them. The peace process moved to Ghent, Belgium, and the war continued as 1814 approached.

The new year brought peace to Europe with the final defeat of Napoleon at Waterloo. The British were now ready to turn their full force against the young country, with punishment and possibly destruction of its former colony becoming a primary goal. The British did not send an imposing invasion army, but they did make several momentous moves. A well-trained force was sent to Canada, ending what appeared to be a successful American effort to capture major cities in that country. The British also sent a naval and military force to the Chesapeake Bay. Fifty vessels, including twenty transports with 4,000 troops, anchored just 35 miles east of Washington, D.C.

Madison had reviewed the defense of Washington with great care and concluded that the leadership and training of American forces were inadequate. America had over 10,000 troops ready to defend the Capital. The British had no cavalry and should have been a force that United States troops could repel. Although the commanding general of the defending U.S. forces was incompetent, Madison trusted his Secretary of War and officers, accepting their opinion that Washington was secure, rejecting his own judgment that the city was in grave danger.

The U. S. troops were made up of militia from neighboring states, and a combination of the governors' failure to give authority to the commanding general to lead the various militias, coupled with the failure of the commanding general to take command led to chaos. On August 24, 1814, the British invaded Washington. They entered the White House, ate the food which Dolley Madison had prepared for dinner, still warm, then set fire to the executive mansion, gutting it. They burned the Capitol building, causing the dome to fall to its total destruction, and they burned almost all of the other government buildings. The British troops departed for their ships the next morning, leaving the nation's Capital in ruin.

Madison had shown considerable courage throughout the ordeal, riding horseback throughout much of a four-day period, giving essential encouragement to the troops and the citizenry, many of whom were ready to capitulate to the enemy. One has to marvel at the strength shown by a frail man of 63 years. Madison understood the threat to the Capital apparently better than anyone else in command, but he bowed to the authority of his officers rather than trust his own judgment concerning the defense of Washington. As early as May, Madison had warned his Cabinet of the potential danger to the seat of government. He foolishly trusted advice given by the secretaries of war and navy and the military, even though he had concluded that a satisfactory defense was not being devised.

The very qualities which permitted Madison to formulate a Constitution which balanced one power against another, spreading authority between branches of governments and states, never leaving final authority in the hands of a single individual, failed him as he led the country in war. He rejected the concept of a strong executive. Reflective thought, balancing of authority, should have given way as advancing forces overtook the army defending the federal Capital.

Madison's rather mechanistic personality, dependent on deliberate rational moves, did not fit the time of war where great flexibility and determined forceful executive actions are required. War did not fit his nature; he was constantly overwhelmed by the reality of war.

But as reality changed, his personality began to work well for him. With all of the destruction and terror and disarray, Madison came out the winner. He overruled Congress and insisted that the government continue to meet in Washington rather than at some safer haven. The government went back to work. While the British sought a failure of confidence within the leadership of the almost twenty-five-year-old country, Madison had denied the British their goal in attacking and burning Washington by providing the confidence which frustrated the British plan. On September 13, American troops successfully defended Baltimore and Fort McHenry, repelling a fierce attack, giving rise to the writing of the "Star Spangled Banner." Remarkably, Madison seemed to have regained some of the confidence and courage which marked so much of his public life prior to his presidency.

While enemy troops were being repulsed near Baltimore, a British naval force supporting an army moving from Montreal toward Albany was defeated on Lake Champlain; and 10,000 British troops, trained in battle against Napoleon, were repulsed prior to reaching Albany. The trouncing of this force, which represented the most potent British effort of the war, was the turning point in the conflict.

In the meantime, Andrew Jackson, in command of the army at New Orleans, beat the Creek Indians and captured the territory which would become Alabama. As a principal part of their strategy to punish the United States, the British had sent a powerful force to invade and capture New Orleans. The British force was arriving at the New Orleans port as Jackson and his troops were headed for Pensacola, Florida. In the greatest battle of the war, Jackson defeated the British, leaving them with the death of their general and 700 troops, the wounding of 1,400 and the capture of 500 others. Seven American troops were killed; only six were wounded.

Although the war had actually ended two weeks earlier in mid-January of 1815, the victory was momentous. Jackson had restored self-respect to the country and rescued the President from disgrace. The Mississippi was open to unchallenged navigation, and the American continent was now without interference from the European powers for the first time in its history.

The peace treaty, which was ratified by the Senate in February 1815, restored American territory occupied by the British and recognized American rights to the Mississippi, the Great Lakes and Newfoundland fishing banks. The two countries were now on equal footing commercially, and, to quote historian Ralph Ketchem,"...the United States, by standing up to Britain, had won a second war of independence".

The war had gone far better for the country than could have been imagined in the many moments of despair during the fifteen months of conflict. The army had won some major victories; the navy gave stellar performances, handling the British its only defeat in twenty years; and the government functioned, though obliquely at times, to fulfill its duties without ever diminishing democratic and individual values and rights. Madison survived the ordeal to become a hero for an America that was on the threshold of great economic expansion in trade and in manufacturing which had grown during the war to fill the void created by a British embargo. Now a victorious nation and at peace, the British navy treated America's merchant ships with respect and courtesy.

Surprisingly to many, Madison became a rather forceful manager during his remaining term of office. Times had changed and he might once again depend on rational ideology in a well-ordered world, where the Constitution and the separation of powers would function without threat of conflict from abroad. He had found the consensus which fostered the reason that he and Jefferson so prized. He dispatched the navy to the Barbary Coast, where the fierce attack on the shores of Tripoli ended once and for all the interference with American commerce in the Mediterranean dating back to Washington's days. He promoted the strong involvement of government in the improvement of roads and canals and in the establishment of a bank of the United States.

There were those who criticized a new Madison for subscribing to Federalist doctrine by embracing big government as his old enemy Hamilton had done. These critics saw Madison as inconsistent and traitorous to his own causes. This negative view is contested by many historians, however, and with justification. Madison's perspective as a Founding Father and compatriot of Jefferson was derived from his experience as a Virginia farmer and by the fact that the majority of Americans were farmers. He was well-schooled in the despotic rule of the British and sought to protect rule by the majority, at that time the farmer. Madison believed that governmental power should expand only with moderate speed, so as not to disturb the growth and freedom of the individual as a self-governing creature. The growth must be slow, allowing government to develop laws and activities prudently, and within the strict interpretation of the Constitution, to serve the common good.

There is no question that this was now a Madison who no longer feared the growth of manufacturing and of a working force without prospects. Times had changed, and he responded rationally to the change. The war gave Madison courage and taught him the importance of strong financial institutions, with a central bank to meet the pressing financial drain of war. He discovered the relevance of domestic manufacturing to the growth of the nation independent of Europe. He held stewardship over a nation that grew in population and geography and understood the need for transportation across an expanding country.

Despite his encouragement of roads and canals and the growth of industry and of a new United States Bank, Madison shocked many in Congress in his last year in office by vetoing a major piece of legislation. Congress had passed a law designed to finance the construction of the very roads and canals which Madison had encouraged. The law proposed a rather unique use of U.S. bank dividends for these internal purposes, and Madison, holding to a strict interpretation of the Constitution, believed that the law so altered the function of government as to require a Constitutional amendment. While Madison had changed his view of industry and commerce and the composition of the majority, he maintained a strict interpretation of the Constitution.

Madison's final year saw the Treasury achieve a ten-million-dollar surplus derived from the duties which trade produced; he retained an army and navy to protect the nation and encouraged the growth of West Point with its training and discipline. He had promoted the expansion of the country, but not at the expense of the Constitution and its "limiting and defined" character.

James Monroe, who had served Madison faithfully as his Secretary of State and concurrently as Secretary of War, successfully won the Presidency in 1820, assuring the continuation of the Republican principles laid down during sixteen years under Jefferson and Madison. Madison relished his final days in office. He almost frolicked at the farewell parties, appearing the proud preserver of the Union he had helped to create.

John Adams, the Federalist former President, wrote to Jefferson, praising Madison in these words: "Not withstanding a thousand faults and blunders..., Madison acquired more glory, and established more union, than all three predecessors, Washington, Adams, and Jefferson, put together."

During his last two years in office, Madison was the beloved Founding Father and President who had preserved the nation's most precious values of a free and functioning government. He had provided peace and prosperity and had moved the country to a new plateau of pride, self-confidence and achievement.

Reader's Score of James Madison

Defense: _____

Economic: _____

Vision: _____

Communication: _____

Lead Congress: _____

Lead without Popularity: _____

Invincibility: _____

Consistency: _____

Self-Confidence: _____

Strengthen Nation: _____

TOTAL POINTS: _____

James Monroe

James Monroe

The struggle between nationalism and agrarian democracy which underlay the conflict between the Federalists and the Democrat-Republicans and their protagonists Adams and Hamilton, Jefferson and Madison continued during the administration of James Monroe. Hamilton supported a strong federal government with a powerful financial and merchant foundation led by the wealthy, educated class. His followers were comprised of a northeast populace with strong ties to England. On the other hand, Jefferson and Madison fought for a broad-based democracy with states retaining more power than the national government.

The political disputes did not deter the growth of the economy of the nation which expanded steadily during the terms of Washington, John Adams, Jefferson and Madison, growth which was accomplished with a minimal involvement of government. In those early days of the republic, international events absorbed a disproportionate share of attention of those who were chief magistrates of the nation.

The war of 1812, which had inspired patriotism, provided an agreeable, though brief, resolution of the conflict defined by Hamilton and Jefferson. Manufacturing had thrived and blossomed in New England.

Southern plantations flourished as well. The peace and prosperity which characterized the last two years of Madison's presidency continued through much of James Monroe's first term, which began in 1817. The mood of the country reflected gratitude over its success in the war and pride in its economic progress. It was a period well named the "Era of Good Feeling." For some time after the war Americans experienced a national purpose and a unity of goals encompassing economic and geographic expansion destined to harness the nation's strengths and resources. Ominously, however, while the national economic and physical expansion was underway with the assistance of an active federal government, the spirit of nationalism was about to run into conflict with regional interests.

The nation was experiencing rapid western expansion. Fulton's steam boat provided transportation on the rivers, but those without access to waterways demanded road and canal transportation for their goods. New England manufacturers cooperated with federal expenditures for these improvements until the tax for such distant access became burdensome. The New Englanders demanded a protective tariff to fend off ever more competitive British goods. The southern farmer had acceded to the westerner's demand for roads and canals and to the northern petition for tariffs until their own interests came to bear. The roads did not help the southern planter nor did the tariffs. For a number of years after the war of 1812, the national interests predominated, but the "Era of Good Feeling" began to unravel as Monroe's first term drew to an end. Sectionalism and regionalism were overtaking the national perspective.

Monroe had been a staunch anti-Federalist during Washington's tenure as President, and he developed a strong dislike of the first President for his apparent support of a powerful federal government. While the United States was expanding, so too was its perception of the role of government. Following this mood, Monroe, like Madison before him, changed his philosophy radically by the time of his presidency, becoming the leader of a wing of the Democrat-Republican Party sympathetic to nationalism. He saw an expanded role for the national government emanating from the expansion of business and industry and from the impact of westward expansion.

He strongly promoted an activist role for the federal government in all manner of economic growth for the country. He encouraged the building of roads, bridges and canals to assist the expanding West, and he fostered tariffs to aid manufacturing in New England. Unfortunately for Monroe, the nationalist wing of the Democrat-Republican party ran headlong into conflict with the old line party members who continued their battle against nationalism and a powerful federal government, continuing their devotion to the farmer, the once dominant economic group in the country. Sectionalism was on the rise. It was soon to be northerners against westerners against southerners, all with a weakened allegiance to a much altered Democrat-Republican party. It was a time of transition for the nation, a transition that would test the character of James Monroe.

Monroe was the last of the Revolutionary War leaders to serve the country as its President. He had served as governor of Virginia, as secretary of state under Madison and had accepted the additional responsibility of secretary of war after the national Capital fell prey to the British. He had conducted himself admirably as a military leader in that debacle, renewing his skills learned during the Revolutionary War where he had served valiantly as an officer under General Washington. Monroe had given Madison unique assistance, acting almost as his assistant, by providing leadership and counsel for all the departments of government during much of Madison's presidency.

Monroe stood about six feet tall, but, being stoop-shouldered, appeared shorter. He had a kindly face which, though deeply lined, was delicate and refined. Although he lacked the great intellect of Jefferson and Madison and many of the great statesmen of his era, he exhibited the steady, patient studious qualities of Washington. Monroe was slow to reach a decision, but was quite decisive once he had reached a conclusion. He was deeply devoted to understanding all sides and then hammering out a program that would incorporate as much as possible of the diversity that was beginning to reveal itself during his first term.

He sought consensus within his cabinet and with Congress during his first term. Washington listened to his advisors and to a wide range of views that surrounded him; but generally he took his own counsel after weighing the alternatives, reaching a decision that was not always a compromise. Monroe rarely permitted his own perspective to prevail over the balancing of forces that presented themselves. His calm deliberation and his compromises to achieve consensus were an effective tool of leadership during his first term. His character was well suited to that "Era of Good Feeling."

★ ★ ★ ★ ★

Early in his administration, which began in 1817, Monroe had secured Florida from Spain, an acquisition passionately sought by both Jefferson and Madison. He supported new nations in South America which had broken from Spanish colonization, and he presided over the Missouri Compromise which held the slavery issue in abatement for thirty years. The expansion westward opened the very sensitive issue of whether slavery would be allowed in new states being formed there. Northern and western states opposed the expansion of slavery; southern states obviously fought for its expansion. Monroe stood by as Congress achieved its temporary resolution of this test of sectionalism versus nationalism.

Monroe believed in giving firm guidance to Congress, the first President to take this stance. He carefully thought through legislative proposals he deemed appropriate for the country and, unlike Jefferson, willingly expended his political influence and prestige to see legislation through to success. A combination of courage which he had consistently displayed in the military, coupled with his political insight and his skills in achieving compromise, set a potentially successful path for Monroe as President. In his first term he was able to select his issues with Congress, thereby avoiding political and legislative failure. Nevertheless, his near unanimous victory in the election of 1820 won him no friends in Congress nor influence over it during his second term, as political combat among the members and jockeying for political position and power took precedence over presidential priorities.

★ ★ ★ ★ ★

Monroe ran unopposed for his second term in the fall of 1820, with electors casting all but one vote for him (he was the only President other than Washington to have run unopposed). This was no indication of ground-swell enthusiasm, however, for the election was of little consequence in the minds of most citizens. Washington had feared that political parties were detrimental to democracy. A strange test of his feeling about party politics would be visited upon Monroe in his second term, for it was, at least in part, the very absence of political parties which produced apathy during the 1820 election. The Federalist party came close to extinction in the last days of the War of 1812, due primarily to their apparently cowardly opposition to the war. The absence of political parties to seek actively party allegiance resulted in voter apathy.

The general disinterest in Monroe's second term election reflected complacency about the national government and the presidency, if not Congress; for there was no spirited competition over who would be President. Americans might have respected Monroe, but he hardly inspired the electorate as did Washington and Jefferson. His reflective and calm deliberate nature did not excite the populace. More to the point, the Republican party now carried under its umbrella the new "nationalist, strong government" wing made up of northerners and westerners as well as the old guard agrarian southern wing. It was actually two parties in one, a challenging and unique set of circumstances for a President who sought compromise and consensus.

During Monroe's second term, Congressmen fought each other for power and over which faction within their own party would prevail. Of the conflict within the party, Jefferson went so far as to state: "The Federalists are with us, only now they are part of the Democrat-Republican party." Henry Clay, that most prominent speaker of the House of Representatives, stated that Monroe might have won the presidency overwhelmingly, but he had not won over Congress, nor would he influence Congress. The ability of a President to control his own party would become a benchmark of success or failure for Presidents. Monroe failed this test during his second term. Only dynamic and assertive Presidents withstand a Congress determined to usurp power, a concern which Madison pointed out in his Forty-eighth *Federalist* paper. Monroe was persuasive, thoughtful and compromising, but hardly a match for the powerful Congress he faced in his second term, a Congress determined to usurp the power of the presidency to advance sectional authority.

★ ★ ★ ★ ★

The difficulties with Congress in his second term notwithstanding, Monroe is most remembered for his skill in foreign policy during both of his terms in office. In this endeavor, he believed firmly in dealing from a position of strength. He promoted an expanded military, navy and coastal defense, at least by standards befitting the small thirty-year-old nation of that day. His military stance and his eminent success in foreign matters reflected Monroe's extensive experience in foreign affairs, his having represented first Washington as Minister to Paris and then Jefferson as negotiator in Paris to help bring about the

Louisiana Purchase. He is credited by some with the swift and successful purchase of that territory. This experience came to bear on the
subject of the developing independence of South American nations.

In his first term, Monroe witnessed the crumbling of Spanish might,
which led to the break-away of Spanish colonies in South America.
The weakness of Spain engendered a fear that European powers, particularly France and possibly England, would step in to assist Spain to
retake its colonies or to colonize them for themselves. Monroe displayed capable diplomacy during his first term when the United States
was forced to walk a tight-rope with the South American revolutionaries, fearing that support for insurgents might threaten the ability to
negotiate a treaty to acquire Florida from Spain. But such a treaty
with Spain was ratified in February of 1821 shortly before Monroe
was sworn in for his second term, giving the United States the freedom to recognize the nations of Buenos Aires, Chile, Peru, Mexico
and Columbia.

Recognition of the new South American nations was more than a
diplomatic act, for this ratification of the new nations reflected
America's self-confidence and national pride expressed as empathy and
kinship toward the freedom-seeking nations which had followed
America's example. In contrast, the nation had lacked sufficient self-
confidence during the French Revolution to give national support for
that revolt. America now could assert itself as free and independent
by encouraging and applauding the liberty of Latin American countries. Latin American policy was steeped in deep seated hostility toward European intervention into the Western Hemisphere, but in
addition there was also some comfort for Americans in Monroe's foreign policy which diverted attention from the evolving sectional disputes within the nation.

As his second term progressed, Monroe was ready for a next step
in Latin American policy. The problems with Spain and France came
to a head as the military and political power of Spain weakened fur-

ther. Once again, Monroe feared for the security of the new South American nations and of foreign incursions on the continent. Would Spain be assisted by its European neighbors in repossessing its South American colonies? Would another European nation assert itself as a colonial power in the Western Hemisphere?

The British suggested that the United States join them in defending the independence of the new nations, a plan which Jefferson and others recommended. Monroe, however, rejected this advice, determined to pursue an independent policy toward Latin America. What resulted was communicated in his annual message to Congress on December 2, 1823. The strongly worded policy, which came to be known as the Monroe Doctrine in the 1850s, was first expressed in the draft language prepared by John Quincy Adams, Secretary of State, and later incorporated in Monroe's speech: "The American Continent by the free and independent condition which they have assumed, and maintained, are henceforth not to be considered as subject to future colonization by any European power." Monroe further stated: "We could not view any interposition for the purpose of oppressing them [the South American States], or controlling in any other manner their destiny by any European power, in any other light than as a manifestation of an unfriendly disposition towards the United States."

The American public enthusiastically supported the policy of recognition and independence for its Latin American neighbors. The nation was displaying its courage and new found maturity in expressing an independence from Europe and from Great Britain, in particular. The declaration that Monroe enunciated was influenced by Adams; but it was Monroe's policy primarily, one which he had enhanced by avoiding a joint pact with England concerning South America. Unlike any European proclamation of similar content, the doctrine was not a statement of imperial intent. Rather, the President was enunciating what historians would refer to as giving the nation "moral character. . .the nation had achieved an American identity." Diplomatic

achievement notwithstanding, while the nation rejoiced over this foreign policy triumph, sectionalism was rising as an ominous threat to
domestic tranquility.

* * * * *

Monroe's final two years in office were significantly overshadowed
by the impending Presidential election of 1824. The candidates seeking the office of the President were John C. Calhoun, Secretary of
War; John Quincy Adams, Secretary of State; William C. Crawford,
Secretary of the Treasury; Henry Clay, the powerful Speaker of the
House of Representatives; and Andrew Jackson, Governor of Florida
and later U. S. Senator. Jackson, Crawford and Calhoun reflected
the sectionalist, anti-big government wing of the party. Adams and
Clay were supporters of the new nationalism, promoting an expanded
role for government.

Jackson, Crawford and even Clay, who were candidates in conflict
with Monroe's policies during his final two years as President, used an
anti-Monroe platform overtly hostile to the President in promoting
their own positions and as a means to discredit Adams and Calhoun,
who remained loyal to Monroe. The open warfare which the three
candidates waged against the legislative proposals and appointments
of the President set the pattern for the final years for Monroe which
John Quincy Adams referred to as the "Era of Bad Feeling." The
rivalries of these candidates gave Monroe considerable personal discomfort and all but destroyed his legislative agenda.

It should be noted that Monroe's Western Hemisphere initiative
was exempted from attack by the three candidates. Clay led the group
in Congress that proposed recognition of Latin American States and
saw to it that the President's policies on South America sailed swiftly
through Congress. But that is where Monroe's accord with Clay and
the legislative branch ended; for during Monroe's final two years, Con-

gress saw fit to cut Monroe's appropriations for the army and the navy and rejected two minor appointees to the army. Of greater moment, however, was the rejection of a treaty with Great Britain involving slave trading and legislation related to the American Indian.

Slave trade had become an American scandal, even among most southerners. It was condemned as inhumane and barbaric in the Treaty of Ghent which ended the War of 1812. During his second term, Monroe proposed a treaty with Britain to permanently settle a wide variety of disputes between the two nations. These included certain border disputes in Maine and Oregon and Britain's right to assist the United States in its fight against slave traders by confiscating that bounty on the high seas. The plan would designate slave trading as piracy, thus permitting any nation, and, in this case, Britain, to halt and search any vessel suspected of being involved in slave trading.

Some members of Congress believed that such searches would violate American sovereignty unless legislation was passed designating slave-trading as piracy. The Senate had previously approved such a concept, and Monroe felt his treaty with Britain would be readily approved as well. Senatorial supporters of Crawford for President, seeing defeat of the treaty with its slave trade measure as a way to embarrass Adams and the President, succeeded in defeating the measure on the first vote, squelching the rapprochement with England which Monroe so desperately sought.

The British were shocked by the Senate's action, as the treaty had been written by the United States and was ready for implementation. British leadership found the rejection to be deeply offensive and refused to consider any renegotiation of the treaty, to settle other matters associated with it or to cooperate with the United States in the reduction of slave trading. Crawford's presidential candidacy was strengthened, while Monroe's worthy plans for enhancing relations with Great Britain were destroyed.

The Crawford candidacy delivered a final embarrassment for Monroe. The President had long suggested a rather unique resolution of the problems related to the settlement of the American Indian. The customary and longstanding governmental policy had been to remove Indian tribes from any area east of the Mississippi, now the focus of vibrant development. Monroe had recommended early in his administration that the Indians be treated as individuals, not as tribes, and that they be provided land for settlement among the whites. He hoped this would engender an assimilation of Indians into the culture, industry and mores of the white community.

The plan was rejected by the Crawford forces and was also rejected by the states, and, in a final battle for Monroe, the State of Georgia demanded the forceful removal of the Cherokee Indians without regard to joint negotiation for the payment of their land. He resisted the petitions for violence against the Indians proposed by the pro-Crawford Georgia leaders. Monroe endured once again the personal attacks from within Congress over his ability and leadership, attacks which had characterized the impending campaign for the presidency.

* * * * *

Surprisingly, none of the candidates received a majority of the electors' votes in the fateful election of 1824. Jackson received 99 electoral votes; Adams, 84; Crawford, 41; and Clay, 37. Without any candidate receiving a majority, the election was thrown into the House of Representatives which elected John Quincy Adams as President, finally removing the burden of the presidential campaign from the shoulders of Monroe.

* * * * *

In retrospect, it is difficult to perceive the tragedy that Monroe felt he had endured in his final years as President. By historical standards, the legislative defeats he suffered were hardly monumental, for much of his time in office Madison had been treated as harshly. But Monroe was a man deeply sensitive to the attacks and criticisms directed against him and his legislation as he became the fulcrum for the presidential campaign. Although Monroe's vast experience in government and his persuasive ability to achieve consensus may well have been the most appropriate stewardship available to the nation at that moment in American history, it was not equal to the challenges of his second term. The power of sectionalism evolved and gained such force in his second term that Monroe became little more than a pawn in the conflict. This festering wound would not respond to the call for a nationalistic spirit elicited by James Monroe.

John Quincy Adams gave James Monroe high praise in his Inaugural Address. He commended the outgoing President for acquiring Florida, for extending the boundaries of the nation to the Pacific, for lowering taxes while reducing the national debt by sixty million dollars, for strengthening the national defenses, for recognizing and encouraging Latin American states and for advancing humanitarian efforts to suppress the slave trade. He had left the country better off than he had found it, which stands to this day as a measure of a President.

Monroe was not one of America's great Presidents; but much of his administration was noteworthy for its political skill, its adroit foreign policy and its enhancement of American self-confidence and pride. James Monroe represented the last of the Revolutionary figures to serve as President, which was almost symbolic, for his administration stood at a crossroads in American history. The apathy of the electorate of 1820 would give way to a reconfigured nationalism and to sectionalism. The nation was on a threshold of a new perspective of democracy and individualism.

Reader's Score of James Monroe

Defense: _____

Economic: _____

Vision: _____

Communication: _____

Lead Congress: _____

Lead without Popularity: _____

Invincibility: _____

Consistency: _____

Self-Confidence: _____

Strengthen Nation: _____

TOTAL POINTS: _____

Andrew Jackson

Andrew Jackson

The nation was forty years old when Andrew Jackson was elected president in 1828. The decades became an incubator for startling changes in the lives of its citizens. The federal government had ruled with a very light hand, with the affairs of Europe usurping much of the efforts of the Chief Executive. The Louisiana Purchase, the War of 1812 and the growth of nationalism within the western hemisphere dominated the first forty years of the nation. Amid these national and international undertakings, the people of the nation were experiencing momentous personal and social changes. The very fabric of their lives was being rent by swiftly moving economic and social upheaval. For many, the secure, predictable agricultural life which most Americans enjoyed through the first decade of the 19th century was being replaced. Young people left home to find new means of self-support. They moved to the cities to become workers in factories or to become mechanics or craftsmen. They risked their lives and that of their wives and children to settle in Kentucky, Tennessee, Missouri, Ohio and Indiana. The underpinning of their moral values, of their comfort and of their self identity based on family, community and religion, was being shaken.

These new generations experienced loneliness, fear, upheaval, a need for effective independence and a need to earn money to "go ahead" as a measure of who they were, as a source of security lost when they left "home." These people no longer felt needed or wanted. They looked to themselves for their sustenance. As a result, it was a materialistic, individualistic, independent and self-reliant breed that made up the mass of Americans by the mid-1820s when Andrew Jackson strode upon the political scene.

Jackson had most of the same experiences as did this new majority. He trusted his own strengths but distrusted government, expanding industry, monopolies of any kind, centralization of banking and paper money. The worker, Western farmer, Eastern craftsmen and mechanic all had similar feelings about government, large institutions and money. They had no ability to create wealth other than by the sweat of their brow or their own hard work and application of skill. They observed the wealthy elitist classes and demanded equality. They saw the "idle rich" benefitting from a government bank; they saw their hard-earned tax payments helping the privileged class, and they were moved to respond. They believed wealth should be for all; they detested special privilege and political privilege. They opposed monopolies and institutions of inequality.

On the other hand, Henry Clay was the leader of a movement in the Senate to coalesce the nation's economic sections. He, along with James Monroe and John Quincy Adams, saw a nation in which a tariff would be levied on imported manufactured goods to benefit the evolving factories of the East. The South would sell its crops to the flourishing North, and the taxes would be spent on the internal improvements of roads, bridges and canals to serve the expanding Western regions.

The concept of Clay and his followers was popular at first, but it soon was opposed by Southerners who felt that the tariff merely raised the price of the goods they bought from abroad without providing significant benefit in their sale of their crops to the North. And the urban worker, the mechanic and the new Western farmer, who were independent, self-reliant and individualistic, could not embrace a program that used their tax money or the tariffs on goods they bought to expand the role of government, whether the new roads served them or not. The fight against the expansion of government took on all of the flavor of Jefferson's battle against Hamilton, but times were quite different. The American System of Clay and Adams and Monroe was a democratic one. These were patriots who wished to promote the welfare of the common man through a government that sought to provide for the common good. They took a national view of the economy, balancing and fulfilling the needs of all. But the new mass of people, uprooted, materialistic, self-serving, self-fulfilling - indeed with a religious and moralistic fervor - looked with disfavor on a federal government that might encroach upon their lives and their money to benefit the privileged few.

This was the setting for the election of Andrew Jackson, the rugged Westerner, as the seventh president of the United States in 1828.

Andrew Jackson had become a national hero by defeating the British troops paradoxically after the War of 1812 had ended. He had shown decisiveness and integrity as a leader of his troops in that conflict, and the American public rallied around him in the election of 1828. He defeated the incumbent John Quincy Adams by 178 to 83 electoral votes. Jackson had run for the presidency four years earlier, winning the largest number of electoral votes; but he failed to win a majority, losing the election to the nation's highest office in a run-off vote by the House of Representatives which chose Adams. Jackson and his followers were furious over the events which denied him the presidency.

The election of 1828 was the first in which the electors were chosen either by state legislatures or mass meetings in each state, replacing the selection by congressional delegations. This change reflected well a nation moving steadily toward greater enfranchisement of the population. The impact of this movement was well-expressed in the election of 1828 with a vast portion of white males over the age of 21 now eligible voters for the first time. The exclusive right of property owners to vote had become a thing of the past.

America was moving rapidly into a new era of economic, political and social mores reflected in the democratization and expansion of the electorate; but another major change characterized this trend in political and social reality as well. Credentials dating to the founding of the nation would no longer bear witness to the leadership skills of a particular candidate, as it had for James Monroe, the last of the Revolutionary War figures to serve as President. Instead, party organization began to replace status as a Founding Father as evidence for selecting a candidate for high office.

Andrew Jackson rode well these sea-changes in the political scene. He gathered around himself leaders from the North, South and West in his political conquest, and he appealed to that new mass of voters swelling the political landscape. John C. Calhoun, from South Carolina, was his Vice-Presidential running mate; and Martin Van Buren, that powerful political strategist, was to deliver New York. The country had expanded westward, and the new frontier states felt quite at home with this man from Tennessee as President.

The economy of the nation had changed to a remarkable degree over its forty-some years. Powerful landowners and New England traders no longer dominated. The workers and small tradesmen, though without property, now made up a significant part of the electorate and were becoming an economic and political factor. Americans had two objectives: equality and money. The landed gentry, the Southern farmer and the big businessman were doing well in attaining these goals for themselves; but the growing mass of the population was now ready to demand equality in all matters, particularly equality of opportunity. They demanded that government no longer give favored treatment to the wealthy elite. Hamilton had affirmed a policy which offered business a friendly and helping hand from government. Now it was the worker, small farmer and middle class that demanded recognition as well.

Jackson had been a successful lawyer and judge in Nashville. His famous military efforts had caused him to be appointed Governor of Florida for a brief period. He had been elected to the House of Representatives during the Washington Administration and became a strong critic of the President over his foreign policy and his handling of Indian affairs. Jackson was later elected to the United States Senate, serving just prior to his Presidential election.

Among his critics, the general had developed a reputation of being hot-headed, vulgar, impulsive and, occasionally, violent. He had fought at least three duels, killing one man in the process. His opponents charged that he had not shown consistency, energy or skill, except in his military duties. As he assumed the Presidency, some felt that Jackson had given little indication of policies or objectives for the country. He had stated that he believed in little or no debt for the country; he had opposed public improvements financed by the Federal government; and he had expressed faith in the common man. Although these themes were hardly the makings of a dynamic new administration, they clearly, intuitively absorbed the very essence and spirit of the new electorate; and they would be the underpinnings of dramatic changes in government.

Jackson had a failed investment experience earlier in his life which gave particular emphasis to his opposition to debt and his hostility toward paper money and debt. He shared this view with many of the newly enfranchised who distrusted the speculations of banks that issued currency so freely that many banks failed, wiping out the savings of average workers and families.

The election of 1828 had been fiercely fought. It was a bitter and personal combat, with the opposition making hay of his brusque and uncouth manner. But the vast majority of voters found him open and vigorous. Jackson, the practical non-thinker, seemed to be the very embodiment of their own ideas and experiences. Despite his reputation, Jackson had acquitted himself with dignity and urbanity as a Senator. And surprisingly, it was this facet of his personality which graced his frequently disciplined stewardship of the Presidency.

★ ★ ★ ★ ★

As Jackson became the Chief Executive, his thick gray hair was turning white. He was a tall man with bright blue eyes whose wrinkled face conveyed the age and pain he endured from old combat wounds. He coughed frequently, having suffered from tuberculosis, and had severe headaches; but he stood erect as the soldier he had been, looking all of his 61 years. His tall and firm bearing had earned him the nickname "Old Hickory" in his military days, a sobriquet which stayed with him throughout his life.

The first term was characterized by careful and diligent management, with Jackson showing perseverance. These qualities clearly surprised his enemies who looked upon him as merely a rough-hewn Westerner. He became notorious to his enemies for the rotation of many government employees, filling offices with citizens who had supported him in the election. "To the victor goes the spoils," or so it was said; and the policy of rotation came to be known as the Spoils System. The move democratized government, enabling newly enfranchised citizens to run the government. The "rich and wellborn" were denied their previous claim to governmental authority, and the mass of people was delighted. The actual number of displaced federal employees was no greater in number than had occurred during Jefferson's administration, but the impact on the future of the nation was resounding. The common man was taking over government, and the Spoils System was its symbol.

Jackson's first term is remembered for three major events. One was the establishment of the Spoils System; the second was his fight over the attempt by South Carolina to nullify a Federal law which it felt to be inimical to its own interests; and the third was the fight which Jackson waged against the Bank of the United States, or the B.U.S. as it was known.

South Carolina opposed tariffs passed by Congress, believing they would be detrimental to the economy of the state. The tariffs were declared null and void by the legislature of South Carolina. Ironically, Jackson, too, openly opposed expansion of the federal government into economic activity to benefit the rich, and this led him to resist protective tariffs that benefitted the eastern manufacturer. Yet this opponent of big government and of protective tariffs used the full power of the federal government to prevent the nullification of federal laws by South Carolina to resist high tariffs. Jackson acted at once to insure the implementation of federal laws by readying troops and ships to send to the state. His statement was clear: "Disunion by armed force is treason" and that blood must flow if the laws were resisted.

Henry Clay averted the confrontation by negotiating a compromise of the tariff rates which both the state and the federal government accepted, but not before the President had shown his resolve to use all of his authority to enforce a federal law. Jackson had moved with dispatch to delay a states' rights' battle which would fester for some thirty years before exploding into war. And he most assuredly gave nationalism a new tone.

It was the Bank of the United States and its charter, however, which marked most clearly the first and second terms of Andrew Jackson.

Shortly before the end of the first term, Jackson had vetoed legislation to renew the charter of the Bank of the United States. That institution, which had been formed in 1816 under James Madison, was part of the American System of Henry Clay, which also included the construction of roads, canals and bridges as a means of assisting the expansion of the nation and its business and commerce.

Jackson and the newly enfranchised voters were anti-monopoly, anti-corporation and anti-encroaching federal government; and some were anti-paper money. But Jackson's very widespread popular support included paper-money advocates, too, particularly from New England. However, in the fight against the Bank, these soft money proponents remained quietly in the background. Jackson and his supporters saw the Bank of the United States as the very embodiment of their discontent with monopoly, big government and institutions of special privilege. The Bank issued paper money, assisting big business, not the common man. It had wide and unfettered governmental authority with an obligation to answer only to its stockholders. The B.U.S. was a monopoly—worse still, a semi-governmental monopoly benefitting the few. It was given the epithet "Monster Bank."

Some allege that Jackson's feud with the Bank dated to a time early in his first term when a Democrat demanded a position in the Bank. When the request was refused, Jackson and the Democrats turned against the Bank. According to Jacksonians, moreover, the Bank had supported Jackson's political enemies and had failed to fund his supporters during the Presidential campaign. It thus became a political and moral, as well as an economic, vendetta that fostered Jackson's determination to discover a means to destroy the Bank. The Bank was anathema to the Jeffersonian ideals embraced by Jackson and his electorate, and Jackson put his entire energy and dedication into the conflict.

Jackson vetoed the renewal of the Bank charter, charging it to be a monopolistic private power usurping the authority of government to the unfair benefit of the rich and the big business community at the expense of the common man, the worker and the small farmer. In a precedent-setting act, Jackson declared the bank to be unconstitutional and contrary to the best interests of the majority. He thus clearly ended the domination of Congress over the presidency, which had prevailed from the last days of Jefferson's administration. Jackson had set a clear path for himself and his administration in his second term.

Jackson's battle to kill the Bank of the United States was a cause with thundering impact upon his second term. It was an issue that brought the President and the common man into a lock step that is rarely offered a President.

★ ★ ★ ★ ★

Jackson made the Bank the issue of his re-election campaign of 1832 when he was the candidate of the reorganized Democratic Party. His opponent was Henry Clay, the candidate of the newly formed National Republican Party. And each fought the battle as the chief spokesman for his respective political and economic interests. Clay appeared to speak for the wealthy and the business community, Jackson, for the common people; and Jackson won the election handily with an electoral vote of 219 to 49. It was the first election in which the candidates were nominated in national conventions, and it was the first election in which the two parties enticed the electorate to get out to vote, exciting them with parades and picnics. Jackson and his Vice President, Martin Van Buren, gained over 55% of the popular vote; but more than numbers were expressed by that vote. Jackson was adored by the populace. He understood the crowd, spoke their language and used the magnificent rallying point of a "Monster Bank" to anchor the attention and allegiance of the common man. But it was primarily Jackson's personal popularity, not the Bank issue, which won him the election.

★ ★ ★ ★ ★

Jackson's second term began with a direct confrontation between the Chief Executive and the president of the Bank of the United States, Nicholas Biddle, who, by some accounts, had done a commendable job of managing its affairs. The Bank's influence had expanded through the development of branches placed strategically throughout the country, while it carefully fostered the growth of money to discourage inflation. The B.U.S. had tight control over state banks, limiting their power to fund the financing requirements of the small farmer and businessman at a time when that economic sector was exploding. On the other hand, according to the Jacksonians, the Bank of the United States did provide ready funds for its clients and friends who controlled large enterprises and the newly developing corporations.

Whether valid or not, the working man believed he could not make ends meet because the rich could borrow so easily. The working man, the small farmer and businessman were persuaded that there was no banking help for them to reach their goals, to "go ahead." The worker without property, the small farmer from the West and East and the small merchant in New England all believed the Bank impinged upon their equality of economic opportunity by diverting funds from their needs to those of the wealthy. A class struggle of sorts was evolving in the country. Certainly sectionalism became a force, as local banks were denied funds while the Bank of the United States thrived. The discontent with the Bank among the majority of Americans was crystallized by Jackson - it was the touchstone for his relationship with the people. It brought them together, it gave them a common language, and it gave meaning and embodiment to the generalized striving for equality by the common man. Jackson preached of the evils of the Bank to his flock, and they listened and cheered him on.

America had a population of approximately fifteen million in twenty-four states as Jackson's second term began. It was a time when the corporation was taking over from privately held business. Morality for the individual no longer applied to the day-to-day affairs of the cold, impersonal corporation as it had for the enterprise run by a man of God, thus alienating the worker all the more and adding to this hostility toward wealth and power. The Bank was the very incarnation of this evolving economic world, and Jackson strode as a giant killer into the midst of a developing economic jungle to slay the dragon, to kill the "Monster Bank." But the veto would not suffice; for although he had prevented the re-chartering of the bank by the veto, the B.U.S. would have all of its full power for the three remaining years of its charter, setting the stage for a conflict of historic proportions in its impact on executive authority.

From the Bank's inception the Federal government had placed all of its funds in the Bank without interest, leaving large reserves for it to loan without government supervision. This made no sense to the Jacksonians; and as the second term began, Jackson began to dwell on the unbridled power of the Bank. One adviser effectively suggested that the Bank was using the government's money to thwart the government. It appeared to its enemies to have the power of a fourth branch of government, unresponsive to the financial demands of the broad spectrum of the population. The Bank was morally corrupt and economically unjust. Jackson became enraged, he exploded, he expressed violent threats against the Bank. Becoming almost uncontrollable in his outburst, he exclaimed that he would remove federal funds from the Bank, remove the deposits!

It was typical of Old Hickory to explode early in his evaluation of a particular situation then quickly shift to calm deliberation. He had full confidence in his plan to remove Federal deposits from the Bank and began its implementation. However, only the Secretary of Treasury had been empowered by Congress to remove funds from the Bank, if he deemed it necessary. He was then to report to the Congress that the funds had been removed, after the fact. Jackson was unimpressed. In a precedent setting move, he ordered his Treasury Secretary to remove the deposits, which the Secretary refused to do.

In an adroit political maneuver to solve the problem of control over removal of funds, Jackson transferred the Secretary of Treasury to the position of Secretary of State. A new Treasury Secretary was sworn in, having first promised the President that he would follow his order to remove deposits from the Bank. Once in office, however, he changed his mind and refused to obey Jackson's order.

Jackson set another precedent and further expanded presidential power by firing the new Treasury Secretary without the approval of Congress, which had confirmed his appointment. He was obviously setting a new standard for presidential authority and power, moving far-afield from the patterns of government established by Jefferson and Madison. His decision to remove public funds from the Bank flouted the authority of the House of Representatives to appropriate funds, as Jackson seized such power for the Chief Executive. Similarly, he shifted dismissal authority over Cabinet members to the presidency by firing a cabinet appointee without congressional approval.

Congress was in recess during the firing of the Secretary of Treasury, giving Jackson leeway to appoint his good friend Attorney General Roger B. Taney to the post on an interim basis. The new Secretary carried out the order to remove funds in September of 1833. Congress did not convene until December. As the new session began, Congressmen raged against the President and the Treasury Secretary. But having little recourse against a President wielding such power, they used the only weapon at their disposal: they refused to confirm Taney's nomination as Secretary of the Treasury. Jackson was undaunted. He successfully continued his removal policy under a new Treasury Secretary acceptable to Congress.

The battle with the Bank of the United States was not over, however. Nicholas Biddle was determined to fight back, to force the President to redeposit federal funds and recharter the bank. His weapon was his absolute authority over the issuance of loans, and Biddle used this weapon as a gladiator would use a cudgel. He came close to shutting down all loans throughout the banking system, affecting all elements of the economy. It took only several weeks to bring economic activity throughout the country to a near standstill. As the months wore on, businessmen and farmers were near bankruptcy. When Jackson was approached by delegations of businessmen pleading for an end to the conflict with the Bank, for some resolution of their plight which resulted from a denial of needed loan funds, Jackson stated that they should visit Biddle since he had all the money.

Jackson no longer needed evidence that the Bank stood as an economic giant outside the authority of the government. But, for a while at least, the Bank continued to utilize and control government funds to bring economic chaos to the nation. Biddle hoped this would turn popular opinion against Jackson, forcing him to give up his fight against the Bank, to redeposit federal funds and renew the Bank's charter. Indeed, the Bank became a rallying point for Jackson's opponents. Those who feared his tyrannical rule, his withdrawal of funds and the financial chaos that might follow the destruction of the Bank, joined with states' rights' nullifiers and Southern Democrats to form the Whig Party under Senator Henry Clay.

The Senate, controlled by the Whigs, fought for the Bank and against Jackson by voting censure of the President for his removal of funds. Jackson, as a man who thrived on public respect and support, was stunned and deeply hurt by the censure, a first in the annals of the presidency. Nonetheless, he would not reverse his decision; the Bank must die. He protested that he was the elected representative of all of the people and, thus, was their spokesman. Once again, he elevated the office of the presidency above the legislative branch.

By the spring of 1834, Jackson took an additional step to destroy Biddle and the Bank. He ordered the removal of Revolutionary War pensions being managed by the Bank, placing them with the Secretary of War. Biddle refused to transfer the pension funds and took the additional and foolish step of refusing to pay out the pensions. He had gone too far.

Congress, finally responding to sustained public support for Jackson's fight against the Bank, acted by voting to support the President in his policy. It began an investigation of the Bank and its possible involvement in the severe financial panic that overwhelmed the country. Jackson won greater control over Congress as his Democratic party gained strength and as his leadership over that party expanded. Biddle was forced to back away from his policy of denying loans, and the country returned to economic health within the year.

The same cannot be said for the Bank. It had neither Federal funds nor the promise of a charter and soon faded from the financial scene, losing its power to state banks and to Wall Street. Jackson had won. He defeated the Bank.

In his fight with the Bank, Jackson shifted financial power from one central institution to a vast array of state banks, thereby diversifying access to financial resources. The country flourished, as a veritable explosion of economic activity swept across the nation with the rapid expansion of industry and farming, both large and small. To an unprecedented degree, states replaced the federal government in building roads, canals and bridges. But as Jackson saw it, the country was expanding to a point of excess. He sought to cut back on wild speculation, particularly in land, which he feared would bring economic havoc to the country. It was a problem which resulted in part from state banks freely issuing credit and notes not backed by gold or silver. Jackson had consistently believed in a far more conservative hard money, backed by precious metals. He equated paper money with the Bank and its excessive expansion of credit to benefit the rich.

In his final days in office Jackson succeeded in requiring gold and silver to be used to buy federal lands in the West and in cutting back on the liberal issuance of notes. This policy and the sudden withdrawal of federal funds from many banks throughout the nation broke the unbridled land speculation, but unfortunately these moves caused the abrupt end of the economic expansion. As his appointed successor Martin Van Buren was elected and took office in 1837, the country was plunged into depression, the most severe the country had experienced to that time, and one which lasted for five or more very catastrophic years.

* * * * *

"Removal" had two separate and distinct connotations during Jackson's second term in office. It referred to removal of funds from the Bank of the United States. But it also defined a policy of removal of Indians from the lands they settled in the Southern section of the country east of the Mississippi. To many white Americans, Indian tribes dwelling in their midst had festered as an open wound, infecting the lives of both the Indian and the white man from pre-Revolutionary days. Indians occupied prized territory located in the path of development and expansion by the colonials and by the generations that followed. In Revolutionary days, the Indians were expected to cede their lands as punishment for siding with Great Britain. When the Indians resisted this proposition, the government pursued a policy of purchasing Indian land. A policy of removal had been the one which most Americans preferred from the beginnings of the nation, regardless of the Indian-British relationship. The striving, materialistic, self-fulfilling new class of whites in America would accept nothing short of the removal of the "red savage" now in the way of their "go-ahead" spirit.

In contrast to the view of the general public, Presidents from Washington to Monroe had consistently adhered to a policy of acculturation and assimilation of the Indians, believing that they had innate intelligence equal to that of the white man, though less-developed. They sought to instill in the Indians American values, the work ethic and their patterns of civilization. Early Presidents understood the insidious effects of hatred upon democratic institutions. Monroe had made a last-ditch and creative effort to have Indians treated as individuals, not as tribes; but his plan suffered political defeat.

Most Americans saw the Indian as "uncivilized" and uneducated, a barrier to the "rightful" growth and expansion of America. It was the popular belief that Indians rejected all of the white man's world and should be removed from his midst and transported to desolate Western lands to carry on as the primitives which white men believed them to be. Although there is some evidence that the Indian might have accommodated to the white man's culture, the effort was never made. Some Indians had, indeed, lived in fine homes and farmed lands with slave labor. They had started their own newspapers and schools. But the white man wanted the Indian territories, he wanted the Indian out of the path of "progress," and he wanted the government to take strong action to rid the Indian from his midst.

Indicative of the conflict with the Indians, Georgia had passed a law forcing all Indian tribes to sell their lands and move west of the Mississippi. The Indians declared that they had rights to their land which were established through a treaty with the federal government. The Indians took their case to the United States Supreme Court where they won their pleading.

While the Bank had been Jackson's primary concern, the Indian problem was possibly the most popular cause among many white Americans at the time; and the President, who was their spokesman, saw to it that this popular objective was fulfilled. Jackson refused to enforce the Supreme Court decision which favored the Indians over the State of Georgia. He would not stand in the way of Georgia's enforcement of its unconstitutional law.

Although Congress had passed laws relative to Indian removal during Jackson's first term, it was in 1834 that Congress passed its most compelling legislation designed to provide Americans with a final solution to the Indian problem. The Indian Intercourse Act set up an Indian Territory in the area which would become the State of Oklahoma. The Indians were to move to the territory and be given land equal in area to that which they gave up east of the Mississippi. No restitution was paid for homes and other improvements which the Indians left behind. In exchange, the Indians were promised perpetual protection from the white man, by the white man.

There is little doubt that genocide would have ensued had the Indians remained in Georgia and surrounding states. But the mass deaths and desolation which characterized "removal" offers scant consolation. Jackson felt that he was giving the Indian the only feasible alternative available to them. They would survive, and they would be permitted to maintain their own culture and way of life in their new land. Jackson used the military to implement his program for Native Americans, and the course he pursued with complete success was a bloody one.

Thousands of Indians who volunteered to move died en route to the West, with countless thousands suffering from sickness and starvation. Those who refused to move were forced into retention camps and were finally sent to the Indian Territory, with tens of thousands dying en route.

Indian culture and, possibly, the Indian nations survived because of Jackson and his forceful compliance with the public clamor. However, the impact of government policy during his second term resulted in the near destruction of a race of people. The Indians became a downtrodden, beleaguered people relegated to desolate unproductive lands, a forgotten and broken people. It is a sad and ironic commentary that this was perceived as the only possible resolution of a difficult impediment to the growth and expansion of the young, vibrant, democratic, freedom-loving America. As one historian points out, however, it may have been the only possible course of action. In a sense, it distracted the nation's attention from that other hate-ridden issue: slavery. The Indian problem was resolved, but the slavery issue would continue to plague the nation.

* * * * *

The rational man was revered by Jefferson; Madison made certain that the Constitution proved to be a vehicle for rational expression; and Washington personified rationality. Those men sought to master the potential for greed and overweaning power by grasping and jealous leaders through a careful balancing of the legislative, judicial and executive branches of government. Distrusting a strong executive, the Founding Fathers established a presidency subject to the checks and balances set out in the Constitution. Of equally great consequence, and possibly without conscious intent, the application of the philosophy of those men implied leadership by the wealthy and educated.

As the nation grew and prospered, if democracy itself was to have meaning, the definition of the rational man had to become more clearly synonymous with the common man. While Jefferson certainly preached the importance of the individual and the common man, one cannot imagine his fighting to enfranchise the unpropertied worker. The growth in the power of the common man, which occurred during the Jacksonian Era, extended beyond the death of Andrew Jackson almost to the election of Lincoln, during which time the common man joined the ranks of the "rational man." He voted; hence, he achieved economic authority.

Jackson displaced the enlightenment of Jefferson with intuitive action, steeped in the emotional strivings of the man himself. His temperament and character led him to abhor the centralization of power, unless it rested in his own hands. The impact of Jackson's nature on American government was both profound and diverse. He enhanced the power of the presidency, while reducing that of the federal government, particularly as it related to big business. He expanded the world of the small entrepreneur and worker along with the authority of the states. This suited well his rugged individualism which proffered a dichotomous America with power dispersed yet coupled with a strong popular allegiance to himself and the office of the presidency.

During his second term, Jackson crystalized his use of the power of the presidency in ways that changed the definition of that office for all future time. Although he enunciated no grand vision for the nation as he entered office, his impact on the presidency and the nation was resounding. Strangely, though he is thought of as one of the very strong Presidents, he used that strength more to remove barriers to the "laissez-faire" life of the country than to inject government into the day-to-day lives of the citizenry. In his fight with the Bank, he was a staunch opponent of an expanded role of the federal government in economic and business activity. There were exceptions, namely in his first term when he confronted South Carolina with the threat of force in its attempt to nullify federal laws and, later, when he managed the Indian problem firmly, bringing the full force of the power of the federal government to bear upon the removal of the Indian. Earlier, he had also caused the French government to settle the long-standing claims this country had with France dating back to the Napoleonic Wars.

His primary use of power, however, was to bring about a shift in emphasis from the use of government as a major support of large enterprise to its recognition of the needs of the small entrepreneur and worker. Indeed, the federal government under Jackson relinquished the major thrust of economic function to the states and private institutions.

Jackson achieved his greatest enhancement of presidential authority in his shift of power from Congress to the White House. There were still three branches of government; but, as one historian said,

"Jackson made the executive branch first among equals." Jackson vetoed twelve bills sent to him while President, more than all of his predecessors together. He altered the concept of the veto from one based solely on strict constitutionality to one based on an interpretation of the Constitution by the people and the Chief Executive. Congress would forever after be on guard that its legislation might elicit the opposition of the President. Jackson, in fact, initiated policy and set priorities for the nation and Congress in a manner not witnessed before in the office of the presidency.

Under Jackson, government became dependent on popular support, but it also became a government with a new definition of executive authority. A two-party system evolved as an additional check and balance of the executive and legislative branches of government. Under Jackson, government moved from being elitist to being a representative institution, effectively reflecting the rise of the common man. The President defined and implemented national goals, with the objective of enhancing individualism and placing limits on the power of big business over the small businessman and government. But in the process, he encouraged a dangerous sectionalism that would impact the nation in its attempt to resolve the problem of slavery.

Jackson departed the presidency with overwhelming popularity and adulation for his forceful, energetic and determined advocacy of individual rights and freedoms. His public support survived his tenure in office to such an extent that when the relatively unimpressive Lincoln and Douglas opposed each other in the election of 1860, there was a sizeable write-in vote for Jackson, twenty-four years after he left office.

Ever the rugged individualist, Jackson fought for the worker and the small businessman with high spirit, but not as thought of in today's world. His administration sought to give the common man freedom of opportunity by assuring greater fairness in his access to economic opportunity, primarily by inhibiting the Bank and by expanding the resources of state banks. Although he gathered great power about himself and his office, he understood the wishes of the electorate. It was the sense of trust in the presidency as the agent of the people which Jackson most clearly passed on to future generations and which most clearly defined Jackson's glorious second term as President.

Reader's Score of Andrew Jackson

Defense: _____   Lead without Popularity: _____
Economic: _____   Invincibility: _____
Vision: _____   Consistency: _____
Communication: _____   Self-Confidence: _____
Lead Congress: _____   Strengthen Nation: _____

TOTAL POINTS: _____

Abraham Lincoln

Abraham Lincoln

Lincoln was twenty-nine years old when he spoke with eloquence to a young men's school in Springfield, Illinois, on the subject of law and the survival of the nation. He recounted the great passion and emotion which had been the underpinnings of the country's founding. He told how the people had put aside greed, envy and jealousy to initiate a political state to prove the proposition that they are able to govern themselves. Lincoln asserted they had, through the fifty years of the nation, demonstrated that, in fact, the proposition had been proven. But he pleaded that the passion which was both needed and exhibited to found the nation was now lost in the pages of history. The nation, he said, must now direct that passion toward adherence to the Constitution and to law for the nation to survive mob rule, greed and sectionalism.

Lincoln pleaded that all Americans support the Constitution and laws by pledging "his life, his prosperity and his sacred honor; let every man remember that to violate the law is to trample on the blood of his father, and to tear the character of his own and his children's liberty." He asked that the observance of the Constitution and laws "become the political religion of the nation." And adhering closely to this dictum which would become his religion, Lincoln asked that reason, not passion, guide the nation.

Lincoln had method in his philosophy. He detected as early as 1838, when he gave that speech, that the nation might split apart someday without adherence to law. Lincoln foresaw, if only darkly, the possibility that sectional interests related to regional commerce in general, and the institution of slavery specifically, might trigger the demise of the United States. Sectionalism was synonymous with the South. The tariff issue had led to nullification and a threat of secession by South Carolina, which Andrew Jackson defused. States' rights and the fulfillment of economic goals in their own way was the essence of Southern politics, where Southern plantation owners benefiting from low tariffs and slave labor, clashed with the New England manufacturer and trader. But it was the institution of slavery that became the final distillate of the irreconcilable differences between North and South, an issue which could not be resolved by compromise.

Lincoln joined the view for the nation that those magnificent documents, the Declaration of Independence and the Constitution, had provided for freedom and equality for all, except Negroes. He detected that a flaw existed in the implementation of those great documents. He repeated the theme many times before he became President, slowly evolving the concept that the nation could not survive "half slave and half free." He saw the evolving political, economic, and social storm having relevance to the founding principles of the country, and he saw the possibility of a role for himself to play in the drama.

Although he never wavered from his primary objective as President, which was to save the Union, this other objective for the nation and for himself evolved slowly. The objective was to correct that flaw of failing to implement the intent of the Founding Fathers, the flaw of slavery which might tear asunder the nation. He had only a glimmer of awareness of this as he began his political career in the 1840s, and he most certainly had no formula to resolve this danger to the Union as he entered the White House in 1861.

Following the principle set down by Clay, Lincoln was a nationalist. But he was more, for his humble beginnings and his simple style marked Lincoln's great strivings in the political arena. He had shown diligence in developing his career as a young lawyer and effectively set a public and political course for himself with the clear realization that his homespun character could be used to his advantage. He was a consummate politician above all, fully aware of his own resources and nature; he was self-confident in the face of adversity and defeat; he understood human nature and was realistic about the opportunities that were presented to him. He was robustly moral and humane; he was a self-made man and wished to be a model for others in this; and he had great ambition for himself that burned and flamed within him and drove him ever onward. He came to have a vision for himself and for America, as he saw grandeur for the nation and for himself in fulfilling the proposition of equality of opportunity and freedom for all.

* * * * *

Lincoln, who was admitted to the Illinois bar in 1836, became one of its most respected and successful members throughout his career as a lawyer. He was elected to four terms to the Illinois House of Representatives in 1834 from his home town of New Salem, giving early vent to his striving for a role in politics. He was elected to the United States House of Representatives from 1846 to 1848, but then, rejecting an offer to be governor of the newly formed Territory of Oregon, returned to build his law practice. While in Congress, he had proposed legislation to free the slaves in the District of Columbia.

As an active member of the Whig Party, he stalwartly opposed the expansion of slavery into territories where it was allowed by the Kansas-Nebraska Act in 1854, returning to the political arena after a hiatus of five years. Although he rejected the Abolitionist stance, he believed that slavery should be fought through constitutional means wherever the federal government had jurisdiction, which it did in the territories.

Lincoln achieved national prominence in 1858 as the candidate for the United States Senate of the newly formed Republican party. His seven debates with the incumbent Stephen A. Douglas, who was the most prominent Senate spokesman for slavery and the author of the Kansas-Nebraska Act, resounded throughout the land, giving Lincoln credibility as a great debater and potential political leader. In the debate he had eloquently expressed his opposition to the expansion of slavery and slavery in general. Despite his loss to Douglas, his notoriety from these debates and lectures at the Cooper Institute in New York propelled Lincoln toward his nomination on the third ballot as the Republican candidate for the Presidency in 1860. An essential part of the Republican platform was its opposition to any extension of slavery. This platform and a genuine fear of Lincoln's antagonism toward slavery caused a schism in Democratic Party ranks that assured Lincoln the election.

The Democratic party nominated Stephen A. Douglas; but the Southern Democrats founded their own party to assure the preservation of slavery, nominating John C. Breckenridge for President, thus splitting the Democratic vote. Lincoln did not win a majority of the popular votes, but he won sufficient electoral votes to be inaugurated as the 16th President of the United States on March 4, 1861. By then, however, seven Southern states had seceded from the Union, causing Lincoln to respond, in his Inaugural Address, that the union was perpetual and the secession void. The Confederate States of America was formed under Jefferson Davis as President, which included a total of eleven states that seceded.

The Civil War began with the fall of Fort Sumpter to the Confederates on April 15, 1861, causing Lincoln to call up first 75,000 then 65,000 soldiers and 18,000 seamen and the blockade of Southern ports. His stewardship of the war became an all-encompassing effort of his administration, with more than a million men under arms in the North as the war concluded four years later. Lincoln, assuming more power than had ever before, resided in the presidency, raised armies, confiscated such property as railroads and wireless and arrested many he felt were dangerous civilians. His actions were approved by a then friendly Congress, determined to defeat the South.

As the war expanded during its early years, the South achieved frequent victories in battle, showing superior generalship and military strategy. It was not until 1863 that Lincoln and the nation began to experience victory in battles at Gettysburg with General Meade and at Vicksburg with General Grant. But by then, the issue of Lincoln's reelection in 1864 became a topic of considerable note.

* * * * *

The re-election of Abraham Lincoln in November of 1864 was one of the more masterful political strategies in American political history. Some 800,000 Northern troops were in desperate combat with a Confederate Army one quarter its size. It was a turbulent time. In retrospect, one must marvel that the election took place at all, for the country was at war with itself. Lincoln had become an unpopular President by the summer of 1864, and many in his party believed he should not run for a second term.

The entire question of a second term for Lincoln was raised in 1863, when party leaders began to ponder the upcoming election. No President had been elected to a second term since 1832, when Andrew Jackson won an overwhelming victory. The second term had fallen into disfavor. But early in 1864, Lincoln announced his intention to break the tradition of one-term presidencies by seeking reelection. The war raged; his task was far from complete.

Lincoln sought re-election, recognizing the groundswell of opposition to him within his administration, his party and the population in general. He had issued the Emancipation Proclamation in 1863 because he believed it would help win the war, to establish his firm opposition to slavery and to rally support among radical Republicans and Abolitionists. But the American public followed its President haltingly.

The voters reacted to the perceived threat of Negroes coming North, but they were also alarmed by the failure of the Union Army to achieve victory or win the war. Although the North had a population of about twenty-two million compared with nine million in the South, the Southern generals out-smarted the Northern troops at Bull Run, Chancellorsville, Chickamauga and Fredericksburg. Recent victories at Vicksburg and Gettysburg had offered hope but had not allayed fears over the competence of the army. The casualties mounted in 1864 as the war entered its third year, and Lincoln knew that he might lose the presidency if the war did not turn in the North's favor. To make matters worse, the government had expanded the military draft in 1863. It was an unpopular move, eliciting a peace movement by the Democrats who had frequently expressed opposition to the war and emancipation. Cries of "racial amalgamation" and "nigger equality" dominated anti-war rallies, particularly throughout the Midwest. Segments of the white population of several cities, including New York, rioted against the draft and against the Negroes, expressing strong hostility toward the black minority. Anti-war rallies, the unpopular draft, the Northerners' fear of negroes and military failures contributed to an uncertain Republican party in 1864, which faced an electorate which had diminished faith in its President.

Nevertheless, Lincoln was a determined, reasoning, thoughtful leader, who never lost sight of his objective to preserve the Union.

And preserving the Union did hold the North together in the battle with the Confederacy. But he also believed that the institution of slavery violated the very essence of freedom and of equality of the individual that the Founding Fathers had promulgated, and, despite its potential hazard as a political albatross, he pursued his anti-slavery stance.

Yet, in ironic contrast to his position on freedom for slaves, Lincoln would not tolerate any strongly organized anti-war activity, equating such with treason and Confederate espionage. He suspended the writ of habeas corpus, instituted internal military tribunals to punish traitorous acts and jailed many who opposed the war, whether political figures or newspaper editors. As many as 13,000 prisoners were rounded up for various reasons, including opposing the draft and assisting the rebellion. By late 1863 and early 1864, Lincoln was being vehemently attacked as a despot, as an incompetent military leader and as a lover of "niggers."

Lincoln did not waiver, toughening his stance on the draft. He promoted the use of black regiments in the army, which inserted that race in combat; and he continued to speak out cautiously and judiciously for the emancipation of the slaves.

The Congress, composed of a large Republican majority, took little consolation in the possible renomination of a man who seemed to vacillate, made decisions cautiously and failed to win battles that were his to win. In 1863, not a single senator supported Lincoln's renomination. The liberals believed Lincoln did not act with sufficient courage to resolve Negro enslavement, and the conservatives thought Lincoln too radical. Several names were mentioned prominently as replacements for Lincoln. Salmon P. Chase, Lincoln's Secretary of Treasury, who believed that Lincoln did not fight effectively for the Negro cause, readily accepted the opportunity to replace his chief. General John C. Fremont, a former commander of Western forces, was suggested as a candidate. U.S. Grant, the prominently successful military leader of Union troops in the West, was offered the nomination, but flatly refused to replace the President.

The Democrats met in Chicago late in the summer of 1864 and nominated General George B. McClellan as their candidate, with both the party and McClellan advocating a reasonable peace with as much haste as possible without sacrificing gains made in the war. In sharp contrast to Lincoln and the Republican party, they declared the war a failure and established the preservation of the Union, at any cost, as their major platform.

A band of radical Republicans had previously met in Cleveland in May to nominate General Fremont as a splinter-party candidate to counter the potential nomination of Lincoln. That rather incompetent military commander led the radical wing of the party until McClellan was nominated by the Democrats, at which time Fremont dropped his candidacy. He and his splinter party so vehemently opposed McClellan's platform that they disbanded to close ranks with the majority of the Republican party.

In a shrewd political move, the Republicans had changed their name to the Union party to attract Democrats who supported the war. Lincoln was nominated by the party at its convention held on June 7 in Baltimore. The unanimous vote for Lincoln was no chance event, however. Lincoln and his political allies had marshaled every political resource they could muster, including patronage and friendship, to corral the state delegations into Lincoln's camp. The Vice Presidency became a bargaining chip, with Andrew Johnson, a border-state governor and "war-Democrat," replacing Hannibal Hamlin. Despite the political challenge to his renomination, Lincoln insisted that the convention platform provide for surrender of the Confederacy and a constitutional amendment outlawing slavery throughout the nation.

In March of 1864 Lincoln had appointed Grant to be Commander-in-Chief of the Union forces. He was moved from his successful command in Tennessee and other Western areas to become supreme commander of the army and to lead the effort to destroy Robert E. Lee's army defending Richmond. General William Tecumseh Sherman, a close friend of Grant, was placed in charge of the Western troops on Grant's departure. For the first time in the war, a joint strategy against the Confederates was planned, with Sherman mapping a drive to split the rebel states by moving his troops to Atlanta, the major rail center of the South. Grant was to attack Lee on the East and capture Richmond, the Confederate capital. After years of military failures, Lincoln was on the threshold of consistent and meaningful victories.

The Confederate forces continued their successful strategies against numerically superior Union forces by frustrating both Grant and Sherman and by sending Confederate forces on a foray almost to the edge of Washington, terrifying the populace of that city.

And all the while the radical Republican Congress feuded with Lincoln over Reconstruction and the means of achieving an anti-slavery policy more liberal than his. The radical Senators were determined that reconstruction of the Southern states would rest primarily in their hands, while the President was determined that such power would rest with him, subject to congressional legislation, creating a potentially explosive and divisive schism.

Congress drafted strong Reconstruction legislation which was introduced in the summer of 1864. Lincoln had used his war powers authority to institute his own form of Reconstruction in Louisiana and Arkansas. He established military authority over each state, outlawed slavery and established rules whereby each state might draft a constitution and become self-governing. Confederate leaders of civilian or military authority were prohibited from voting, as were Negroes, and an oath of allegiance to the Union by ten percent of the population was a requirement. The legislation proposed by Congress, which was similar to Lincoln's although more punishing of Confederate activists, easily passed both Houses and soon became a popular cause of the Republican leadership. The act required that a majority of citizens pledge that they had taken no active role in the war and required Senate approval for all state governors. Lincoln vetoed the measure, however, asserting that Congress had exceeded its constitutional authority in outlawing slavery. The President asserted that he had war power authority to outlaw slavery, but that a constitutional emancipation amendment would be the only legal way to permanently abolish slavery. The Republican leadership was outraged over Lincoln's veto and over his clearly stated intention to retain authority over Reconstruction.

Lincoln firmly held to his position for two reasons. First, he followed his humane nature and his understanding of human motives in placing responsibility for the war upon the entire nation and not on the South alone, as the Congress was determined to do. He began his quest to return the South to the Republic, to restore its function within the Union. His second reason for his firm stand on Reconstruction harkened back to the speech in Springfield, Illinois, in 1838. He consistently returned to the need for the rule of law and of the Constitution at a time when passion would destroy the nation. Although his critics alleged that Lincoln intoned the Constitution only when and where he saw fit, he stated that Congress had neither constitutional nor legal authority to outlaw slavery.

By August, military and political defeat filled the air. A new group of dissident Republicans planned a convention to be held in Cincinnati in September to elect a "competent" Commander-in-Chief for the nation, one with administrative skills and liberal policies, one who would direct the nation to a successful conclusion of the war. Members of Congress demanded Lincoln's resignation, as did some of the delegates to the Cincinnati convention.

By the late summer of 1864, Lincoln himself felt that his election was in jeopardy. Conservatives pleaded with the President to distance himself from emancipation and to become reconciled to the preservation of the institution of slavery in the South. As fall approached, there were moments when Lincoln doubted his own leadership. The war was being fought to save the Union, but that effort now was paired with the abolition of slavery; and, at times, it seemed that the slavery issue would overwhelm his ability to persuade the nation that both the war and abolition must go forward. He contemplated a peace mission in August to settle the war and leave open the issue of slavery, but that desperate move to stop the war and possibly save his candidacy was quickly extinguished as Lincoln opted to merge principle with expediency.

The Democrats, the liberal Republicans, the anti-Negroes, the anti-war and anti-draft partisans all took turns issuing attacks on the President. They referred to him as a "dictator" and as a "nigger-lover." The opposition had a hey-day until the tide of battle turned in early September.

Atlanta, the rail center of the South and the vibrant business hub of that cotton empire, surrendered to Sherman on September 2. The Union now controlled the city second only to Richmond in reflecting the power of the Confederacy. Every city in the North celebrated the resounding victory. One hundred gun salutes sounded in the eight largest cities of the nation.

By late September, General Philip Sheridan had succeeded in destroying the forces that had threatened Washington only two months earlier. The navy had routed the Confederate Navy off the coast of Alabama. Victory in war seemed assured. Lincoln stiffened his stance to preserve the Union and to abolish slavery. He brought his case to the people in every platform that was open to him without directly campaigning. He issued letters and spoke to soldiers; he asserted that the American heritage of freedom of opportunity for all must be preserved by winning the war. He preached patriotism and allegiance to the values the Founding Fathers had instilled in the Declaration of Independence and in the Constitution. Lincoln himself stood as a living example of that freedom of opportunity; and the country listened, as the election would soon demonstrate.

Lincoln played the political game fully to win the election. He offered patronage and horse traded major political appointments to elicit support from dissident minorities. The major opponents within his party were being quieted, and the Democrats were being silenced by the victories that Lincoln's generals were producing. Soldiers who voted within their regiments or were sent home to vote, supported Lincoln en masse.

Lincoln defeated McClellan by an electoral vote of 212 to 21, with Lincoln winning by five hundred thousand out of the four million votes cast. Although the vote had been a resounding victory for Lincoln, it left some serious questions unanswered. The slavery issue had been muted by the Republicans generally, if not by Lincoln, even though abolishing slavery was in its platform. The country had been diverted from the slavery issue as the Republicans charged the Democrats and their candidate McClellan with treachery, preaching peace at almost any price. To some, it seemed that the vote was more anti-McClellan than pro-Lincoln.

Unfortunately, Lincoln was not rejuvenated by his election victory. At 55 he seemed worn out, melancholy, if not ill. The task of bringing the nation together after a victory in the war that now seemed visible over the horizon was a burden the towering President did not relish. Did he have the stamina to prevail against the forces that would be waged against his stewardship? He was about to win the war; could he win a fair peace?

★ ★ ★ ★ ★

In December, Lincoln won his last great non-military battle. The Thirteenth Amendment outlawing slavery was introduced in the House of Representatives to provide constitutional underpinning to his Emancipation Proclamation. Lincoln believed the amendment must be accomplished before the war itself ended, terminating his war—power authority to free slaves. Every possible political connivance was employed by the President. He personally persuaded and cajoled old friends and political associates. He pleaded the case for abolition through the halls of Congress, finally producing a two-thirds vote plus three in favor of the amendment in the House. The Senate had voted for the amendment earlier, and only state ratification was needed. As a great political strategist, Lincoln understood fully that all his energy must be applied to winning congressional support of this historic amendment. And he succeeded.

Congress would not allow him to rest, however. As his second Inaugural approached, the battle with Congress over Reconstruction erupted, draining the life blood of the President. The burdens of the presidency had always weighed heavily upon his shoulders, his primary diversions being trips to the battle field to converse with his generals and witness the war first-hand and occasional evenings at the theater.

With victory his, Lincoln knew full well the stark reality of what lay ahead. He faced the tribulations of political office seekers, the massive responsibility of filling cabinet posts, the staggering cost of paying for the war, waging the peace and Reconstruction with a hostile and determined Congress and winning over popular support for a program for freed slaves.

The morning of March 4, 1865, was overcast and rain-streaked. Lincoln spoke before the throngs gathered at the Capitol for the Inaugural to hear his concluding words of that address: "With malice toward none; with charity for all; with firmness in the right, as God gives us to see the right, let us strive on to finish the work we are in; to bind up the nation's wounds; to care for him who shall have borne the battle, and for his widow, and his orphan—to do all which may achieve and cherish a just and lasting peace, among ourselves, and with all nations." It was Lincoln, the spokesman for humane and moral values, communicating his belief in a whole nation sharing responsibility both for the war and peace—a peace to fulfill the principles set down by the Founding Fathers.

It was truly a time of triumph in Washington and on the battlefield as well. After capturing Savannah, Sherman cut off Lee's supply and rail lines from the South and approached Richmond; but it was for Grant and his army of the Potomac to smash Lee's army and take Richmond. Grant succeeded, and Lee surrendered at Appomatax Courthouse on April 9.

But the precious, fleeting exhilaration for the victor faded as the battle over Reconstruction raged between Lincoln and Congress. His plan, which varied from state to state, was based on military supervision over the states. He believed this would be the only way to prevent a minority of Union loyalists from being overrun by a majority of Confederates who would undo the emancipation of the slaves and frustrate their slow evolution into economic self-sufficiency. His proposals would permit the South to rule itself, while Union forces stood guard to protect the freedman. There could be no restoration of slavery, and emancipation must be fully enforced. The freedman were not to be given the vote, however.

Radical Congressman fought to enfranchise the Negroes immediately. They rejected his plan for Reconstruction, preferring to limit the authority Southerners would have in their government. Lincoln was willing to compromise, but he was not certain that the nation was ready to give Southern Negroes the vote. Lincoln would heal the wounds, if Congress would follow his lead.

Lincoln advocated gradualism in Reconstruction and the rehabilitation of the former slaves. His plan for the post-war era reflected a deep understanding of Northern whites, of Southern Unionists, of the freedman, of the defeated Confederacy and of the need for strong executive control. He understood the thinking of both liberal and conservative and concluded that military supervision of the South was a necessity. His was a national perspective, which would take all of his powers of persuasion, of tact and patronage, to bring the disputing factions together. Once again, he would have to withstand the attacks from all those who opposed him. The defeats, the victories—all he had faced in the war—he would now meet in peace and Reconstruction. Only now there were times he felt frail and ill. Only now there would be no war powers to sustain him in unpopular moments.

As the war neared its end, Lincoln revived and regained some of his strength. He joined Grant at the battle front to witness first hand the wounded soldiers. Six-hundred thousand had died in the North and the South, more than two-thirds from disease. He walked through the ravaged city of Richmond, now quiet. It was a sullen and devastating end to the courageous and proud rebels.

As the war ended, assassination was feared by a few of Lincoln's protectors and advisors. They worried about the possibility that some Confederate might see the death of the President as the only way that the South might somehow yet win the war or improve the peace. Although Lincoln would not heed the warnings of his guards and cabinet, he at last agreed to have a cavalry guard with him when he rode the streets and finally permitted a guard when he went to the theater. Lincoln believed that a freedom-loving political system could not offer absolute protection to the President from some crazed assassin.

Nonetheless, Lincoln had become morbid about illness and death. He reported with marked distress the dream in which he arose from sleep, hearing sobs. He wandered downstairs to enter upon the sobbing people, but the mourners were invisible. He went from room to room, with no living person in sight. He continued walking, arriving finally in the East Room. There before him was a catafalque with a corpse lying on it, wrapped in funeral vestments, with soldiers all around it acting as guards. All the onlookers were weeping pitifully. "Who is dead in the White House?" he demanded of all of the soldiers. "The President," was the answer; "he was killed by an assassin!" As Lincoln recounted the dream, he was pale and in his most morbid of moods. His sleepless nights turned into moments of nightmare and so, possibly, did his days as he pondered the tasks of healing the nation's wounds.

On April 14, Good Friday, little more than a month into his second term, Lincoln was cheerful and happy and readily recounted a dream he had, one which he had before on occasions of military success. In the dream, a phantom ship moves quickly toward a dark and indefinite shore. Was the dream an omen of success again?

He met with his cabinet in the morning; Grant joined them. Lincoln announced that Reconstruction should continue under military law, under presidential, not Congressional, control. The administration's plan must be implemented at once, since Congress was not in session and could not interfere with its program. The military would stand as a bulwark, protecting the small band of Union loyalists in the South and the freed slaves from the Confederate rebels who could quickly overwhelm them and restore an ante-bellum South. The Negro vote was considered, but once again postponed rebel leaders would not be hanged or jailed.

The Grants could not join the Lincolns at the theater that night, and Mary Lincoln substituted a young officer and his fiancee as their guests. Lincoln almost canceled the theater plans at noon; but his presence at the theater had been announced in the newspapers, and he stated that their plans should be carried through.

The President and his wife went for a ride in the late afternoon, which turned out to be the most pleasant time the two had spent together in a very long time, planning their lives and travels after the White House days. Upon returning, Mrs. Lincoln developed one of her severe headaches, which led her to change her mind about going to the theater. But Lincoln, despite his fatigue, said he needed a night out full of cheer and laughter, so Mrs. Lincoln agreed to go.

Lincoln and his chief guard, detective Crook, spent some moments on war matters, at which time Crook pleaded with Lincoln not to go to the theater or at least to permit him to accompany the Lincolns as an additional guard for the President. Lincoln refused his offer.

During the play, John Wilkes Booth entered the unguarded, unlocked presidential box and fired his derringer into the head of the President at very close range. Lincoln was fatally wounded, dying the next morning; his masterful presidency ended.

Epilogue

The ages will forever debate how Lincoln would have fared in this second term. One can only speculate. His unique character would certainly have served him as he would grapple with Reconstruction, a radical Congress, the defeated South and the freedman.

Although Lincoln had much of the dignity and self-prepossessing nature of Washington, he was not aloof as was the first President. He stood his ground with Congress; but, having the benefit of experience on his side, he departed from the first President in his relationship with Congress. Lincoln was the powerful, undaunted leader of the nation, permitting little usurpation of his executive authority. He took the counsel of his cabinet as did Washington, and, as with Washington, he made up his own mind. Lincoln was not a military leader; but to many of his generals, he was their general. He personally studied military strategy, utilizing the Library of Congress the better to prepare himself to assist in the war effort; and assist he did, over and over again. He was vilified, as was Washington, but he never experienced the widespread adulation that Washington had received from the populace. Only in death did he receive such admiration.

Although Lincoln was not the philosopher and political thinker that Jefferson was, his writing was the equal of Jefferson's. Lincoln's command of the nation in time of war and his clear comprehension that slavery was anathema to American freedoms as set down by the

Constitution and the Declaration of Independence surpassed any of Jefferson's administrative and leadership skills. Unlike Jefferson, Lincoln risked his political power, spent his political influence whenever and wherever he deemed it necessary if he believed the cause was right. But he was also the political strategist, so that he considered the odds before he acted, frequently influencing those odds by leading his cause, by communicating with the electorate brilliantly and with unique insight.

The Abolitionist Movement brought the nation to crisis and decision over slavery. Without Lincoln, the resolution of the conflict would most assuredly have been the dissolution of the United States.

Lincoln probably understood the intent of the Founding Fathers in drafting the Constitution and the Declaration of Independence as well as they did. He was responsible for implementing the fulfillment of individual freedom and equality of opportunity more than any President before or after. He is the benchmark for the measure of the presidency, but, unfortunately, he did not serve very many days of his second term. Had he lived, it would have been a time when his strong and determined nature would have collided with the will of Congress, with the hatred and fears in both the South and the North, with his own waning health. Without great popular support, conflicting forces would have torn at his soul, but he would have persevered, applied reason, and political cunning. He would have sought support among the electorate with his great persuasive powers.

One can only speculate how this articulate, thoughtful, driven man would have fared in his battle with Congress and the South over Reconstruction. One thing is certain, he would have applied all his great skills and energy to achieve his objective for the nation: to bind up the wounds, to bring together the warring faction, to find no blame.

But such speculation aside, in his brief second term Lincoln had achieved fulfillment of the task he had set for the nation and for himself. The war to save the Union had been won. But the war was also to correct that failure to implement fully the Declaration of Independence and the Constitution. The failure left by the Founding Fathers was to be wiped away. Freedom and equality of opportunity for all was complete. Slavery would be no more. The Constitution had been expanded; the rule of law over passion might now prevail.

Reader's Score of Abraham Lincoln

Defense: _____   Lead without Popularity: _____
Economic: _____   Invincibility: _____
Vision: _____   Consistency: _____
Communication: _____   Self-Confidence: _____
Lead Congress: _____   Strengthen Nation: _____

TOTAL POINTS: _____

Ulysses Grant

Ulysses S. Grant

Tragedy was visited upon so many who trusted Ulysses S. Grant that one must marvel at the popularity of this great warrior. If it was not tragedy that accompanied him, then it was the disappointment of those who were dependent on him for leadership, stewardship, judgment. The tragedies for the soldiers in battles at Cold Harbor and at Spotsylvania were, in reality, casualties of war and must be evaluated in the context of the great victories which Grant most certainly delivered to save the Union. But he also was witness to tragedies visited upon the freedmen of the South and upon the American Indian and upon the workingmen who suffered from the panic of 1873.

Grant himself, however, was not a tragic figure. He was, in fact, a survivor of some considerable magnitude. He endured, he persevered, and in great measure he was a raging success from near his fortieth birthday until his death some twenty years later. Although he experienced only failure when he tried his hand at farming or in his father's tannery business or in real estate, his lot in life turned around for him with the advent of the Civil War, for he was blessed with a natural genius for military command.

Grant had entered West Point at the age of seventeen, hardly distinguishing himself except for his considerable aptitude on horseback and for an intriguing indication of skill in a painting course. He remained in the army long enough to serve as a lieutenant in the Mexican War, displaying an acute ability to learn how the army and combat worked and what distinguished a good commander.

He was Civil War commander of all American forces from early 1863 through 1865 when the war ended. He earned the post by his victories in the West in such battles as Vicksburg and Chatanooga. He not only mounted a mighty siege of the army of General Lee in Virginia, but he also masterminded and directed successful battles fought in Tennessee. He conceived the thrilling combat plan which General Tecumseh Sherman wrought upon the armies and the citizens of the South with his march into Atlanta, to the sea, and then north almost to Richmond. Grant was among the great military strategists of all history.

Grant is a study in contrasts, however, for his great military acumen was both preceded and followed by significant failure. His military efforts had shown some glimmer of achievement during the Mexican War, where he expanded his responsibilities as a quartermaster officer to encompass battle leadership of troops in minor combat. But that military career ended in his resignation when he was in his thirties, with the stigma of excessive drinking embedded in his record. During his years as a civilian, he was barely able to support his family in the various pursuits he followed. His father's assistance and support was not adequate to sustain Grant in the pursuit of the endeavors in both business and farming he attempted.

He reached the pinnacle of success in his years of startlingly rapid rise through army ranks from 1862 to 1864, when he became the first Lieutenant General since George Washington. He further distinguished himself when he wrote his acclaimed Memoirs, shortly before he died. His innate brilliance lay in his military prowess and in writing. He evidenced far less natural affinity for the presidential arena.

* * * * *

II.

Grant was a rather short man of about five feet seven inches, slender, pale and shy in social situations. He listened intently; he was a common man himself and, although shy, mixed well with others of his background. He was given to depression and drinking when he was separated from his wife, Julia, and from his family. He rarely would allow for such a separation after his first stint in the army, even at the height of combat in the Civil War. Grant desperately needed to be loved, perhaps adored. His feats of glory in the war provided this and, of course, his two-term tenure as the 18th President of the United States was the stage for the adulation he and Julia prized most dearly. Some men seek presidential office for the power over people or money which ensues. For Grant, all of his power and authority was directed toward one goal: to be accepted. Although he was a man dedicated to fulfilling the functions of the office of the presidency, when circumstances or his own shortcomings made success unattainable, Grant became unable to marshall forces within himself or his administration to alter the course of events. He lacked political shrewdness, but as telling, he rarely persevered in carrying out his own judgement in matters of policy.

Lee surrendered to Grant on April 9, 1865, just five days before Lincoln was assassinated. Andrew Johnson became President, but Grant became the most popular man in the country among Northerners for having saved the Union and among Southerners for having given Lee and his soldiers most gracious surrender terms. Johnson contended with this hero by including him in his inner-circle of advisors and by thrusting Grant's support of the administration before the public whenever possible.

Johnson fought with Congress over Reconstruction, pursuing rather mild limitations and restrictive measures on the former rebels. In contrast, the radical Republicans, dominant in Congress, demanded harsh control over the South. Congress enacted legislation assuring that the human rights and civil liberties of former slaves would be guaranteed by the government. Johnson had no such strict agenda, and it appeared that Grant sided with him. When the Secretary of War, Edwin Stanton, a radical Republican, followed the leadership of Congress and not the President, Johnson fired him, replacing him with Grant on an interim basis. After months of wrangling between Congress and Johnson, Grant turned against Johnson. He relinquished the office of Secretary of War, restored the position to Stanton, and set about to become the presidential nominee of the Republican party. He displayed more political sophistication as a candidate than he would as President.

★ ★ ★ ★ ★

III.

It was an easy nomination victory for Grant, for the party needed his candidacy as much as Grant craved the office. The election of 1868 was surprisingly close, however, even though Grant carried 214 electoral votes against 80 for his Democratic opponent, Horatio Seymour. A swing of not quite 30,000 votes in the 5,700,000 popular vote would have elected the Democrat, who represented the party which had considerable clout in large Northern cites as a carryover of anti-war sentiment.

Grant began his tenure with a show of independence from the Republican party through his selection of cabinet members from among his old military associates and from among business tycoons he had come to respect. He avoided party politics. His generally successful first term was noteworthy for its peaceful tenure on almost all fronts.

In foreign affairs, Grant pressed for and won a satisfactory settlement of a Civil War dispute over Great Britain's involvement with the construction and outfitting of the *Alabama* and other Confederate warships.

The Fifteenth Amendment to the Constitution was passed with

Grant's strong support, giving suffrage to all without "regard to race, creed, color, or previous condition of servitude." There were civil rights' laws passed to protect the rights of the freedmen in the South, but few of these were strongly enforced. With Grant's encouragement Congress established the Justice Department to implement these laws. The majority in both North and South preferred only that order be preserved in the reconstructed South, which Grant's first administration provided. Congress found the politically untutored Grant an easy mark, however, beginning a siege of the President's programs by defeating his proposal for a civil service system to diminish the graft-ridden spoils system. Grant's attempt to annex Santo Domingo as a state to which the Negro might emigrate failed to carry the Congress, despite his concerted effort throughout his terms to win their support. It was an idea he cherished throughout the balance of his life.

As a hint of events to come in Grant's second term, there was a brief economic panic over an attempt by financier Jay Fisk, Jr., to corner the gold market, with the assistance of Grant's brother-in-law. The President and his Secretary of the Treasury personally interceded with Wall Street to defuse a potential collapse.

It was a time of scandals in the national, state and local government, when the divisive activities of the ilk of Tammany Hall in New York City effectively diverted attention from the plight of the South. Corruption in government had been festering and growing from the 1820s with the enactment of a Tenure in Office Act, limiting the power of the chief executive to discharge federal employees. The Spoils System fostered dishonesty; and, by Grant's time, spoilsmen in government held a special relationship with entrepreneurs who benefited from the tariff, enticing graft among office holders. To all of this must be added Grant's unusually trusting qualities in judging his friends and associates. He was no judge of honesty, and, when confronted with evidence against those whom he had appointed, his nature would not permit him to distrust their service to him and to the nation. Fortunately for Grant, a major scandal in his first term relating to a railroad barons' payments of graft to federal officials, known as the Credit Mobilier, did not reach the President. He escaped that fiasco unscathed.

Despite his shortcomings, Grant enjoyed success in his first term, maintaining his popularity with workers and the common man. He had settled a festering feud with Great Britain. Although the Negro was being denied his civil and political rights by the K.K.K., the South seemed relatively quiet. He had sidestepped scandal. The nation was at peace, and Grant seemed above reproach, a hero.

★ ★ ★ ★ ★

IV.

The Republican party readily renominated Grant. A group of dissenters and very liberal Republicans formed a splinter party which nominated Horace Greeley, the editor of the *New York Tribune* as its presidential candidate. Strangely enough, the Democrats joined the bandwagon by nominating Greeley as well. It was to no avail. Grant won re-election hands down with 286 electoral votes to three for Greeley. Only in a few southern states, where the black man had no vote, did Greeley receive any support.

Ulysses S. Grant was an inspiring general; he was always a popular President; and he also could be a surprisingly wise judge of political reality in some unexpected ways. For example, he said that the freedman's problem was one of class struggle. Although Grant showed flashes of having a fine intellect, unfortunately, he only rarely employed this quality effectively as President. His failure to apply his intellect, perseverance and insight to meet the challenges of the presidency would characterize his final four years in office.

By the advent of his second term, the movement to help the freed slave as led by abolitionists and the radical Republicans had all but evaporated. The populace would now turn inward to fulfill their own economic goals. Radical Republicans were replaced by liberal Republicans who sought only to determine how one might assist the educated middle and upper classes to thrive in their *laissez-faire* pursuits. The difficulty which Grant experienced with Congress in his first term worsened in his second, as the authority of the office of the President itself diminished as the nation sought to place power and authority, not in government, but with businessmen and the growing number of tycoons of industry. The nation's economic prowess was growing at a geometric pace. And as it did, the presidency and Grant's authority waned, and it seemed to do so with Grant's acquiesence.

In the South the freed slaves were making amazing strides winning such political positions as sheriff and other local offices. They were showing potential for success at farming and in entering the white man's world in many ways. But class acceptance was not to be theirs, not for a hundred years. The dominant white population was being displaced in their customary leadership functions by northerners sent in by Congress and by blacks as well. Whites banded together to murder blacks who tried to assemble, who voted, who held themselves as equals. Grant became incensed, sending General Philip Sheridan to Louisiana to prevent further violence. But his troops only temporarily quelled the anti-democratic forces of the white supremacists. The President spoke eloquently to Congress in January of 1875 pleading for additional legislation to protect the freed men. It was an honest and sincere effort on the part of the President, but it all soon became an empty gesture, as southern state after southern state implemented white supremacist governments and mores, using violence and murder wherever necessary. The country no longer cared. Their attention was directed toward personal success. Congress, at one time more aggressively for the freedman than Lincoln, did not care. Grant's Cabinet, and particularly its most influential voice, Hamilton Fish, the aristocratic Secretary of State, gave only advice to avoid controversy, to allow the southern states to run their own affairs. Thus occurred the tragedy for the blacks of the South which Grant felt powerless to prevent.

Could Grant have changed the course of history for the freedmen? One thing is certain, in the long run he did not persevere. Reading the sense of the nation, he retreated. The task most definitely would have required great reason, political skill, intelligence and the expenditure and risk of his popularity to withstand the hatred of southern whites and to suffer the indifference of northern white supremacists. Lincoln had all of the qualities for this fight, but would he have fared better? Grant showed many of these leadership qualities in the war. Lincoln predicted and Grant understood that massive force and diligent legal prosecution would have been required to quell the white mob and the likes of the K.K.K. Might there have been another Civil War only with dreaded guerilla war overtones? Probably not, but Grant was in no mood to find out.

Grant was a great general when he had command of forces he understood, when he had the support of Lincoln and others of authority in Washington. The war gave him an opportunity to make his mark in the world in a sphere he understood, to achieve the adulation he craved. Grant showed less proficiency or, more to the truth, no propensity to lead an admittedly reluctant Congress or nation in a direction which was counter to popular sentiment or to his own self protecting interests. There is no question that in his first term Grant promoted civil rights' legislation and encouraged the development of the Department of Justice to implement civil rights' legislation. But as his second term evolved, he did not carry the fight to the trenches in the South as he had done in the Civil War. One could argue that the government and its people needed a rest after its bitter conflict. Southern white hatred against the blacks was almost insurmountable. But Grant failed to assist the freed slaves during his second administration, and no one, for a hundred years, would have his moment in history, his power or his imagination to improve their lot. Unfortunately, failure characterized much of Grant's second term. It is a discerning general who strategically retreats. It is a reasoning President who knows when his constituency will follow. Yet, there is no following without strong leadership. Possibly the times were not ripe for Grant to lead with firmness, but there was no firm leadership in his second term.

* * * * *

V.

As his Presidency advanced, Grant became a man who lived to preserve his own world. The blacks were in no position to assist in this pursuit and neither were the Indians. During his presidency, the army fought hundreds of conflicts with the Indians. These culminated in that most infamous battle at Little Big Horn with Custer's last stand during Grant's last year in office. To his great credit, Grant had been, from time to time, a tireless and understanding fighter for the Native Americans, striving to diminish the endless massacre of Indians. Although it was Grant's primary view that the Indian should be integrated into the American culture and way of life, in a manner once proposed by President James Monroe, the advancing white movement Westward overwhelmed the plan. Grant finally proposed placing them on reservations where they would be protected from white incursions. These also provided the ever expansion-minded whites protection from Indian forays. He successfully fought the extermination of the Indian, but he was helpless in his endeavor to improve their lives or to interrupt their rapid fall into abject poverty when, as farmers of infertile land, they were denied their true skill as hunters in the vast open territories they had once roamed.

* * * * *

The year 1873 brought tragedy to North American workers as the disastrous financial crash of that year hit with its full fury. It began with the failure of the financial tycoon, Jay Cooke, to sell securities of his Northern Pacific Railroad. Grant traveled to New York that September as the panic increased to allay fears on Wall Street and to try to restore economic stability to businesses. But the house of cards had collapsed, the business community was in a state of siege, wages fell precipitously and a depression which lasted no less than six years was in full force.

Grant was torn between two conflicting and very opposite economic policies which were touted as the solution to the business community. One was to inflate the money supply by increasing the printing of greenbacks. Dollars would go into the hands of the Western farmers, the Eastern entrepreneurs and the working men. The opposing argument pressed for deflation, a "sound currency," backed by gold, one which would earn the respect of foreign countries. Grant supported a hard currency and deflation. He vetoed a bill which Congress had passed which would have increased money by $64 million, siding with the conservative bankers and the wealthy. He had once been a failed businessman and farmer himself; but now his closest friends and advisers were the rich and wellborn, and he would not turn against their advice. He sought and received approval from the wealthy. He trusted that the masses would not blame him for their economic plight, and he was correct!

* * * * *

Ironically, it was not the demise of Reconstruction or the failure of Grant's Indian policy or the devastating depression, but corruption and scandal that are the hallmark of Grant's administrations. These festering wounds were most evident during his second term. The spoils system had flourished with the defeat of his Civil Service proposals. Trusted old friends who had served him during the first term were no longer at his elbow, and they were replaced by those whom Grant wished to trust, but who misused him. In some situations his friends of years past took advantage of their friendship to pocket money from whiskey and other taxes.

Grant responded to investigations into his administration as would an embattled soldier defending a fort. He took personal offense to indictments against his appointees. Resignations were rife. His Secretary of the Treasury resigned under suspicion and a court martial was held for one of his old comrades who ran off with whiskey tax money.

Although, surprisingly, Grant's personal popularity was generally unscathed by the endless investigations, his party believed him to be a political albatross, and refused his hints for a third term. The Grant administration came to a rather ignoble end in 1877 with the disputed election of Republican Rutherford B. Hayes, whose victory was dependent upon voiding votes of Southern states which were not legally constituted.

*   *   *   *   *

VI.

Grant was a man with brilliant insights into and understanding of human nature and travail. Yet, in the final analysis, his actions were determined by the truly difficult issues facing the nation as they coupled with his need for acceptance and his desire to avoid politically dangerous conflict. He had once observed that the timing of the Civil War was fortuitous, for it allowed the nation to rid itself of the fierce dispute associated with the institution of slavery in time to permit the country to compete economically with a Europe which was thriving with an unfettered industrial revolution. He understood that the Mexican War, in which he took an active part, was a precursor of the Civil War in that it was about extending slavery, exemplifying the theory that war is an extension of politics. In war, he had recognized the freed slave as a group in need of government and military protection.

He believed they had the innate skill to contribute in a very construc- tive and positive way to the war effort. He, perhaps better than any President before him, understood the plight of the Native American. In the end, these were all futile insights. He inadequately committed his authority to stop the massacre and subjugation of the black man in the South or the Native American in the West. Grant's great power and prestige were visited too lightly on the problems of the worker, the freedman and the Indian to affect their plight.

His administration was wracked with corruption, yet he did not have either the courage or the temperament to face squarely the pos- sibility that he must act to rid himself of scoundrels who fed upon his nondescript administrative authority.

Grant gave a surprising farewell State of the Union message in December of 1876, which gives some credence in his own words to the assessment of his presidential performance as troubled and fre- quently ineffective. After reciting his minimal experience with politics in childhood and his insulation from political matters, he went on to recount how appointees, whom he said were not personally loyal to him, had been the players in corrupt episodes during his administra- tion, omitting any references to corruption by his personal friends. Further, he quite accurately referred to the difficult challenge of bring- ing together the divergent factions and interests created by the war and its aftermath. The times were unique and worked against him. His political innocence saddled him with the mistakes of weak associ- ates. With all of this, he pleaded that he had made a conscientious effort, that he had done his best to uphold the Constitution and the laws. Grant's natural impulses and intuitive genius flowed during the Civil War but did not sustain him in his presidency, and he under- stood this.

Possibly no President faced the resolution of such momentous social issues as Reconstruction and the peaceful settlement of the Indian without any constituency within the electorate or Congress to sustain courageous and statesmanlike action. In this, Grant stands alone in American history. His effectiveness, particularly in his second term, is tarnished by his many failures. He appeared to "give up" as events overcame solutions. For Washington, Jefferson, Madison, Jackson and Lincoln the office of the presidency had somehow been the vehicle for their use of power, of reason and authority, for influence and guidance. The office itself became an instrument for self-expression, for leadership. In a manner of speaking, the office of the presidency fell slightly into the shadow of these men when they held that office. With Grant, the office seemed to overshadow the man.

Reader's Score of Ulysses S. Grant

Defense: _____
Economic: _____
Vision: _____
Communication: _____
Lead Congress: _____

Lead without Popularity: _____
Invincibility: _____
Consistency: _____
Self-Confidence: _____
Strengthen Nation: _____

TOTAL POINTS: _____

Grover Cleveland

Grover Cleveland

The presidency seemed to be in an almost dormant state from Grant's tenure and the end of Reconstruction through the terms of Hayes, Garfield and Arthur. The conflicts of the war and sectionalism, and the challenges of the freedman and the Indian and the intrusions by foreign powers receded in prominence and in memory as the nation grew and prospered. Power was becoming vested in massive organizations of industry, business and finance, overshadowing the presidency and the federal government, in general. Almost three million immigrants came to the United States in the 1870s and an additional five million arrived in the next decade. Many of these new arrivals moved to the West, significantly expanding that region. Manufacturing thrived and the corporation became still more powerful, expanding their influence to monopolize whole industries. Railroads crisscrossed the nation, opening wide the nation and the perspective of its people. The worker began to form unions to match the authority of the ever-expanding work force with that of even more powerful businesses interests.

Mark Twain referred to it as a "Guilded Age," depicting the appearance and pomp of the newly rich. There was great expansion of urban living, resulting in severely overcrowded cities. Although industry and manufacturing flourished in the East, farmers of New England were faced with the impact of more productive land in the Midwest and West, forcing many off their farms. Meanwhile, the South achieved a remarkable comeback in its restoration of productive farming, but it also attracted textile mills and other manufacturing to its economic base.

While industry, finance and big business flourished, the new immigrants moved West and so did farmers from Ohio, Indiana and Pennsylvania, attracted by more fertile land. The nation grew from fifty million in 1880 to over sixty-two million in 1890, as the railroads and grange roads provided access to such newly opened western areas as Kansas, Nebraska, Iowa and Minnesota. Banks were lending money freely, and rainfall provided unexpected fertility. But disaster hit the farmers in the late 1880s when a severe draught and the onslaught of grasshoppers destroyed the crop of many of those who had experimented with the new West. Farms were foreclosed, while prices dropped for those who survived. Money flowed from the borrower in the Midwest to bankers in the East as interest rates spiraled. The railroads, subject only to state regulation, charged far more for short hauls than for long ones. The farmer, customarily conservative and self-reliant, turned to the federal government to regulate the rates of railroads which were, in fact, engaged in interstate commerce. They demanded the unlimited coinage of silver, which would make money cheaper for the borrower and more available to Western farmers. A radicalization of mood was to overtake the nation from the 1880s through 1920, with the farmer joining the laborer and the urban dweller demanding that the federal government redress their grievances.

Industries had consolidated during the 1880s and 1890s, picking up slack left by the failure of the less efficient producers, reducing competition and allowing them to become more able to obtain the capital required for the new equipment of the industrial revolution.

But such expansion led to the alienation of the worker, while strikes became a response to discontent. Immigrants joined the factory workers already in place to become citizens of the ever growing urban one-third of the nation. The tensions of the struggling farmers, of workers seeking self-esteem and some control over their destiny, together with the over-crowded city dweller characterized an America in transition. The weak Presidents who had served after Ulysses Grant were slow to respond to the discontent.

The national government, which had been Republican from Lincoln's election in 1860, operated with a growing treasury surplus during the 1880s, when America's economic success and accompanying imports produced a large tariff income for the expanding nation. The government confined its focus to matters of tariff legislation, civil service reform and the minting of silver, in addition to gold, and with little else.

Republican Presidents had been relaxed in their management of government and their looseness encouraged a continuation of the questionable morality and resulted in scandal which characterized the Grant administration. The weakness of the federal government and the growing social frictions which resulted from overcrowded cities, dissatisfied workers and struggling farmers led to an undercurrent of public discontent with their government. This was the mood, despite the improved life that the industrial revolution provided for many. With all of this, there was still much of the feeling of self-reliance and independence that had been widespread since Jackson's day, although it was now often the uprooted immigrant who would look to himself for fulfillment, having left his familiar surroundings far behind in Europe.

It was a time of significant changes in the values and economic status of the American people, whether their families dated to the landing of the Mayflower, or they were those who most recently docked at Ellis Island. But the changes were so sudden that their impact was yet to be absorbed fully by the nation. Jobs and money were relatively plentiful which calmed the stress of change. On the surface, it was a quiet, almost sedentary, transitional period, which welcomed Grover Cleveland into the White House in March of 1885.

* * * * *

Cleveland had an unglamorous career as an attorney in Buffalo, moving into politics as sheriff, mayor and governor of New York. He maintained a reputation of being impeccably honest, hard working to a fault and a good administrator. The latter two qualities merged unevenly as Cleveland delegated very little of his assignments, working until three or four in the morning to pay bills personally which emanated from his government position. He was a man of great pride and personal self-confidence; he believed his own judgment to be fail proof. Cleveland greatly admired Thomas Jefferson and Andrew Jackson, adapting their views on limited government, constitutional allegiance, hard currency and the inherent necessity for man to care for himself without any dependence on government. While respecting the economic might of business, he opposed excessive power in the hands of monopolies, particularly the railroads. He appreciated the great natural resources of the West and moved to preserve them. He respected the unions being formed but would not permit the government to assist them.

* * * * *

Cleveland's first term, which he won in 1884, was relatively uneventful, despite a fiercely fought campaign that was as bitter as any in American history. Cleveland successfully rode the storm that broke over his having fathered an illegitimate child over a decade earlier. He diffused the issue by readily admitting the charge, stating that he, as a bachelor, had acted honorably in caring for the child. Possibly because of the excitement caused by the campaign, almost 80% of the eligible voters cast their votes. It was a time of great enthusiasm for

America, and Grover Cleveland personified much of the ideals of the populace with his own pride, self confidence, self reliance, honesty and forthrightness.

Cleveland, who ran on a platform of lower tarrifs and reform in national finances, the civil service and in administrative departments, narrowly defeated his Republican opponent, James G. Blaine, with an electoral vote of 219 to 182. He was the first Democrat to be elected to the presidency since James Buchanan won in 1857. Immediately demonstrating his administrative skills, Cleveland carefully appointed his cabinet selecting qualified businessmen from whom he demanded a strong dedication to public interests over their private concerns.

During his first term, he successfully promoted the expansion of Civil Service, adding almost 12,000 to their ranks. He vetoed over 400 bills passed by Congress, many of which were private pension bills or bills which granted special privileges to select industries. He signed the legislation setting up the Interstate Commerce Commission, beginning the regulation of railroad rates across state lines, and he restored to public ownership vast acres of unused land granted for railroad rights-of-way. Cleveland opposed any expansion of public doles to private citizens. He recommended legislation which would provide a labor commission to settle disputes, a measure which was defeated by Congress.

The federal treasury swelled during that first term, primarily due to high protective tariffs. Cleveland was not a proponent of free trade, but he did encourage legislation to reduce the tariff on many goods to benefit the working man and small business man who depended on foreign products. His efforts to reduce tariffs threatened protected industries and their employees, turning voters, including many Democrats, against him. In the election of 1888, Cleveland was defeated by Benjamin Harrison by an electoral vote of 233 to 168, even though he had received a popular plurality of more than 100,000. Cleveland retired to private law practice in New York, believing his days in public office had ended.

Meanwhile, the Democratic party, which was comprised of a group of sectional factions, struggled with local issues more frequently than national ones, while the Republicans were only slightly more national in their viewpoint. The Republicans, under Benjamin Harrison, increased tariffs and spent money freely, causing a growing concern among the populace over an administration thought to be spendthrift. The splintered Republicans, protective of their own self-interests, became disenchanted with Harrison.

★ ★ ★ ★ ★

Cleveland gathered together the various factions of the Democratic Party, gaining its nomination for President in 1892, running on a platform of economy in government, lower tariffs and hard currency. He defeated Harrison 277 to 145.

Cleveland was a big man, weighing over 280 pounds. He was of average height, with a drooping brown mustache and a double chin. His movements, as would be expected for a large man, were lumbering, yet he could display consistent energy. He portrayed dignity and self-confidence, and it was for these qualities, coupled with the trust that citizens placed in him, that won him a second term. Although he was a man who lacked imagination and was without a plan for the nation, he conveyed a spirit of security and stability which attracted the people to him. He overcame sectional in-fighting within the Democratic party, defeating the platform of a sizeable element of Western farmers who fought for easy credit through the rapid expansion of silver dollars. The People's party was the outspoken proponent of free silver, the nationalization of the railroads and an income tax. He defeated "radical Democrats," the Republicans and the People's party, becoming the only president in American history to come to the office after having been elected and then defeated as President. The electorate gave him a Democratic Congress as well. He was a proud man and felt fully vindicated.

The spoils of victory would not last, however. Cleveland was sworn into office on the fourth of March, 1893. In the spring of the same year, the Reading Railroad failed and the National Cartage Company, a product of intemperate financial expansion, went bankrupt. The agricultural depression worsened, and banks in Europe and England suffered a gold crash. Stock prices fell, banks panicked and called in loans, credit became scarce, business failures multiplied. Cleveland responded to the crisis, demanding that Congress repeal the bill mandating the purchase of silver, which was depleting the treasury of its gold reserve. The liberal wing of the Democratic party believed this action damaged the farmers by increasing their debt further, while benefitting the financial interests and big business. But he believed that financial stability would be restored by improving confidence in the United States Treasury and the American dollar. Cleveland also proposed the reduction of tariffs, believing that cheaper prices for imported goods would benefit the consumer and the common man. His most dramatic effort to resolve the depression was to float hundreds of millions of dollars worth of government bonds through the J. P. Morgan Company. His purpose was to bolster the Treasury and the cash reserves of the nation. But the depression was not affected, and the President appeared to be embroiled with Wall Street power brokers. To many, he seemed to lack any perception of the struggles of the farmers, unemployed workers and failed small businessmen.

Cleveland was a controversial man with many contradictory personality traits. He was personally assertive, yet he believed in a highly limited government. His assertive nature was frequently abrasive, haughty and authoritarian. He fought bitterly with Congress, without regard for party. While he succeeded in repealing the silver purchase bill, he failed in his attempt to reduce tariffs. He had used all of his political clout in the silver purchase repeal, and none was left for the tariff reduction which might have benefited those enduring economic hardship. The Democratic Congress effectively turned on this determined and assertive Chief Executive. Although he himself was reluctant to impose governmental solutions to solve the nation's problems, his ability to govern was diminished by his assertive nature which lost him control over his own party and Congress.

★ ★ ★ ★ ★

Cleveland and the Democrats had offered themselves to the working man as his benefactors through lower tariffs and a secure dollar. But workers lost confidence in their Democratic President early in the second term when Cleveland, a strong supporter of business interests, sent the army to Pullman, Illinois, to break a strike against the Pullman Company. A group of outside unions joined the striking workers at the Pullman plant out of sympathy for their protest against a wage reduction. Rail service to Chicago was halted by their strike. A Federal court injunction was issued to stop the strike, which the court alleged prevented the delivery of the U.S. mail, and Cleveland sent in troops to enforce the court order. The Democratic governor of Illinois protested that the President had challenged his authority by sending in troops without the governor's request. It was labor as well as a Democrat governor against the President. Cleveland, acting upon his assertive nature, breaking both with his belief in a limited government and with the working class, brought an end to the strike. The conservative President ran headlong against the growing dissension among the working class, grappling neither with the symptoms of discontent nor with any of their causes.

Cleveland remained stubbornly committed to his policies. The Western farmer demanded relief from low prices, financial failure and foreclosed mortgages through the expansion of silver-backed money. Cleveland refused, believing in the "sound" restricted currency of gold. He accepted the guidance of Eastern financial interest over that of the farmer and small businessman.

In the face of the depression, Cleveland squandered the popularity he had enjoyed in the interest of morality, self-reliance and noninterference by government into matters he felt to be in the private sector. Jackson and Grant held the same perspective during previous depressions, but they managed to convey a posture which kept intact their great rapport with the common man. Cleveland might well have cooperated with the Democratic governor of Illinois to stop the strike at Pullman. He might have spoken to workers; he might have found some manner to hint of even-handedness between labor and management. But he remained a stern task master to labor, to the farmer and to the small business man. He believed that the free coinage of silver was heretical and the populace turned against him, condemning him to depart his second term of office as one of the most unpopular Presidents in the history of the country.

★ ★ ★ ★ ★

Despite the economic hardships facing the President and the nation during his second term and despite the fact that foreign affairs were of minimal interest to Cleveland, several episodes of historical moment occurred. Interestingly, Cleveland's brief forays in foreign matters foreshadowed a more aggressive America in such affairs, but they also reveal some of Cleveland's conflicting nature. His assertive personality would do battle with his views on the limited sphere for government.

President Benjamin Harrison had approved the annexation of Hawaii to the United States as one of his last acts in office. The small nation had undergone a coup, probably masterminded by American interests in the Pacific Islands. Cleveland, who opposed the concept of manifest destiny extending beyond the shores of the United States, withdrew the annexation bill before it could be approved. This was a clear example of Cleveland's hostility to an expanded power of government.

In great contrast, however, he successfully employed considerable saber rattling, threatening war with England if it failed to accede to binding arbitration in a border dispute it had with Venezuela over its common border with a British colony. Cleveland appeared jingoistic in his protection of the Western Hemisphere from incursions by European powers, calling upon the Monroe Doctrine as the authority for his actions.

Finally, Cleveland refused all support for the uprising of the Cubans against Spain. He believed the insurgents to be hot heads without substance. The independence of Cuba was a popular cause for many Americans and would soon surface in America's nationalist foreign policy. But Cleveland sided with Spain, believing it would maintain law and order on the island. He refused to apply the Monroe Doctrine to Cuba. It must be said that Cleveland was inconsistent in his foreign policy at best, displaying antithetical facets of his nature and philosophy of government, a government at first assertive and then withdrawn.

* * * * *

Cleveland left office in March of 1897. The Democratic party had nominated William Jennings Bryan, a man whose policy and spirit were diametrically the opposite of his. Bryan was for free trade, the unlimited purchase and coinage of silver, for the farmer and laboring man and against power in the hands of the wealthy industrialists and financiers. Though with less precision than Cleveland, he spoke eloquently, passionately and intuitively. Although he was not running for reelection, Cleveland felt bitterly defeated by the nomination of Bryan. Cleveland could well have been a secret supporter of his Republican opponent, the victorious William McKinley, who believed in a hard currency backed by gold and in the sacred role of business and finance in the welfare of the nation.

* * * * *

During his second term, Cleveland added 44,000 places to the Civil Service classified list, a larger number by far than had ever been brought into that service, which numbered over 86,000 at the end of his terms. His Justice Department pursued five cases under the Sherman Anti-Trust Act, winning in only one. Cleveland considered this to be reform, and for his moment in history, it may have been as much reform as the country was ready to accept. He served at a time when the forces of economic and social change produced by the industrial revolution, the consolidation of businesses, the rapid expansion of financial authority, the subjection of labor and the rise of unions were not yet at critical mass. Cleveland had little imagination and intuition and even less farsightedness about the future of the nation. He was a rigid, disciplined and rather cold administrator who, nonetheless, restored authority to the office of the presidency. His times and the social and economic tools at his disposal would hardly have led him to be a great reformer in the tradition of either of the Roosevelts or a Wilson, were he to have been so inclined. Cleveland, in his second term, missed the opportunity to work with his party and with his broad constituency made up of all economic sectors of the nation to resolve very challenging problems. Cleveland, a man at the crossroads of American history, lacked vision and creativity. His response to his world was conscientious yet sterile and without impact.

Reader's Score of Grover Cleveland

Defense: _____	Lead without Popularity: _____
Economic: _____	Invincibility: _____
Vision: _____	Consistency: _____
Communication: _____	Self-Confidence: _____
Lead Congress: _____	Strengthen Nation: _____

TOTAL POINTS: _____

Theodore Roosevelt

10

Theodore Roosevelt

Theodore Roosevelt was an imaginative, driving leader, dedicated equally to his political career and to public service at a time of transition and social and economic upheaval which followed the industrial revolution and the closing of the frontier. Cleveland, Harrison and McKinley had all shown some recognition of the changing times, but it was Roosevelt who grasped the meaning and significance of change. It was he who would climb the bully pulpit of the presidency to alter the essence of the times, as he presided as the chief magistrate of the nation from 1901 through 1908.

The rugged individualism of the Jackson era, with its celebration of limited government and the spirit of "go ahead" for the small businessmen and farmers, evolved through the Civil War and the industrial revolution to full blossom some seventy years later. At the turn of the century, individualism had its most intensive expression in the tycoons of industry and finance. A handful of business leaders accumulated such wealth and power as to rival the authority and power of the federal government.

Railways were dominated by E. H. Harriman and James J. Hill; finance, by J. P. Morgan; steel, by Andrew Carnegie; oil, by Rockefeller.

The meat packers controlled prices and so did the sugar barons. Unions began to form, with over 2,000,000 members in the American Federation of Labor. Democracy was being subverted by the greed and power of great assemblies of industries, utilities and financial managers. Prices were being set by the railroads, by the meat industry and by others without the benefits of competition. Special rebates were given to favored large customers, to the detriment of small producers.

In its legislation, Congress was pro-business, with such rare exceptions as the passage of the Interstate Commerce Act under Grover Cleveland in 1887 and the Sherman Anti-Trust Act under Benjamin Harrison in 1890. However, industry, flaunting its power, sidestepped the impact of such legislation, sensing that neither Congress nor the White House were inclined to pursue violators.

The nation had grown from 16,000,000 in Jackson's day to almost 90,000,000 as the century drew to a close. The last states to enter the union, Oklahoma, New Mexico and Arizona, would close Western expansion and divert attention to a wider world in which America might assert its influence. South and Central America and China, Japan, the Philippines and Hawaii took on greater attraction.

Presidents Grover Cleveland and William McKinley were not unmindful of a United States in transition. They were, however, comfortable with a status quo which fostered the growth and power of industry and business, disregarding their impact on the common man. Despite sweat shops and child labor, the economy thrived. In the late 1890s the nation, including labor, supported the legislative and executive branches of government in promoting high tariffs and in granting favors to big business. But there was growing unrest among small businessmen, the Western farmer and the laborer, unrest which young politicians such as Theodore Roosevelt believed might tear the very fabric of America.

Roosevelt had been rather sickly as a child, but with the encouragement of his father he developed great physical strength and endurance, spending several years as a rancher and cowboy in the West, earning a reputation for his horsemanship, stamina and bravery. Roosevelt earned a degree at Harvard where he achieved membership in Phi Beta Kappa, was an editor of one of the campus newspapers and continued his habit of voraciously reading a wide variety of books. At Harvard, he expanded his sophisticated acquaintanceship with social Darwinism which preached survival of the fit among man and its institutions. Roosevelt understood that there were disadvantaged individuals, groups, sections and institutions within the nation. He had a strong sense of fair play and of equality of opportunity for all people.

Theodore Roosevelt abandoned law school at Columbia so that he might enter Republican party politics in his early 20s. His wealthy New York family backed his efforts, though at first reluctantly. He was a state legislator, achieving uncommon success; he served as a civil service commissioner for the United States, expanding that merit program substantially; he became a crime busting police commissioner of New York City, widely know for his fearless courage, stamina and skill. He was Assistant Secretary of the Navy and then led the Rough Riders in the Spanish American War. He was elected governor of New York, sending chills along the backs of party regulars as the popular leader encouraged legislation to assist the downtrodden laborer and limit industrial excess.

Roosevelt was a man of fervor with a religious dedication. He was, above all, a moralist. While in college, he began a book on the naval battles in the War of 1812, which stands to this day as an authoritative source. He would be a rare breed in the White House, a scholar, an intellectual, a professional politician, an amateur prize fighter, a strict moralist, a militarist, a reformer who was anti-revolutionary, a political compromiser. Yet, he was not a great political theoretician. He was more guided by the "rightness" he saw in public affairs than he was by some broad philosophical concept.

T.R. had initiated social legislation as governor of New York that so infuriated the Republican party leadership that they nominated him as the Vice Presidential running mate for William McKinley's second term in 1900. It was a way of getting rid of the political gadfly. Roosevelt was a national hero by this time, having earned his spurs in the field of battle as a colonel in the Spanish American War, not an uncommon source of hero worship for Americans. But he was also loved for his reputation as a fighting governor and police commissioner. The party wanted this thorn plucked, and the Vice Presidency seemed the correct instrument. He was nominated and McKinley was re-elected. McKinley, however, was assassinated, dying on September 14, 1901, just six months into his second term, elevating the outcast party rebel, Theodore Roosevelt, into office as the 26th President of the United States. At forty-three, he was the youngest man to serve as President.

Roosevelt was a popular, persuasive man who loved a good battle, and now he had the ear of the county, his party and of Congress. With religious zeal and moral invective, he almost vengefully pursued the excesses of business and corruption in politics and commerce. With equal verve, he advanced the centralization of governing in his executive branch. The various programs and platforms for which he is remembered appear almost secondary to their use as a stage for his show of great power and authority. But whether it was for self or country, Theodore Roosevelt was a successful nationalist and internationalist. He was a man who sought equality of opportunity for Americans and who tended to dislike any great show of wealth. He was a politician who would win many a battle in the White House.

He soon expressed his concern about the spread of crime, corruption and urban squalor; but it was the trusts that engaged his primary interest. Roosevelt waited five months before acting upon his concern over the power of big business and the trusts, but then he took action. He stoutly attacked the trusts and what he believed to be greed in business by directing his attorney general to bring action against the Northern Securities Company for violating the Sherman Anti-Trust Act. The action shocked Wall Street and his fellow Republicans. The Democratic President Cleveland had pursued six such cases with success in only one. But the impact of a Republican turning upon his own, and the magnitude of the target, put the entire nation on notice. The Northern Securities Company was a trust made up of the majority of the railroads in the United States, which had been controlled by E.H. Harriman and James Hill. Their merger was assisted by J. P. Morgan, and it was destined to dominate transportation in the country. Roosevelt ordered his Attorney General to dissolve the Northern Securities Company and to do so with all due speed and dispatch. Despite the hue and cry of J. P. Morgan, Senator Mark Hanna and others, T.R. waged war on trusts using the Northern Securities as his foil. One year later, the Supreme Court upheld its dissolution.

Big business remained flexible in the face of the attack and simply reoriented its strategy in response to Roosevelt's onslaught. New combinations of business avoided the clustering of trusts, but growth continued unabated. Government moved to regulation as the solution, passing legislation increasing the power of the Interstate Commerce Commission over rates and special rebates. More disclosure of industry's financial data was mandated.

As industry grew, so did labor unions. In Pennsylvania, members of the United Mine Workers Union began a work stoppage in the anthracite mines. The nation faced a very cold winter and a disastrous impact on the railroads and on production of iron and steel. The event was ideal for the activist Roosevelt. He brought together industry and labor, with government acting as an impartial third party, to implement an arbitrated settlement. It was the first time that government had not acted as a protector of business against labor. As with his challenge to the trusts, T. R., a modest reformer, not a revolutionary, was determined to preserve the institutions and values he believed were basic to America's freedom. The trusts were developing powers which rivaled those of the federal government and threatened to crush the worker and small businessman, while the militant union might bring upheaval to business and radicalize the populace. He feared both. He had no interest in subverting or hampering business, for he believed America's prosperity and world position required strong enterprise. He challenged excess and unfair domination from any quarter.

Roosevelt expanded the economic function of government by adding the Departments of Commerce and Labor to the Cabinet. He also expanded the role of the Department of Agriculture into the investigation of disease of plants and animals and the suitability of various soils and the production of better seeds. He began his great quest for conservation through the preservation of national forests and the expansion of the National Parks system, retrieving vast acreage from the hands of big business which had subverted the Homestead and other laws which were designed to grant government lands for private use.

In foreign policy, Roosevelt embarked on a path toward strong nationalism and internationalism begun with Cleveland and his Venezuelan foray. The United States became economically and politically involved in China, Japan and the Philippines. And following a pattern begun by James Monroe, the country expanded its economic influence over Puerto Rico and Cuba as a result of the Spanish American War. This far flung expansion of the nation's economic horizon led to a growing conviction that a canal was needed across the Isthmus of Panama to permit the navy and merchant ships to traverse more easily the Atlantic and Pacific Oceans. France and England had each been active in such a venture, with France having gone so far as to have designed and nearly financed such a canal. Roosevelt firmly seized the venture for the United States, making construction of the Canal a totally American enterprise.

His manner of dominating the South and Central American nations, particularly Columbia, was one which earned for Roosevelt and the United States the reputation for very heavy-handed and belligerent manipulation of its affairs with these neighbors. Gun boat diplomacy and T.R. became synonymous in the minds of many in South America and also in the minds of many of Roosevelt's enemies in Congress. He used the blunderbuss, according to his enemies. But the canal became the emblem of Roosevelt's success in international affairs, achieving the nationalistic strength which he sought for America. Roosevelt further affirmed his belief that the United States was on the threshold of greatness in his programs for the Philippines, where he encouraged enlightened economic growth and the development of governmental skills. T. R. pursued a path which straddled anti-imperialism on the one side and old guard colonialism on the other.

In a further enhancement of American's reputation as a growing power, Roosevelt settled an Alaskan boundary dispute with Britain, sending troops to the region to emphasize his determination. He won a stand-down with Germany and Great Britain as they threatened the independence of Venezuela over the non-payment of debts. Roosevelt employed the navy with great acumen and forced those European countries to acknowledge T.R.'s corollary to the Monroe Doctrine which stated that no European nation shall gain any control over any American Republic. He implemented a similar policy in regard to Santa Domingo, exhibiting his "speak softly but carry a big stick" diplomacy. But all of this was in his first term. It was in his second term that he truly hoped to make his mark.

★ ★ ★ ★ ★

T. R. was not comforted by the throngs who supported him. He was a man who suffered from anxiety that was revealed in his campaign to win a second term. He had reduced his verbal assaults on Wall Street to curry the favor and financial support of big business, and he promoted an expansion of veterans' pensions to gain votes from the massive pool of Civil War retirees. Not surprisingly, he won the presidency by the unprecedented popular majority of over 2,500,000, which was 57% of the vote. It was a great personal triumph, one that gave credence to the tactics and strategy he had mustered for both the nomination and the election. But his own party had little confidence in him, despite the fact that the American public adored his pluck, his courage, his outspoken honesty, his strong leadership, his drive to do battle, seemingly for them, against the giants of industry and commerce.

Teddy Roosevelt was the most popular president since Andrew Jackson, but he lacked the clout and influence and control over his own party that Andrew Jackson finally secured in his second term. Like Jackson, he attempted to restore equality of opportunity for the common man in the face of the encroaching power of big business. Congress set out at once to bottle up his recommended legislation for railroad regulation, tariff relief and employee disability. Roosevelt was a maverick Republican, and the old guard in the Congress would do its best to thwart his moralistic reforms, despite the adulation of the mass of voters.

Surprisingly, the President entered combat with glee and good spirit. He had learned to "rough it" in his days on the range in the West, in his prize-fighting training at college and after and in his confrontation with the enemy in the Spanish-American War. Although he did not win all of his legislative program, he did maneuver the hostile Congress over a year and a half to win approval for a bill, revolutionary for its time, regulating railroad rates and rebates. Many laws would be passed subsequently regulating monopolies and excesses of big business, but, like breaking the four-minute mile, it was his precedent-setting success that established a pattern. To his great credit, T.R. compromised and horse-traded, cajoled and argued his case relentlessly to achieve his goal. He brought the Republican party to approve reform legislation it vehemently opposed. He had stood up for the common man and for small business with pronounced success, thereby setting in motion the trend that would place unfettered *laissez-faire* business under the yoke of government.

The first two years of his second term were exciting for both T.R. and the nation. For the first time in the nation's history, laws were passed which required accurate labeling of foods and drugs and the inspection of meat. A Children's Bureau was created. He called the nation's governors together for the first time, and they met annually thereafter.

Roosevelt viewed his reform legislation as necessary to preserve both the American economic system and the social order. The Founding Fathers had created a political system which was to allow freedom and liberty to reside side by side with prosperity and the accumulation of wealth. The opportunity must be there for all. The authority of the government must be there for all, although some might profit more than others. The system of representative government, with its checks and balances, would be preserved. As Roosevelt came into office, the wealthy had come very close to controlling the courts, the Congress and the White House. Roosevelt sought to restore the representative government and democracy devised by the Founding Fathers. He was no revolutionary, but he moralistically sought to restore the right of freedom and prosperity for the many, not just for the few.

There were critics of Roosevelt who found him crass, self-serving, rambunctious and, in the words of Henry James, "The mere monstrous embodiment of unprecedented resounding noise." But was T.R. essentially bluster and illusion? The noise and bluster was, in fact, the sound of change, for Roosevelt brought the nation to a new plateau in the evolving expression of the Constitution. He set in motion the means whereby competition would survive, but it would be regulated. The nation would be headed in the direction in which the common man would once again find that equality of opportunity coupled with freedom. It was a remarkable concept, and Roosevelt sought to reaffirm it his own rather moralistic, non-theoretical way.

★ ★ ★ ★ ★

Roosevelt, however, was not willing to confine himself to the arena of domestic politics. He brought a temporary end to the isolationist policy for the nation established by George Washington in his Neutrality Proclamation and in his Farewell Address. During his second term, he effectively acted as the mediator of the war between Russia and Japan, earning a Nobel prize for peace in the process. With great ingenuity and resourcefulness, he resolved a conflict between Britain, France, Germany and Spain over Morocco, which might have ended in war but for Roosevelt's cogent diplomacy. He encouraged the second Hague Peace Conference to promote world peace by limiting the size of armies, a plan which was rejected but which was certainly the precursor of the League of Nations and the United Nations. He somewhat clumsily maintained an open door policy in China, utilizing a sizeable naval and military force to do so, and he settled a dispute with Japan over immigration. In a dramatic show of the American flag and its military strength, he sent America's now vast navy around the world, establishing for all to see the military authority of the United States, placing the nation squarely among the world powers.

★ ★ ★ ★ ★

In the eyes of many, it was in his domestic policy of conservation that T.R. gained his greatest accomplishment. He established the Forest Service in his first term; in his second term, he advanced conservation dramatically by rebuffing the incursions of utilities and the mining industry into public lands. Water resource plans were developed and he initiated five national parks and sixteen national monuments. The American people were given the gift of the country's natural beauty and grandeur, and Roosevelt was its benefactor.

* * * * *

Teddy Roosevelt's second term demonstrated his adroit governmental management, and this was especially true when one considers the hostility of Congress toward the President and his programs. During the last two years of his presidency, T.R. faced a Congress which had found its voice and its courage and a formula to thwart the President. It passed laws limiting his authority to conserve the nation's open lands, and child labor legislation was blocked.

Further challenging Roosevelt was a severe financial panic in 1907 which might have induced a fire storm of protests against the administration and the President himself. The people might blame his anti-business programs for the collapse of markets and business. But Roosevelt went on the offensive. He addressed the nation and assured them that policies he had recently advocated to regulate business were in their best interest. He expanded the money supply through government effort and enlisted J. P. Morgan to place $25 million in national banks. The panic was soon brought under control.

Roosevelt compromised with Morgan, big business and financiers to maintain economic stability and jobs, and he preserved the economic and political institutions of the nation in the process. With the economic panic over and his legislative program in trouble, Roosevelt compromised with Congress, with good spirit, maintaining some control and influence over his party. He seemed to thrive on crisis and conflict and to relish great challenge. It brought out the best in the man.

The Founding Fathers had harnessed the belief that men are greedy and have great self-interest. They coupled this with the drive for freedom and equality to bring about an engine of democracy, freedom, liberty and prosperity. This concept was not in serious jeopardy until the industrial revolution had reached its fruition in the early 1900s, permitting greed and self interest to be unfettered by the countervailing force of representative government. Industry might have curtailed freedom were it not for changes introduced by Roosevelt. He conserved American values as an anti-revolutionary who loved business and industry and national power, but who hated the massing of great wealth among the few. Roosevelt fought for the common man and a classless society just as he fought for the preservation of a militarily strong nation, and as he fought for business. He led the nation toward a somewhat less *laissez faire* state to preserve those most innovative values on which the nation had been founded. It was an outgrowth of that same conflict which arose between Hamilton and Jefferson. It would not be settled in Roosevelt's time, but he did grapple openly with the relationship of government and equality of opportunity. Interestingly, he utilized a powerful federal government which Jefferson detested, to improve the status of the majority.

★ ★ ★ ★ ★

Roosevelt had stated at the beginning of his second term that he would not seek a third term, a decision he most assuredly regretted many times. As he turned the beloved power of his presidency over to his self-appointed successor, William Howard Taft, the most popular President to his day reluctantly released his hold over his stewardship of America and its grand design. Roosevelt would be remembered for his charisma, his moralistically encased ministrations, his impetuous pursuit of causes, his great concern for conservation and, most certainly, for his appreciation for the common man. In his triumphant second term, he overshadowed the office of the Presidency as only few would do.

Reader's Score of Theodore Roosevelt

Defense: _____

Economic: _____

Vision: _____

Communication: _____

Lead Congress: _____

Lead without Popularity: _____

Invincibility: _____

Consistency: _____

Self-Confidence: _____

Strengthen Nation: _____

TOTAL POINTS: _____

Woodrow Wilson

Woodrow Wilson

It was a solemn and holy enterprise which brought Thomas Woodrow Wilson to the presidency from 1912 to 1920. Wilson was a man of considerable intellectual achievement. He was a political philosopher who envisioned democracy enhanced by the leadership of an elitist presidency, probably seeing himself at the helm. While he espoused the good of the common man, he found personal friendship almost unattainable. He was a man who spoke with unusual oratorical skills to move and lead his audiences, but he never became one with them.

Throughout his life, Wilson needed reassurance of his own personal worth. His presidency, his public speaking, his writings, his political stance, his support for such causes as the League of Nations—all contained some of the plaintive wail of a child pleading for love, affection and approval. Most frequently, for him to find any solace at all, acceptance had to be absolute, without a hint of reservation. Wilson was a man who sought desperately to control his world, to be its master, to be a pharaoh answerable to no one. Although he was a voracious reader and wrote many books, he rarely read newspapers. He would glean only enough of the current popular sentiment or trend to devise his platform. Wilson readily expounded his theories of government as well as their implementation, sometimes getting bogged down in theory. He surrounded himself with people who would say exactly what he wanted to hear on any subject. He refused the interplay of the executive and legislative branches of government, behaving contrary to his own theories on the subject.

This sketch of the presidency of Woodrow Wilson, hopefully, will illustrate the role of character in effective Presidential leadership, for his traits of character and temperament were played out most dramatically in the melodrama that was his second term.

* * * * *

II.

Wilson was raised in the post Civil War South where the violence of war was indelibly imprinted in the impressionable mind of the young son of a Presbyterian minister. Wilson's father was a stern, uncompromising task master to his striving boy, and there are those who attribute Wilson's compulsive need to find love, affection and approval to his relationship with his father.

The young Wilson tried law first, abandoning it as too personally confrontational and combative, despite his great love of debate and oratory. He married and entered Johns Hopkins, earning one of the earliest PhDs in political science. He then became a teacher, first at Bryn Mawr and then at Wesleyan, finally moving to Princeton at the age of thirty-four, to become a full professor of jurisprudence and politics. His career had advanced because of his reputation as a teacher and scholar and as an author of books on government. But the intellectual life held little satisfaction for the man. His only fulfillment had been in the expression of ideas, but this gave him no gratification of the magnitude he sought. From the time he had been in his late teens, he had seen himself in politics as a leader of men, somewhat as his father had been from the pulpit. However, he saw himself as a great statesman, a molder of men's minds and souls; but for the younger Wilson, it would be from the sphere of government, rather than the pulpit.

* * * * *

III.

Princeton served Wilson well. He published six books and became a popular figure with students, faculty and alumni. In 1902, he was unanimously elected president of Princeton. He quickly expanded the curriculum, the faculty and staff, as well as the endowment of that prestigious university, assuming over time absolute authority over both the administration and faculty. His strong outspoken leadership and his public addresses on such subjects as politics, government and the excesses of wealth brought the attention of state and national conservative Democratic leaders. They were seeking various alternatives to the populist and almost radical William Jennings Bryan, who had dominated the Democratic scene as the presidential candidate throughout recent elections.

Wilson had never been a reformer in his political views. He had rather been a student of governmental institutions and how they might function more effectively. His greatest interest was in the restoration of individualistic leadership, which his great facility in writing, oratory and organization might provide. He believed in a strong federal government, but he was not opposed to large and successful business enterprise. Nor did he support a powerful union movement. His philosophy reflected more nearly the Whig or Federalist view of government than it did a Jeffersonian or Jacksonian perspective. Conservative Democrats found in Wilson the kind of leadership they were seeking in a time of industrial expansion and progressive pressures.

* * * * *

Wilson was nominated as the Democratic candidate for governor of New Jersey and won the office on November 10, 1910. During the campaign, he had carefully sidestepped political positions that might cost him the support of the political bosses, while posing as one who was not under their control. It was a shrewd piece of political maneuvering for one so new to that arena.

Although he had been a political conservative, Wilson, observing the winds of progressive change being demanded by the Democratic loyalists, effectively rebuffed the political bosses of the state and won his entire progressive legislative program in the first legislative session. Laws were passed providing for utility regulation and school reforms, the direct election of U.S. Senators, an end to corrupt practices and a beginning of workers' compensation. He achieved these momentous results reflecting the reformist mood of the state and of much of the country by marshalling his great moralistic powers to cow the political bosses of both parties and by winning a spirit of cooperation between Democrats and Republicans in the legislature. Wilson, the conservative, had become the reformer. He had integrated his need for dominance, control and absolute authority with a theoretical and goal oriented platform, compatible with his spirit of moral authority. Wilson was a power-hungry man whose self-esteem required the testimony of applause and adulation, cloaking his strivings for power in the mantle of service to mankind.

★ ★ ★ ★ ★

The Democrats wavered but nominated Woodrow Wilson as their candidate for President on the forty-sixth ballot that summer of 1912. Wilson had overcome the opposition of Democratic bosses to win the nomination. He won the election because he faced two candidates who split the Republican vote. The incumbent, William Howard Taft, represented conservative Republicans. Theodore Roosevelt ran on the Bull Moose ticket, attracting his loyal Republican followers and the radical progressives. Wilson usurped the middle of the road, attracting Democrats and liberal Republicans. His platform, "The New Freedom," was centered upon the restoration of a competitive economy. He encouraged big business, but he staunchly opposed the stifling power of the trusts. Communicating a concern for the common man, the campaign became a moral crusade. His emotional oratorical style served him well, and he succeeded in maximizing the political polarization in the Republican party. He was elected President of the United States on November 5, 1912, with an electoral vote of 435; Roosevelt received 88; Taft, 8. Although the vote was a sizeable plurality for Wilson, the nation gave him less than a majority of the votes in the three-way split;but they did give Wilson a Democratic Congress.

Wilson very quickly set about implementing his newly found liberal and reformist Democratic platform. In his first thrust of power at Princeton, then as governor of New Jersey, and now in his first term as President of the United States, he displayed a very vital sense of the possible. He intuitively absorbed the reformist tenor of the times, and he grasped the impact of a Congress of his own party, swept in with his victory. His sense of political timing and of the correctness of his own power-oriented temperament for that moment in history boded well for his first term. He was both the bold leader and tyrant. He demanded and received the very subservience of a Congress which perceived the popularity of the President and of his program. One could not find a previous presidential term which produced so much legislation. This, however, can not be credited totally to Wilson's power for, except during the Civil War and during the tenure of Theodore Roosevelt, there had hardly been the opportunity for strong government intervention into economic and social matters. Now the growth of big business, the expansion of great wealth and the urbanization and industrialization of the nation evoked such incursions.

That trend, which began with the Civil War, found its way through T.R. to Woodrow Wilson, with his crusading nature, to the espousal of change and reform, at the very moment when its time had come.

The newly created Federal Reserve injected public authority into the banking system and the credit markets. Tariffs were reduced. The Clayton Act was passed, greatly expanding the power of the federal government to control trusts, while simultaneously exempting unions from anti-trust suits. The farmer received expanded credit through the Federal Farm Loan Act, while railroaders were given an eight-hour day. The Federal Trade Commission was formed to investigate and outlaw unfair trade practices. A compensation law was passed for Civil Service workers as was a child-labor law. Wilson worked toward greater regulation of business to limit monopolies and foster competition for the benefit of the middle-and small-sized businessman and farmer. It reflected the old effort to restore economic opportunity to the common man, to restore the American ideal. Expanding the precedent set by Theodore Roosevelt, he implemented his legislative program, setting a new measure of presidential authority.

Wilson's victories were not without cost, however. He had employed the most stringent political measures in his ramrod of legislation. He withheld patronage. He was ruthless in his demands on the members of his own party to support his legislative program which he foisted on Congress with minimal consultation. He might address Congress, as he did, breaking a precedent set by Jefferson, and he might meet with members of Congress; but he did not seek their advice. Instead, he authoritatively expounded his views. He won his legislative battle; but many in the legislative branch, including members of his own party, were resentful toward, if not irate at, the President's dictatorial manner. Wilson was fulfilling his thirst for power in the name of human good. In his religious zeal, he suffered no remorse overruling any petty opposition that failed to comprehend his "altruistic" motives.

* * * * *

Since Wilson had spent most of his adult life dedicated to the study or practice of government, logically it was primarily domestic policy that held his primary interest as President. This was to be altered, however, first by events in Mexico and then in Europe. The President decisively settled a dispute with Mexico with forceful intervention. But the war in Europe which began in August of 1914 was another matter. The nation and its President wanted to have nothing to do with that foreign conflict. The President sought a neutral course, despite his own strong pro-British sentiments. The nation was experiencing a rather severe recession in 1914, and the increased demand for U.S. goods was a boon to the economy. Sales to the allied countries exceeded those to Germany, but trade with all of the warring nations continued conforming with the nation's neutrality. As the war intensified, the British established blockades against shipments to Germany, while German submarines torpedoed U.S. ships destined for Britain and France.

The administration feared that defeat of the Allies would change the balance of power in the world and require vast armies in the United States to protect its democratic form of government. Yet, neutrality prevailed. The President offered to mediate the war, but the combatants rejected his offer. He had proposed that there be no victors, a resolution which the British and the French could not contemplate, given their hatred of the dreaded Kaiser.

In the meantime, Wilson had permitted his domestic program to languish during much of the last half of his first term. It was only as 1916 and the time for his reelection approached that Wilson once again proposed further reformist legislation to assure support from the progressive wing of the Democratic party, which was still the minority party in the country. But it was the war in Europe and America's possible involvement in it that was the chief election issue.

"He kept us out of war" was the slogan of many of Wilson's support-ers, despite his own hesitance to employ a slogan that might not prove to be accurate. The preservation and implementation of law and or-der in world affairs was actually the basis for his foreign policy.

Wilson won the election, but only by the slimmest of margins, defeating the Republican candidate Charles Evans Hughes by an elec-torate vote of 277 to 254.

* * * * *

Resentment built in Congress against the authoritarian, dictato-rial President, but this was defused by the rising trend toward patrio-tism which followed the nation's slow drift toward war. Shortly be-fore the election, Wilson used the threat of war to enjoin the Germans to cease their attacks on shipping, which were intensifying American sentiment toward joining the Allies in the war. Americans who were benefiting from shipments to the Allies rallied behind their cause. There was rising pro-Allied feeling among those who feared a break up in the old balance of power which might pit America's freedom and its way of life against the authoritarian and despotic Germany and Aus-tria-Hungary.

But it was a different view which carried the nation most signifi-cantly into a pro-war mood. It was, to some significant degree, ideal-ists who pleaded for morality in world affairs and who wished to make the "world safe for democracy" whose perspective drew the country toward war. When the Germans reneged on their agreement to limit submarine warfare and when their underwater force began again to disrupt Atlantic shipping, the country went to war. Wilson, the altru-ist, could overcome his distrust of war to do battle in the name of freedom and a lasting peace.

War was declared on April 16, 1917. During the war, Wilson

became the spokesman for people throughout the world who sought a peaceful and law-abiding world. A great ground swell of patriotism spread across America, and Wilson was America's acknowledged leader and spokesman for the "holiness" of a war to achieve peace. But Wilson was also the all-powerful Commander-in-Chief, not only of the armed forces but also of the entire nation. He demanded and obtained legislation which gave him authority to run the war but which also granted him powers customarily reserved for Congress.

Some in the legislative branch attempted to withstand the authoritarian usurpation of power, but Wilson was uncompromising. His power would be absolute and no force would stand in his way, despite very well substantiated charges that Wilson ran the war ineptly. Congressmen charged him with dictatorial rule, but he dismissed such allegations as petty and divisive.

As victory of the Allies became more assured, Wilson expanded his role as the altruistic leader of a nation and of all nations that selflessly and without desire for gain, without greed, would seek a fair and lasting peace. The foundation for his stance was expressed in fourteen points for peace which he communicated in a speech to Congress on January 8, 1918.

Wilson's proposals had a pious tone, but little basis in the real world of global politics. He pleaded for a fair peace, self-determination among nations, an impartial resolution of colonial claims, freedom of the seas, reduction of trade barriers and the establishment of a League of Nations to assure lasting peace. The Germans asked Wilson for an Armistice in October 1918 based on the fourteen points. Reluctantly, the Allies acceded to the Armistice on Wilson's terms, excluding a Freedom of the Seas Clause and any reference to minimal reparations. The war ended on November 11, 1918.

★ ★ ★ ★ ★

Surprising everyone, Wilson took absolute charge of peace negotiations for the United States. His delegation excluded members of
Congress and, most particularly, the powerful members of the Senate
Foreign Relations Committee which would have to approve any treaty
that would ensue. He failed to heed the counsel of any members of
his delegation, who were hardly the prominent leaders of the calibre
expected to assist his effort.

Wilson's counterparts, Lloyd George of Great Britain, Clemenceau
of France and Orlando of Italy, who at first opposed the idea of their
direct involvement in the negotiations, succumbed to Wilson's position and joined the conference. The peace was seen quite differently
from each side of the Atlantic. Wilson set out to engineer a peace
among equals based on security and the removal of the economic
causes of the war. These had been the basis for his attempt to mediate
the war prior to the U.S. entry into the conflict, and it remained his
consistent perspective; yet he failed miserably to negotiate that end in
his protracted stay in Paris.

Wilson left the United States for Versailles as the popular spokesman for future peace. He was heralded in the streets of Paris and
London as the great leader of all mankind in the pursuit of a secure
future. He carried a mandate for leadership into the treaty rooms in
Paris. But despite his understanding of the causes of unrest and war
and the need for conciliation with Germany, Wilson came to Paris
with only one firmly held position. That program was the approval of
a League of Nations to assure lasting peace and bring to the world
freedom of opportunity and freedom from oppression. It was a view
that was altruistic and destined to make him a revered prophet throughout the world, despite the fact that it was a utopian view at best.

Clemenceau and Lloyd George supported the League almost as
strongly as did Wilson, but they did not bring with them the excessive
baggage of moral authority and mission which Wilson applied to the
concept. The British, the French, the Italians and the Japanese, all

victors in the war, sought national gain from victory. They demanded inordinate reparations from Germany, and they asserted their right over certain of Germany's territory and colonies. They sought and won a re-establishment of old spheres of influence which would fuel their respective self-interests and assure the failure of the peace.

Wilson, the great altruist, a man with a mission of good, desirous to instill morality in the management of governmental affairs throughout the world, would not stoop to crass negotiations or bargaining in so holy a cause. Principle and rationality must prevail. Wilson's great skill was in oratory and in inspirational leadership. Finding face-to-face negotiations difficult, he sidestepped the tedious fight over reparations to gain approval of the League. His British and French counterparts were dismayed by the naive Wilson, garnering concessions for their countries that demolished the peace in exchange for a League they would support under any circumstances.

Wilson failed to marshall his great economic influence over the Allies because of sizeable American loans to them. He had popular support among the peoples of America and Europe, yet he would not muster this great influence to improve the treaty. He surrendered his fight for a peace among equals, providing for a practical resolution of the day-to-day functioning of Germany as a defeated power, and he gave up his fight for the economic survival of newly formed European nations. He retreated from his fight for a just peace to achieve a League of Nations which had unattainable goals in a world steeped in self-interest and greed. He ultimately sowed the seeds of unrest, conflict and war by acquiescing in a harsh, unrealistic settlement, a sad commentary on one so dedicated to peace. Although Wilson was not in himself responsible for the catastrophe that followed some twenty years later with World War II, he was the only individual who was in position to have made a difference in that outcome. And he failed to do so, believing that the League would resolve all conflicts and ameliorate the harsh German peace settlement. But Wilson did compose a League of Nations covenant that was approved as a part of the Peace Treaty of Versailles.

Wilson worked tirelessly on the document, frequently typing his own rough drafts late into the night for presentation to the next morning's session. The covenant contained some segments which, when they reached the press—as they did daily—were not well received in the United States. Article X, which provided military intervention by member nations to prevent national conflicts, was of particular concern to many Americans who feared that the country might be surrendering its sovereignty to an international authority. Other sections seemed to violate the Monroe Doctrine. Sentiment against the League as drafted was building in America, even though, by far the dominant view favored the League to achieve permanent peace.

As the war drew to a close in that summer and fall, the mid-term election of 1918 had become a necessary distraction to Wilson. The President stumped for Democratic candidates for Congress, but he did so in a dangerously pugnacious fashion. He demanded the election of Democratic candidates and the defeat of Republicans by asserting that he needed the absolute loyalty of Congress to finish the war and complete the peace. The campaign backfired. The Republicans had supported the war and were loyal to the wartime President. They demanded they not be turned away from office simply to place more Democrats in power. The Republicans won both Houses of Congress in 1918, providing Wilson with a Congress led by the opposing party during his final two years in office.

To make matters worse, the Republicans and many Democrats were smarting from the autocratic and dictatorial manner in which Wilson had treated Congress during his first-term legislative onslaught and during the war. Further, Wilson's plans for peace became the focus of the now very powerful chairman of the Senate Foreign Relations Committee, Henry Cabot Lodge of Massachusetts. That Senator, an old ally and very close friend of Teddy Roosevelt, had many political vendettas to settle with Wilson. Lodge was a political scholar and an authority on world affairs, and he was certainly a supporter of T.R. in the 1912 election. Wilson had overshadowed the Senator in all matters of political and diplomatic dialogue. He had defeated his friend Roosevelt and had failed to take his or, for that matter, any Senator's advice on legislative matters. Wilson had ignored the Senate, particularly Lodge, in the peace process, and Lodge was fully prepared to even the score. Roosevelt and Lodge had plotted against the League prior to Teddy Roosevelt's death, and Lodge and a group of Senators who were particularly isolationist in their views teamed to destroy the League and embarrass and damage the all-powerful President.

The nation continued its generalized support of an international organization to preserve peace, but the growing criticism of the formula devised in Paris brought confusion to the ranks of Wilson's supporters. The Senate, which is constitutionally empowered to approve treaties and must do so by a two-thirds vote, was in the mood to approve some form of League membership. A movement was growing to make recommendations to modify the treaty approved in Paris, however, and it was this revision that Lodge brilliantly intended to use to destroy both the League and the President.

Lodge cleverly perceived Wilson's obsessive nature. He observed correctly that the authoritarian President would demand absolute adherence to his precise plan for the League. To experience that self-esteem and adulation he so desperately required, Wilson would tolerate only the most unflinching acceptance and approval of his plan for the League. Lodge simply suggested, with clarity and reason, that the concept of the League was fine but that it needed some amendments. The Senate was divided into small groups: one that totally opposed the League, another that supported the League without change and another that wished to make changes. Lodge discreetly fought the battle against the world organization on the grounds that he was fighting for the integrity of the United States and for the preservation of its sovereignty.

Wilson was too rigid to compromise. His inordinate self-confidence and his need for absolute obedience were such that he would not allow the League Covenant—as passed with the Treaty of Versailles—to be altered. Wilson asserted that the Treaty had to be approved as it stood, believing it would open a Pandora's box of changes by other nations were it to be sent back for amendment. European leaders stated that they would accommodate the Senate's changes to assure the participation of the United States in the League, but Wilson refused to listen. He refused to hear the pleading for compromise by Senators friendly to the League. Wilson would not budge; he would not allow the friends of the League to vote for the Treaty with one iota of change.

Wilson clearly understood that he was in a do-or-die struggle with the Senate over ratification without compromise. When petitioned by his closest friends to bend, he stated that it is the Senate which must bend! When he understood that the Senate would refuse to ratify a Treaty without amendment, Wilson fought back. He would redress his grievance with Lodge and the Senate by taking his case to the American people. Despite his great fatigue from having traveled to Paris where he had personally spent gruelling hours in pursuit of a treaty, he determined to make an extended speaking tour for his unamended League. He left Washington on September 3, 1919, traveling eight thousand miles and delivering forty speeches to countless thousands in the process. It is unclear what he expected this audience to do for the League.

The dispute was quite technical and many Americans had grown weary of the feud over a world organization that might jeopardize America's self-interest. Senators generally supported the League in some form. The American public was not the instrument for calm resolution of the Senate debate. Wilson's exhausting tour would be of no avail as fatigue and illness overtook him. He collapsed and returned to Washington on September 28, 1919, an ill and defeated Don Quixote. Four days later, Wilson suffered a stroke that left him debilitated and bedridden, with his wife, Edith, fulfilling many of the duties of the Presidency for the remainder of his term.

The fight for the League was not to be settled quickly in the Senate, however. Despite his failing and bedridden state, Wilson had several opportunities to have his dream realized, but he refused. The full treaty came to a vote in the Senate on November 19, 1919, and would have passed easily if Wilson had allowed the Democrats to vote for compromise, but he would not. The Treaty was defeated. Wilson, though ill, directed the vote. The nation was dismayed and saddened by its failure to join in this momentous effort for world peace. The sentiment was such that the Senate agreed to vote again on the issue in March of 1920. But once again, the President remained undaunted. He would not allow compromise, and America's participation in the League went down to defeat for the last time.

★ ★ ★ ★ ★

The final years of Woodrow Wilson's second term had some of the elements of a Greek tragedy. It seemed that Lodge manipulated the tragic figure of Wilson as did the ancient gods. Wilson had achieved momentous success in his first term, maneuvering his power thrusts to benefit mankind, tolerating no infringement of his authority. His need for absolute adherence to his will to feed his self-esteem and well-being was an effective tool for progress for the mass of Americans. The war years brought together the driving force of the President and the goals of the nation at war. All of Wilson's plans and his dreams unravelled, however, as the war ended and peace returned.

Congress did not turn on him, as it had other Presidents; the sentiment of the people did not suddenly become his enemy. Foreign powers and foreign conflicts did not overturn his grand plan. It was Wilson himself and his deep-seated, obsessive hunger for unstinting adherence to his judgment that undid him. Wilson actually was not a shadow from a Greek tragedy, for he would not acknowledge his own responsibility and involvement in the pathos and drama. His plan for a world without war faded with the implementation of an unjust peace and a League struggling without United States' membership. The American people, now tired of conflict, elected Warren G. Harding in 1920 by the widest margin given any President to that time, setting aside, for a period, the cares and concerns of domestic change and world strife.

Reader's Score of Woodrow Wilson

Defense: _____

Economic: _____

Vision: _____

Communication: _____

Lead Congress: _____

Lead without Popularity: _____

Invincibility: _____

Consistency: _____

Self-Confidence: _____

Strengthen Nation: _____

TOTAL POINTS: _____

Calvin Coolidge

12

Calvin Coolidge

The 1920s were a time of individualism, materialistic extravagance, a time when responsibility was shirked for pleasure-seeking pursuits. There were actually few pressing problems at home or abroad to distract a self-indulgent society bent on fulfillment of greed, of gain, of a new life free from war and Victorian mores. It was strange, indeed, that Calvin Coolidge would minister, with their adulation, to this throng of Americans as their President from 1923 to 1929. It appears as an incongruity, a historical anachronism. But was it? Who was Calvin Coolidge? Was he the man for his time, this quite shy, self-confident, modest, loyal, lucky, opportunistic, rigid yet shrewd politician?

Coolidge was born in a small village in Vermont, to parents who were both attentive and kind, yet with a pressing need for frugality which fitted well with spartan New England values. Coolidge's father owned a small store and a farm across the road, where young Cal willingly assisted in the chores. His father was a successful politician in his own fashion, serving three terms in the state house of representatives and one term in the state senate. The son obviously inherited his father's political savvy.

After the death of his mother, Coolidge completed his high school education at a private school nearby his home. He went on to obtain his degree at Amherst College where he graduated *cum laude*, despite some early difficulty with his grades. From the very beginning of his college days, he conveyed strong interest in political affairs and in public speaking, despite his very shy demeanor. He joined a law firm in Northampton, Massachusetts, passed the bar and soon opened his own law office in that small western Massachusetts community.

The enterprising, diligent and determined Coolidge joined the Republican party in his small, chosen community, quietly learning the tenor of things politically. There was an economy of motion about Coolidge. He was elected to the city council, became the city solicitor, was elected to the state house of representatives and was reelected. He became a two-term mayor of Northampton, and then went on to the state senate where he served two terms as the lieutenant governor. In 1918, he became the governor of the state of Massachusetts. A rather dazzling array of political successes for a man who was reputed to speak only infrequently to anyone at length, usually limiting his conversations to a few brief phrases, sometimes spoken in dry humor and jest. Calvin Coolidge had a devilish streak, though not malicious, which would bubble forth unexpectedly, though frequently not perceived.

Coolidge's wife, Grace, whom he married while beginning his career, was a charming, warm, out-going, cheery woman who would contrast with the introverted Coolidge their entire life. Yet she complemented and encouraged her self-directed husband, a man who translated Dante's *Inferno* from the Italian during their honeymoon. Not a typical politician for any time, but also not a Jefferson nor a John Quincy Adams, nor a Lincoln. He was a man who respected vision in others, but he was not a man of vision himself; he was too rigid, too much the puritan, too prudent, too reflective, too opposed to take action.

★ ★ ★ ★ ★

As governor, Coolidge was quite active for him; even so, his actions were no more than he deemed absolutely necessary to meet the occasion or fulfill a pressing mood of the electorate. He was well-regarded by labor, despite his rock-solid conservatism. His legislation which attempted to reduce rents, which imposed a forty-hour week on certain industries, controlled the power of landlords and established laws which provided dwellings for the poor. He initiated laws limiting rental increases, and required landlords to maintain services to tenants. He fostered laws permitting cities to operate public street railways. It was a time when the national mood was for reform in government, a time to care for the welfare of all. Wilson had followed the call, and Coolidge, too, gave redress to the mood of the nation. He moved toward progressive action in response to his sense that his electorate wished him to do so.

Events were said to carry Calvin Coolidge in an uninterrupted line toward success. Circumstances did serve Coolidge well, but he certainly perceived the meaning of each and never failed to maximize their impact or the enhancement of his own career. One illustration stands out. As governor, he was to intercede in a police strike which had taken on national prominence. The Boston police struck in 1919, after first having joined the American Federation of Labor. They had defied a police commissioner rule against joining the union and that affiliation caused the commissioner to fire nineteen union leaders. The ensuing strike, which affected 75% of the 1,500 policemen, led to some vandalism and fear of rampant crime. Calvin Coolidge quietly waited for the conflict to fester while the police commissioner and the mayor faltered. Finally, Coolidge acted minimally, yet, decisively, sending in the national guard, declaring that "There is no right to strike against the public safety by anybody, anywhere, anytime." He became a national figure overnight.

Coolidge was reelected governor in 1919 by a record vote and became a presidential contender in 1920, receiving a small vote for that office; but he was nominated for the Vice Presidency on the first ballot. The Republican ticket of Warren G. Harding and Calvin Coolidge easily defeated the Democratic contenders, James M. Cox and Franklin D. Roosevelt. The nation was ready for a return to "normalcy," to the "good old days." Harding and Coolidge seemed an ideal team to restore life uncomplicated by war, international drama and full of self-fulfillment.

Coolidge had been trained in the legislative process as a state representative, senator and lieutenant governor, honing his parliamentary skills to a fine point. As Vice President, he chaired the Senate of the United States with uncommon impartiality and good judgment. He lived quietly and out of the limelight, avoiding society. On the morning of August 3, 1923, Warren G. Harding died, thrusting the silent, shy, ardent politician into the White House to become the 30th President of the United States. The man of few words was quoted as saying "I think I can swing it." And swing it he did.

The Harding administration had been freewheeling, with rumors of late night poker games and martinis in the White House, despite prohibition. Members of Harding's cabinet had taken large sums of money in exchange for the sale of oil rich navy owned tracts of land to an oil company at unreasonably low prices. Revelations of impending scandal whirled around Washington and the nation as Harding died. Coolidge took little time in asserting his own authority, but he was cautious about casting any aspersions on the memory of his friend and benefactor, Warren G. Harding. Coolidge was severely loyal, but not to a fault. After months of investigation and revelation, the newly installed President caused the resignation of the Secretary of Navy and the Attorney General, effectively separating himself from a scandal that sent several prominent men, including Harry Sinclair, president of his prominent oil company, to jail.

Coolidge was unalterably honest, a good judge of appointees, without any political baggage by way of commitment to any man or group, and he became a man who rather quickly won the hearts of America. He had a quiet New England wit, which sneaked up on those he confronted. He was full of playful devilment, surprising the White House staff by ringing all of his buzzers at once to see how quickly they would respond. He would ring for the elevator and then duck downstairs. He would inspect the kitchen at unexpected times. This rigid, apparently sterile, rudely quiet, loyal and yet wily politician, loved being President. He never failed to see the irony of the modest, small-town boy whose innate good judgment, common sense and savvy, put him in the nation's highest office. He never flinched at the task, but he did fulfill his role with a strict code of frugality and sparsity in government and with an allegiance to all things of business, which some believe led the nation headlong into the most disastrous depression in the history of the nation. He said, "The business of America is business." He and the Congress maintained that philosophy unswervingly through the terms of Calvin Coolidge. He had been trained and firmly believed that a greater spirit looked over man's destiny and assured his success. He connected this belief to the capitalistic system and its ability to bring about the maximization of the good for all, unfettered by government.

It was the best of all perfect economic worlds, and there was no reason to tamper with the American economic system which would divinely bring success and comfort to all. Coolidge was no materialistic worshiper himself. He believed that the fruits of economic and financial success must be the foundation for broadened education, science, culture, enhancement of family values. Economic gain, to Coolidge, must never be an and unto itself, but a means to an end— namely an enriched and full life.

* * * * *

The Congress responded weakly to the newcomer and outsider who now occupied the White House. Harding had been the selected choice of powerful Senators, who suddenly found no welcome mat at the presidential office. The progressive wing of the Republican party, led by Robert LaFollette, had an agenda of its own. It would be a challenging legislature for the novice President, with little more than a year before the national election. But Coolidge, relying on his patience, his common sense, his astute political understanding and courage, effectively engaged the battle with Congress. He vetoed a bonus bill for all veterans, which was sustained; he vetoed a bonus for World War I veterans, which was overridden; and he proposed lower taxes, which were approved with modification. He sought membership in the World Court, but was repulsed by Congress, which also excluded Japanese immigration, despite Coolidge's fight for the Japanese. The administration and Congress approved lower reparations for Germany. It was a time of compromise and modest achievement, with the upstart President gaining strong support from the American public and press for his independent and effective stewardship, albeit spartan in scope and perspective by contrast with an administration of Roosevelt or Woodrow Wilson.

The test of Calvin Coolidge as a political strategist came at the Republican convention held in June of 1924 at Cleveland. The President dominated the process out-of-hand; the old guard was deposed by forces supporting Coolidge, giving him victory on the first ballot. Robert LaFollette and his progressive followers formed a third party, but neither they nor Democrats were a match for the now popular President who won the election by the widest Republican majority in history. It had been an uninspiring and most undramatic election, but that was what the American public sought—no distractions from the day to day pursuit of personal fulfillment, of extravagance where it could be afforded, of individualism, of greed, of expansiveness on a personal level. The government had its place—a small one—and that is how the President and the people wanted it—and that is where it stayed for four more years. Rarely have the American public and its President had a greater rhythm in concert. The need for government was at a minimum, and the philosophy of the President was perfect. He had no crusading heroism in him as did T.R. and Wilson—nor were there causes about which to be heroic. It was a time when synergy meant quiet acquiescence by the government in business expansion and private existential desire.

Coolidge had the support of a wide variety of Americans. The educated and blue collar worker alike found comfort in the unintellectual, fiercely honest, patriotic and uncharismatic leader. He represented a return to fundamental values; he was unspectacular, but he was trusted.

Calvin Coolidge was an efficient administrator whose desk was quickly cleared, who delegated authority to worthy appointees, occasionally without regard to party. He would nap in the afternoon; he would take short walks through the White House in the morning; he would inspect the kitchens. Coolidge studied in great detail any matter that was to confront him in an impending meeting, frequently overwhelming his quest with facts that supported his own position.

During his second term, Coolidge promoted business as the means to advance the nation in its quest for material comfort, for expansion of science, for education, for culture, for charity. He brought about an elimination of the federal debt, and, as the federal surpluses grew, he reduced taxes. He opposed the involvement of the federal government in building of roads and most public improvements, believing these were the responsibility of the state and the local community. He felt the same way about welfare. As governor of Massachusetts, he had promoted welfare and labor legislation. As President, he was for such programs—but not for them in the hands of national government. He reduced appropriation requests for all such programs, lightening the tax burden.

Coolidge and his agenda were inheritors of the Jefferson-Madison-Democrat-Republican philosophy. The war and the fiasco over the League of Nations had disillusioned the people about government, and the sustained economic expansion of the '20s abetted the feeling of independence. Coolidge reigned supreme, with only a handful of liberal and progressive Senators and newspapermen and economists pointing to the excesses that were cropping up as weeds among the bountiful fields of private flowering. The farmers and their supporters in Congress sought a redress of their sinking prices and the deterioration of their standard of living, but Coolidge countered with the exclamation that their individual efforts were to be their salvation. They should seek solace in the character their farm lives built; their quality of life should sustain them. He believed that a God-spirited economic plan would resolve their problems. His address to Congress in December 1921 contained no mention of any social need which the government might try to assist, despite the growing spectre of unemployment, slums and child labor. Tax cuts and unfettered business were the order of the day—even if it meant excess and an impending wild speculative fever.

In the years of 1926 to 1927, the Congress passed an act providing for the mediation of railroad labor disputes, the extension of the Federal Reserve Act and twice voted to assist farmers with an act that would allow the government to buy surplus farm products to support eroding farm prices. Twice the bill was vetoed by Coolidge, with the demand that the farmer must care for himself.

America flourished, but Europe was suffering. Tariffs restricted sale of their goods to the United States, at the same time U.S. banks were extending vast credits to European businesses. As the European businesses expanded with American funds, surplus products built up. The nations of England, France and Italy found it difficult to repay their debts to the United States. Germany could not meet its even reduced reparation obligations to the allied nations. An equation for failure was evolving in the public and private treasurers of Europe at the same time that a wild frenzy of unrealistic stock market expansion was evolving in America. The American President refused to relieve the allies of their war debts. The seeds of devastation were sewn, and Calvin Coolidge would or could not see.

* * * * *

Coolidge had traveled very little during his life. His views of the world were not cloistered, however. He had intuitively supported Wilson in the League of Nations, though he observed its political futility and acted accordingly. He supported the World Court in the Congress without success. He most effectively defused an evolving conflict with Mexico through this appointment of Dwight Morrow as ambassador to that nation, giving that capable statesman a free hand and full support to resolve the issues that were hampering American business interests in Mexico. He did equally well in the appointment of Henry Stimson to resolve similar difficulties with Nicaragua and the Philippians. He used diplomacy in reducing disharmony with China. Coolidge may have provided protection for American business interests, but his critics accused him of employing "gun boat" diplomacy in his dealing with China and with South America. He maintained a peaceful, yet unfriendly, atmosphere in America's relationship with most nations. It was a period of dollar diplomacy in Europe and South and Central America.

Frank B. Kellogg, as Secretary of State for Coolidge, succeeded in the adaption of the Kellogg Pact signed by sixty-two countries, which stipulated that the signatory nations renounce the use of armed force to settle disputes. It was an Utopian idea, but it did receive the support of the American Congress and people. The rigid, conservative Calvin Coolidge had a world view for his time that was both cosmopolitan and self-serving for the business of America.

* * * * *

The United States Treasury had a large surplus of 400 million dollars by 1927; credit was cheap. But industry was experiencing a slow down in demand. Farmers were experiencing a recession, money was piling up in the banks, and bankers were anxious to lend. Money flowed freely to strange investments in Europe and other parts of the world, to mortgage backed securities to promote a real estate boom in Florida and elsewhere. It fueled the now wild speculation on Wall Street through easy, low cost broker loans to buy and promote stock sales. Total stock shares traded in 1920 were 223 million. By 1928 the number reached 920 million.

The price of stocks in many prominent companies far exceeded their worth. In late 1927 the Federal Reserve Board lowered interest rates and made money more readily available for wild speculation. In January of 1928 Calvin Coolidge stated publicly that he believed the broker loans were not excessive. The unbridled speculative fever was nearing a crisis point. A weakened agricultural economy, European loan defaults, a bust in the real estate boom, a collapse in the stock market all would combine to bring down the economic house of cards that the 1920's had produced, but not until Calvin Coolidge would be out of office for six months. He would be lucky once again.

The Congress which now returned to Washington in 1928 and 1929 was pro-Coolidge and was responsive to the wishes of the President who had announced a year earlier that he would not seek a third term. Legislation was limited to approval of the construction of fifteen new naval cruisers, a new customs treaty with China and, ironically, the allocation of funds to build Bolder Dam—which would later have its name changed to that of his successor, Herbert Hoover.

* * * * *

Coolidge reflects almost a caricature of the Republican party in its most *laissez faire* philosophy. He believed that business is the source of the sustenances which flow to society. It is not at all clear that governmental intervention alleviates the threat of economic collapse. The fact remains, however, that Coolidge and his administration refrained from any effort to grapple with the elements of the economic upheaval that lay over the horizon.

There is no question that Calvin Coolidge rejected any counsel toward inhibiting the wild speculation in the nation. He preached and practiced frugality for himself and for government. But he could not bring himself to inhibit the free rein of business, despite its violation of every principle of frugality, savings and hard work he preached. His political side—"do not interfere"—his religiously zealous, conservative bent, the conviction that the spiritual hand of God will lead the way—were abdications of leadership. He retreated from his own values, and, by permitting the nation to violate his own principles of careful management and frugality, aided and abetted the economic collapse of the nation that began in 1929. It is a sad commentary that he understood, better than almost anyone in public office, the requisites of common sense and careful husbanding of one's affairs; he had the allegiance of the nation; he could have moved upon the impending debacle without spending government money. But he would not. Coolidge was said to embody a philosophy of inaction. That may well explain his failure to respond to the impending crisis that overtook the nation.

Reader's Score of Calvin Coolidge

Defense: _____   Lead without Popularity: _____

Economic: _____   Invincibility: _____

Vision: _____   Consistency: _____

Communication: _____   Self-Confidence: _____

Lead Congress: _____   Strengthen Nation: _____

TOTAL POINTS: _____

Franklin Roosevelt

Franklin Delano Roosevelt

Few Presidents in American history have intuitively sensed what the American people wanted and then had the opportunity, the drive and the paternalistic wish to fulfill those desires as did Franklin Delano Roosevelt. He was a man uniquely timed in history, opportunistic to the hilt and imbued with a wide-ranging uninhibited curiosity that permitted flexibility in solving fiercely challenging problems. Interestingly enough, his curiosity lent a dilettante air to his character, so that his programs seemed to lack focus, a long-range plan or a theoretical or even goal-oriented content. Roosevelt was a man infused with charisma, indomitable self-confidence, unflinching optimism and an encompassing understanding of America's history. He was a man of action, and his temperament and character were particularly well-suited for the times. The catastrophic Depression and the world war were a stage set for the drama which Franklin Roosevelt would play upon for twelve years as President of the United States, dominating his era as no one else would do in the twentieth century and few had done in the nation's history.

Roosevelt was not a deep thinker, but his spirited curiosity led him to an unusual breadth of awareness in a wide range of subjects. He saw patterns and relationships in events with great perception, which to some is a measure of intelligence. He absorbed facts and feelings and their relevance. Unafraid of change, he loved novel ideas and, on impulse, frequently ordered them to be implemented. He was not a master planner in the days of the New Deal, but it is doubtful that anyone could have devised a disciplined plan to resolve so complex a crisis as the Depression with its twenty-five percent unemployment. Roosevelt was a man who kept his fingers on the strings of all phases of government. He was a frequently charming and an outwardly warm-hearted man; but he had a will of steel and used it in controlling his administration, his party and the electorate as a benevolent master and, with two exceptions, was devoted to democracy and to the ful-fillment of the Constitution. While he came to be rejected out of hand by his own class, his greatest accomplishment during his first two terms of office may have been in restoring the confidence of the vast majority of the populace in the American political and economic systems.

★ ★ ★ ★ ★

The initial hundred days of Franklin Roosevelt's first term are leg-endary and equally so are the stories of the pampered life that sur-rounded him as a child. It has been said that his mother would have bought the U.S. Navy for him if she could. Raised in a spacious Hyde Park, New York, estate, Roosevelt had his own pony as a child, was assisted by a governess and was educated by private tutors; he owned a twenty-foot sailboat, and he traveled to Europe eight times before his teens. He was paralyzed from the hips down with polio when he was thirty-nine, and the ensuing helplessness did much to transform the effects of the great indulgence he had known as a child. All of this would come together at the very beginning of F.D.R.'s second term, however, to make that period one of the least illustrious for the

President who dominated the American political scene of the 20th Century.

Roosevelt had been raised to pursue his athletic prowess with a lusty dedication. He found similar pleasure in naval history and with anything nautical, and he collected stamps. Preparatory to Harvard, he had attended Groton, the elitist private school, but was no scholar. In college his interests centered on social clubs and in the college paper the *Crimsom*, where he played an active and honored role. He was fairly popular at Harvard, but hardly the student that his cousin Teddy had been many years before. The only interest he showed beyond his self-indulgent, fun-loving existence was his support for the underdog Boers in their South African fight. He entered Columbia Law School after Harvard, married his distant cousin Eleanor and passed the Bar without completing his degree. He joined a law firm for a brief period, but found the routine not to his liking. F.D.R. had shown an interest in politics at Harvard and, after college, participated somewhat casually with the Democratic Party (his father had been a Democrat) in his home area near Hyde Park. In 1910, Roosevelt was the successful candidate for the state senate after a truly vigorous campaign in which he drove his automobile to visit every corner of the district.

Roosevelt became a leader of the progressives who were swept into office that year, fighting Tammany Hall's candidate for the U.S. Senate. The political fighter was being revealed for the first time in the young reformer who supported the standard fare among liberal programs of that day, embracing women's suffrage, direct election of Senators, direct primaries, expanded Civil Service and conservation. His strong support for Wilson in 1912 led to his appointment as Assistant Secretary of the Navy in World War I. He was thirty-one years old at the time and a novice in politics.

Roosevelt's love of ships and deep knowledge of naval history, combined with his drive and ambition and his take-charge nature, turned the assistant secretaryship into the aggressive office it had been when his cousin T.R. occupied it prior to the Spanish-American War. Roosevelt sought to expand the navy and its role in warfare.

His charm and the Roosevelt name led to his nomination as the Vice-Presidential candidate with James M. Cox in the election of 1920. The result was a devastating loss to Warren G. Harding, which led to Roosevelt's retirement from politics and public life at the age of thirty-eight. One year later, while vacationing at the family summer home at Campobello, Roosevelt was stricken with polio, apparently bringing the final, crushing blow to his political ambitions.

He refused to give in to the paralysis which destroyed the use of his legs and which, by any measure, should have made him an invalid. He courageously and tenaciously restored as many of his daily activities as possible. He learned to walk with crutches and developed great upper body strength through swimming. It appears that Roosevelt's impairment made him more sympathetic to the plight of the common man though he had certainly understood the agenda of the progressives. He developed patience, and his invalidism may have added to his attractiveness to the voter. In any event, he returned to political life in 1928 as the Democratic candidate for governor of New York. His name-recognition and charisma as well as his engaging speeches all combined to win him the governorship.

* * * * *

Roosevelt was an effective, popular and administratively skillful governor who carefully gathered together all interests, including opposing Republicans, to implement his legislative program which included such liberal causes as unemployment insurance, old-age pensions and legislation favorable to labor. Roosevelt was never interested in theories, and this particularly applied to economics and finance. The Depression began shortly after Roosevelt's first term as governor; but he had not foreseen the impending disaster anymore than had other political leaders, nor did he excel in proposing legislation to alleviate the crisis other than humane and liberal moves toward relief and public-sector spending. Roosevelt was easily reelected as governor in 1930, and his name began to spring up regularly as a Presidential nominee in 1932. He struggled through the nominating campaign, going to the Chicago convention with a majority of the delegates, but well short of the two thirds required for nomination. After pulling in John Nance Garner of Texas as his Vice-Presidential partner on the ticket, F.D.R. won the nomination on the fourth ballot. Roosevelt may have been weak in theory, but he understood drama and politics. He broke all tradition by flying to the convention to deliver his acceptance speech in person. It foreshadowed the image and format which Roosevelt would use throughout his presidency. He would be innovative, responsive to popular sentiment, forceful in any situation, dramatic, free from tradition, politically astute.

★ ★ ★ ★ ★

Herbert Hoover had quietly attempted to break the free fall of the economy by cutting taxes, increasing spending and loosening the money supply. He established the Reconstruction Finance Corporation to lend money to faltering businesses. But he drastically increased tariffs which practically destroyed international trade by 1932. Yet, it was not policy alone which defeated Hoover; it was style. Hoover was reclusive, defensive, distant and aloof. He refused to call a special session of Congress; he appeared inert to the general public. In contrast, Franklin Delano Roosevelt communicated his indomitable warmth, good spirit and optimism; he appeared to offer a plan to get the country going again. While he did not propose specific solutions for the nation's ills, he inspired confidence in his ability to be a strong leader who would bring the nation out of its morass. Herbert Hoover was soundly defeated by 57% to 40% in the popular vote, and the Democrats won control over both houses of Congress.

When Roosevelt was inaugurated on March 4, 1933, the dream of the Founding Fathers as expressed in the Declaration of Independence, that freedom and prosperity could blossom together, seemed a failed memory. Roosevelt injected a renewal of faith and spirit with his famous words indicting fear, reassuring an America that had been conservative, individualistic and pro-business for most of its history. In their own respective times, Jefferson and Jackson, Lincoln and Wilson had made inroads in the conservative and individualistic political atmosphere seeking to expand political and economic opportunity to a wider franchise. By 1933, however, a vast segment of the people were suddenly and tragically excluded from economic opportunity. Americans had not changed, but their economic condition had. Their objective was to reenter the secure economic and political environment they had known. F.D.R.'s New Deal programs and the public response to them must be seen in that context.

Legislation during that now famous first hundred days was directed toward saving and restoring confidence in the banking system. The country went off the gold standard. The Federal Deposit Insurance Corporation was created. Welfare measures, but more accurately government-created jobs programs, were implemented through the Civilian Conservation Corps (C.C.C.) and the P.W.A. which undertook all manner of public works, from roads to sewer plants. The Tennessee Valley Authority (T.V.A.) was established. But to many, the major thrust of the early New Deal was the enactment of two principal legislative programs to induce scarcity in manufactured and farm products. The Agricultural Adjustment Act (AAA) was designed to increase farm income by reducing over-production by farmers through the withdrawal of land being farmed and the purchase by government of surplus crops. The National Industrial Recovery Act (NIRA) and its administrative expression, the National Recovery Administration (NRA), were designed to combine industry into groups which would cooperate to impose production limits to control prices and wages, interestingly, a concept borrowed from the Hoover administration. These concepts were popular with labor but also received support from farmers and business organizations. The purpose of these programs was to implement an artificial market of scarcity which would induce higher wages and profit. Unfortunately, the NRA was an ill-conceived program, patched together almost abruptly. It contemplated the cooperation of both small and large business and labor to establish standards for production, wages and hours that were primarily contrary to the self interests of the respective parties.

Roosevelt was given near dictatorial authority over legislation, as Congress frequently sidestepped committee review, passing legislation within hours of presentation and after only minimal consideration. Congress was overwhelmingly behind the President and willingly cooperated in the drive to confront the nation's crisis during that first hundred days. Washington became a center of experimentation, frequently with conflicting and contrary solutions all being implemented simultaneously under the overview of the benevolent, charming, yet controlling, F.D.R. Bureaucrats vied for authority and power and for the blessing of their leader, who was not above playing one against the other or changing his opinion on a subject based on the last person with whom he had talked.

The nation and the economy rallied, though modestly, as a restoration of confidence outdistanced the recovery in jobs. The 1934 mid-term election gave the Democratic party still greater control of both the Senate and House and, with that, an expansion of the party's power. But F.D.R. did not experience any such enhancement of his authority over the legislative branch. It was an election year; there were votes to be gained. As the nation's crisis was perceived to have diminished, the independence of Congress from the executive branch once again was restored, and it overrode the President's veto of a

Veteran's bonus. It had been Roosevelt's initial policy to cut severely regular government budgets, shifting those funds to support emergency programs. The rebuke from Congress was minor, however, compared to the vituperative personal attacks against Roosevelt from the wealthy and from newspaper publishers. A deep and abiding hatred of the President and his programs arose, reminiscent of the worst attacks on Washington or on Lincoln. Roosevelt took the criticism quite personally. He was shocked and disappointed with this reaction of people from his own class, and he responded to the onslaught by targeting the rich for much of the balance of his first and second terms. Earlier, Roosevelt had shown an equivocal, almost anti-labor view; but as industrialists and big business opposed him, he embraced labor and incorporated its fight into his own, integrating that ever more powerful electorate within his Democratic constituency.

At the same time as the nation was attempting to right itself, Adolph Hitler had voided the Versailles Treaty and had retaken German territory given to France at the end of the First World War. Japan had invaded China; Mussolini would invade Ethiopia; Spain would have a Civil War, with the rebels aided by Germany and Italy. Since the rejection of the League of Nations in the early 1920's, America had turned inward and became isolationist, which the economic debacle of the 1930's only intensified. Consequently, the U.S. responded to this military adventurism by passing a neutrality act (with Roosevelt's approval) which put an embargo on arms sales to any belligerent, giving the totalitarian states a green light to their plans for aggrandizement.

As 1935 evolved, political life for F.D.R. became still more complex. The Supreme Court declared both the NRA and the AAA to be unconstitutional. Despite the fact that the NRA was proving to be unmanageable, Roosevelt was incensed that the "nine old men" of the Court could subvert his objectives and those of the electorate without having to answer to any authority but themselves. Further complicating 1935 for F.D.R. was the rise of a third-party force con-

trolled by Senator Huey Long of Louisiana, who sought to gain political power by promises of broad new programs for labor in particular. Roosevelt responded to this and other competing forces and to
the court's rebuke of the NRA and AAA by expanding the New Deal
to include Social Security, the Wagner Labor Act to replace sections of
the NRA which protected labor, farm legislation to replace the A.A.A.,
the WPA as a pump-priming economic stimulant and stringent new
taxes on the wealthy. Unemployment dropped. Roosevelt, ever the
pragmatist, had now set a still more liberal, more confrontational,
more defiant, more pro-labor, more anti-business course for himself
and his party as he entered the campaign for the election of 1936.

★ ★ ★ ★ ★

The electorate had little difficulty making up its mind that Fall,
giving Roosevelt the largest plurality in history, all but eight electoral
college votes and a towering dominance in both houses of Congress.
But the second term for Roosevelt was in some respects a gift of the
devil. The Democrats—as in James Monroe's time—had no need to
coalesce their goals against a common, opposing political enemy. Factions within the party vied for power at the expense of the authority of
the Chief Executive. Northern liberals faced off against Southern
conservatives. Of far greater note, however, were two mistakes made
by F.D.R., one political, the other economic, which visited political
damage to his authority, to the well-being of the nation and would
have adversely impacted his image in history, were it not for World
War II.

The election landslide served to reinforce Roosevelt's bitterness
over the Supreme Court rulings declaring the NRA and the AAA unconstitutional. Although the Court ruling relieved the administration of programs, particularly the NRA, which were actually functioning rather badly, as his second term began, F.D.R. was determined to

dilute the authority of the Court with its power to subvert the wishes of the executive and legislative branches of government, each of which is responsible to voter influence. In Roosevelt's view, the Court was insulated from public opinion and blatantly overturned legislation that underpinned the New Deal. The Chief Executive would not tolerate such subversion of public sentiment or of his authority.

Roosevelt announced to his Cabinet early in his second term that he intended to introduce legislation that would expand the number of Justices on the Supreme Court, allowing him as many as six appointees. The great political strategist, the man who had avoided confrontation, the man who sensed so perfectly the authority and leeway he had with Congress and the voters appeared suddenly to have become politically tone deaf. He would permit no criticism of his idea from either cabinet or Congress. It was to be a *fait accompli*. The backlash that ensued was not against a Wilson who had brought the wrath of Congress down upon himself by too authoritarian a relationship with the legislators. F.D.R. had been dictatorial during his first term, but those times were ripe for strong leadership, and Roosevelt had maintained his rapport with Congress, despite a growing dissatisfaction with the authoritarian nature of the man and his reputation for vindictive and devious acts. This was not the basis for the intense opposition to the "Court-packing" proposal. This was no revolt of Congressmen who sought to take back power from a too strong executive. The fight against the "court bill" was one based on preservation of the Constitution, of judicial tradition and of the separation of powers. Unfortunately for his legislative agenda, F.D.R. had not had a single opportunity to appoint a Supreme Court Justice during his first term, a rare situation by historical standards, producing a Court without the influence of any of his own appointees. Several justices actually wanted to resign; but the economic legislation of 1933 had reduced their pensions, so they could no longer afford to retire.

Complicating the Court-packing proposal was the fact that a number of quite progressive justices on the Court opposed it. Further, the Court had upheld several major pieces of liberal New Deal programs, after having found the NRA and the AAA unconstitutional. All of this led many Congressmen to believe that the Court was far less conservative than F.D.R. had alleged. Finally, Congressmen had obtained a commitment from several aging justices who expressed a willingness to retire, allowing the President to make his selections for the Court. But with Wilson-like intransigence, Roosevelt refused to alter his plan to pack the Court. The nation and Congress turned against him and his plan.

Roosevelt truly failed to perceive the political reality which surrounded his Court-packing plan. He had won a resounding victory at the polls, and the Democratic Congress had won additional seats; he saw the Court's opposition as a subversion of the program of the Democratic majority in Congress and of his authority to lead. But Congress would not submit to the resolution which F.D.R. proposed. The solution—the penalty—did not fit the crime. As Congress debated, the Court found several more New Deal programs to be constitutional. Congress passed a bill providing the justices with full retirement pay for life, assuring the resignation of several conservative Justices, with one Justice resigning as Congress prepared to vote. The Social Security Act was declared to be constitutional. But F.D.R. continued his intransigence; he wanted six justices of his choosing. It was July 1937 when he would be denied this right, as the Senate, refusing to vote on the matter, returned the legislation to committee, where it died. It was an ignominious failure for the popular and innovative and powerful Chief Executive.

Roosevelt rankled under his defeat. It was now 1938, and he sought vengeance against those conservative Senators and Congressmen who had opposed him. It was to be a purge, and Roosevelt pulled out all stops to promote and support those who might defeat his political enemies. It was a petty and unproductive effort, and he failed. His influence with Congress was now at a low ebb. He had weakened his ties to powerful members of the Congress, diminishing his credibility with legislative leaders in his own party.

Having mismanaged his dispute with the Supreme Court, Roosevelt became petulant, apolitical, unthinking in his drive to resolve a stumbling block he believed the Court would be for his economic solutions to the Depression. Jefferson and Jackson had each found the Court to be unresponsive to the democratic process. Each had believed that the Court did not follow the will of the people. Further, Roosevelt had won a resounding vote of confidence in the 1936 election. He understood the electorate! Congress was on his side! The economy continued to struggle along with massive unemployment, and Roosevelt had only four years to complete his task; his legacy for America must be accomplished in his final term in office. All of this might explain why he so desperately wanted a Supreme Court that would respond to his plan for the nation; but why did he pursue his goal so ineptly? The spirit of invincibility induced by his convincing victory in the election, coupled with the thought that he must succeed in his final term in office, might suffice as explanations. It is possible, however, that a hidden bent in his character and temperament came into play as well to hamper his judgment.

F.D.R. apparently could not integrate the Court's opposition, which was beyond his reach. He could neither charm, nor cajole nor woo the Court's allegiance and support. Losing his impressive patience and political savvy, he lashed out and irrationally attempted to control the Court. It is possible that in a drive to be master of his world, now emboldened by the landslide victory, he believed he should not have to negotiate, to placate, to compromise with any of the body politic. He acted as though he might now wield absolute authority, failing to incorporate the objectives of those who had put him in office. It was the gravest mistake of his political career, a petulance that would haunt his second term.

Meanwhile Roosevelt faced another problem: 1937 brought the economy to its greatest level of recovery since the Depression began. Employment expanded, the economy showed signs of flourishing, the stock market rallied. Following surprisingly conservative principles, Roosevelt and his economic advisors became fearful of too strong a boom ensuing. This was unwise, in retrospect, since seven million were still unemployed, and the standard of living of many who were employed left a great deal of room for improvement. But the Federal Reserve, following Roosevelt's guidance, drastically reduced credit, and Congress acquiesced to cut half of the W.P.A. rolls. The economy promptly slid into a "Roosevelt Depression," throwing almost two million more workers into the ranks of the unemployed. It was the result of an impulsive, non-theoretical action by Roosevelt, who readily implemented spur-of-the-moment decisions. By many standards, the New Deal had been a failed machine, for the unemployed seven million in 1937 was hardly evidence of success. The economic crisis of 1937 and 1938 gave no comfort to the planners in Washington. The administration, which by this time was actually following the leadership of liberals in Congress, quickly reversed itself by loosening credit and significantly expanding government programs and spending to alleviate a depression that was suddenly intensifying.

(As an aside, there may be some clue as to one reason for the failure of the New Deal in Lyndon Johnson's courting of business in his administration. He believed that Roosevelt was too adversarial toward private enterprise.)

★ ★ ★ ★ ★

The President was struggling with a particularly hostile Congress by 1938. Taking responsibility for leadership from the President, the

Congress had passed the last of its New Deal legislation, establishing a minimum wage and a forty-four hour work week. Although it approved a watered-down version, it had defeated F.D.R. on a government reorganization plan which appeared to be another attempt to expand his power. It was a now more independent body facing a liberal, anti-big business President whose control of the Democratic party had been weakened. Moreover, it was a time when the President, who had previously shown the spirit occasionally to attack totalitarianism in both East and West during moments of greater popularity, now followed public opinion most carefully. Because the nation was in an isolationist mood, his leadership on foreign affairs was cautious; he would follow this popular isolationist sentiment until events forced the nation's hand.

Although he retained his huge popularity with the electorate, the economic failure, sit-down strikes that were closing auto plants and the Supreme Court debacle weakened F.D.R. both politically and physically. He was increasingly the target for abuse in the press now that he appeared vulnerable. His fishing trips on naval vessels were constantly exposed and ridiculed in the press. The man who relished his first term in office as few presidents were allowed, became crestfallen, dejected, tired and nervous. He would gather his strength slowly, but not to do battle for New Deal legislation, for that experiment was slowly, steadily falling into disrepute. He would muster his strength now to venture into the arena of foreign affairs, where Hitler's Germany, Italy and Japan were developing an agenda that the world would heed.

Roosevelt had equivocated on developments in Europe in the 1930s. He had failed to assist the liberal, legal government of Spain, encouraging an embargo of armaments to the nation defending itself from the rebel Franco, who was supplied with arms by Germany and Italy. He failed to oppose Italy's conquest of Ethiopia. He hinted privately that he detested Hitler and feared that the nation might face a totalitarian Europe if England and France were to fail, yet it was not until 1938, as Europe neared war, that his full attention was directed toward the impending crisis. Germany invaded Austria; Japan expanded its war with China; Franco would win; Italy would conquer Ethiopia; the Munich Pact would provide allied sanction of Hitler's partition of Czechoslovakia, postponing war. Roosevelt shifted from a passive role to one of leadership, making those moves which would assure his place in history. He would make America "the arsenal of democracy," but first he had to move the public from its commitment to isolationism. Although his initial belief was that assisting England with war material would allow the nation to stay out of the war, Senate leaders pleaded the case for a "fortress America," which would care for itself while avoiding foreign conflicts. Roosevelt displayed renewed self-confidence, meeting with Senators to work out a program to help Britain and France defend themselves. He reestablished the working relationship with Congress he would need to arm America.

In March of 1938 the Germans overran Czechoslovakia. F.D.R. failed to have the Neutrality Act amended to remove the arms embargo. On September 2, 1939, Poland was invaded, offering Roosevelt his opportunity for action. Britain and France declared war on Germany. Roosevelt was now the man he had been in his first term. He utilized his political prowess to the full with a recalcitrant, isolationist Congress, which finally amended the Neutrality Act in October. Military equipment would be sold to the allies on a cash-and-carry basis. Selective Service was enacted, as was a program of lend-lease of military hardware. The President and the nation were trusting that the allies, now better armed, might stave off the growing might of Germany and Italy, and keep America out of war.

Roosevelt was to demonstrate again his innovative temperament. At Einstein's suggestion, he ordered the research begun which resulted in the atom bomb. Denmark and Norway fell to the German forces in April of 1940. In May, the German blitzkrieg began in full

as their troops ripped through France. On May 16, F.D.R., addressing Congress, asked for a massive buildup of American military planes
and ships. Congress, hoping the measure would keep America out of
war, approved his plan. Belgium and the Netherlands fell, and by
June 14, Paris was in German hands. But Congress would not permit
the administration to transfer warships to the British. Churchill, now
in close contact with Roosevelt, pleaded for the warships needed to
forestall an invasion. In August, Roosevelt announced his plan to
trade fifty over-aged destroyers for British bases. It was a courageous
act on the part of Roosevelt in the face of an isolationist Congress, a
move which gave the British a sorely needed boost to their morale.

Through all of this, the political pot boiled. It was a presidential
election year, and Roosevelt had affirmed that he would not run for a
third term. The Republicans nominated Wendell Wilkie. There were
no serious contenders for the Democratic nomination; and, despite
his public protestations, his own political maneuvering resulted in his
nomination on July 17, 1940. But it was a nomination given without overwhelming acclaim due to reservations concerning a third term
for any President. As the war clouds gathered, Roosevelt wrapped
himself in the incumbency, giving only few political speeches, stating
that he would keep America out of war. Many who had supported
F.D.R. turned against him, as isolationists, Communists and conservative Democrats voted for Wilkie or for splinter candidates. But
Roosevelt won 449 electoral votes to 82 for Wilkie. The third term
taboo had been broken, but it took the popular appeal of Franklin
Roosevelt and the impending world conflict to do so.

The wartime triumph of the nation under the leadership of Franklin
Delano Roosevelt did much to wipe away the blot which his second
term might have been for the only President to have been elected to
the office four times.

F.D.R. rose to heights of leadership during World War II. He
inspired confidence; but more, he inspired a belief in eventual victory

and a feeling of cohesiveness in the nation. He chose his military and domestic leaders wisely, and, with equal wisdom, he gave them the free hand and the tools to win their battles. He became the leader of the free world, as Wilson wished to have been. His plan for a United Nations would be adopted; and he had a vision for peace which may have been flawed, but was, nonetheless, far reaching. Yalta was intended to bring Russia into the family of nations and, by their insertion into Europe, hopefully end the divisive war-producing envy and power-seeking which had been the bane of America from Washington's day.

But all of this was during his third and very brief fourth term. What were F.D.R.'s accomplishments based on his first two terms and to what qualities of the man are they to be attributed? The plan to pack the Supreme Court and a faltering New Deal haunt his second term. Of necessity, his faults of vindictiveness, self-righteousness and pettiness have to be acknowledged. His management by impulse, sometimes contradictory, compromised his reputation. His steadfast and insatiable curiosity, coupled with his opportunism, resulted in the perception that there was a lack of focus in his programs during the New Deal. It gave his efforts at that time an aura of dilettantism. Yet with all of his faults, there is a distillation of his intelligence, his character and temperament and his time in office that defines his success during his second term. The Depression had devastated many Americans. Individualism and *laissez-faire* which blossomed in the '20s had failed. The promise of America was denied to countless millions. If Roosevelt had any great plan for America during his first two terms, as Jefferson did in his drive for democracy or as Lincoln did in his desire to save the Union and extend the franchise, it was to seek intuitively to preserve the nation and its economic and political institutions and to provide economic security to the people. Roosevelt had a kinship of understanding for the underdog, a dedication to fair play. He restored hope and confidence, even though he did not adequately restore jobs in his first two terms. He most assuredly expanded for all time the role of government, introducing the concept of the safety net for the worker through New Deal programs, expanding the role of government in the resolution of individual economic problems. And quite unintentionally, he introduced government spending as a device to counter recessions.

Franklin Roosevelt's achievements for an America in Depression were recognized by the throngs of Americans who idolized him. He put people to work, the business climate improved, and he restored confidence in the political and economic system. The devastating Depression had no precedent and no cohesive body of economic theory to utilize in its resolution. Consequently, Roosevelt's highly flexible, intuitive and experimental approach may have been the only course available. But all of this and, particularly, his impaired second term might not have served well to burnish the name of Franklin Delano Roosevelt in the annals of history. It would be the Second World War which offered F.D.R. that rare second chance. It was the war with its opportunity to implement military discipline and to incorporate the lessons of history that permitted him to focus all of his brilliance, his charisma and intuitive leadership to win the war and begin the process of world peace which fostered the legacy of Franklin D. Roosevelt as one of America's outstanding Presidents.

Reader's Score of Franklin Delano Roosevelt

Defense: _____

Economic: _____

Vision: _____

Communication: _____

Lead Congress: _____

Lead without Popularity: _____

Invincibility: _____

Consistency: _____

Self-Confidence: _____

Strengthen Nation: _____

TOTAL POINTS: _____

Harry Truman

14

Harry S. Truman

"**G**ive 'em hell, Harry!" That encouraging shout from the voices of his supporters during Harry S. Truman's whistle stop campaign says a great deal about the 33rd President of the United States. Truman's self-confident, up-hill battle for re-election and the robust response of his audience was reminiscent of Andrew Jackson and the throngs who cheered him on. Truman spoke the language of the common man and inspired the broad support he needed to win his first elected term in 1948.

Truman was a politician by profession. He was a diligent student of the tasks set before him, honest to a fault in a field frequently lacking that quality, fiercely loyal to his party, to his friends and to his allies. He was extremely well-versed in history, with a deep understanding of the American presidency and the objectives of the Founding Fathers. He was a man of courage, unshaken by criticism or adversity or crisis. He was resolute, decisive and methodical, yet, on several occasions, he made momentous decisions with too little planning or insight. To many, he appeared an average Midwesterner, a modest man who almost seemed to wear the presidency as a mantle of authority and honor as a means of carrying out his stewardship. He

217

had been rather soft spoken until well into his tenure in the White House, when he developed a confrontational and acerbating tone. He had extraordinary self-confidence. He was a political realist who understood the electorate, but, uniquely for a presidential office holder, he did not choose to follow the mood of the voter; he chose to lead.

* * * * *

II.

Truman was raised in or near Independence, Missouri, in a matriarchal family steeped in Southern tradition. He was the son of a strong-willed, educated and cultured mother who engendered a taste for reading and piano in her boy. His poor eyesight restricted his athletic ability and made him appear to be a "bookworm." His father was a farmer who tried his hand at business from time to time, providing adequately for his family, despite some reversals. Although he was not raised in wealth, he was never aware of poverty or deprivation. It was not until he graduated from high school, well near the top of his class, that financial adversity hit. His father had speculated and lost heavily in grain, causing Harry to give up any thought of college. He spent several years as a bank clerk in Kansas City. He then joined his father to farm his maternal grandfather's nine hundred acres for ten years of physically arduous work.

World War I pulled Harry Truman from the farm into a field artillery unit in France, where he served as an officer with some distinction. He developed valued self-confidence from his success in courageously leading his men into dangerous combat. When the war ended, Captain Truman returned to Kansas City to join an old friend in the haberdashery business; but the severe economic recession that occurred after the war caused the bankruptcy of that fragile enterprise. Truman then decided to enter politics, a love he shared with his father who had held modest political offices in the area. He successfully ran for county judge, an administrative office with responsibility for such matters as building roads and bridges, receiving the endorsement of the Pendergast family, power brokers in the Kansas City Democratic party. He was defeated for a second term in the office, but successfully ran for the office of presiding judge two years later and was re-elected in recognition of his honest, diligent, frugal and meticulous fulfillment of the post.

In 1934, Harry Truman became the successful candidate for U.S. Senator from Missouri, riding into office on the coattails of the widespread support for F.D.R. and the New Deal, and also because of his own grueling campaigning and the avid support of the Pendergast machine. He was a staunch New Dealer, although he voted to override F.D.R.'s veto of the veterans' bonus. Truman developed a close relationship with many of the inner circle in the upper House and was known as a hard and loyal worker for innovative New Deal legislation such as the Civil Aeronautics Board, learning well how politics worked at the national level. He became a fighter against big business, concentrating on combinations in the railroads, siding with labor in their disputes. He was known as a trust buster, and his view of the overwhelming power of big business led him to support F.D.R. in his battle with the Supreme Court and his effort to expand its membership. Truman concurred with Roosevelt that the Court was pro-big business, although he clearly understood the grave error Roosevelt had made in failing to win over Congress to his point of view.

Truman's support of Roosevelt and his policies was not significant enough to win the President's backing his bid for reelection in 1940. F.D.R. gave his support to the governor of Missouri who was running for the office of Senator, believing that the governor could deliver more votes for Roosevelt. But Truman gained the nomination with diligent campaigning and support from the railroad union and minorities, going on to win his reelection. The victory returned him to Washington as the war in Europe was heating and American military preparedness was escalating.

As his new term began, he initiated an inspection tour of defense installations and production facilities, detecting significant waste and mismanagement. His speech to the Senate on the subject led to the formation of a watchdog committee of five Senators to oversee defense contracts and the appointment of Truman as its chairman. The committee was particularly appropriate for Truman, following, as it did, upon his experience in building roads and bridges in Missouri, where he developed a reputation for proficiency and honesty. Fortuitously for Truman and the nation, the committee's efforts resulted in billions of dollars in savings for the war effort, propelling the name of Harry S. Truman before the American public and before the Democratic party. The exposure led to his nomination and election as Vice President in Roosevelt's fourth term in 1944.

* * * * *

III.

The allied forces were moving toward a meeting with Russian troops in Berlin and American forces were in combat with the Japanese in Okinawa when F.D.R. died on April 12, 1945, just three short months after his inauguration. Harry S. Truman, one of the few who enjoyed being Vice President, suddenly became President of the United States without having been involved in or informed of the myriad of events and decisions he would face as Chief-of-State. He was catapulted into unexpectedly having to make decisions that would soon drive the war effort toward its conclusion in Europe, that might have led to a potentially cataclysmic invasion of the mainland of Japan, that would lead to the impending April 25 meeting in San Francisco to formulate and enact the United Nations and that would perfect the atom bomb and test its effectiveness.

The Yalta Conference—the gathering of FDR, Churchill and Stalin early in 1945—which was to have set a pattern for Russian, British and American cooperation for a free and independent Europe, came unraveled just four months after the meeting, as Russia asserted its own authority over governments in Poland, the Baltic and the entire Eastern European sphere it occupied. The Congress had rebelled against Roosevelt as his new administration settled in, angered by a lack of involvement with the decisions of Yalta and with a President who had all too frequently bullied his way with the legislative branch. Truman, the grass roots political realist who had spent ten years in the Senate and who was an exacting student of American history, set about to effectively rectify that impaired relationship with Congress.

Although sympathy for the new President abounded, confidence in him was slow in coming, for he followed a master communicator whose voice was the stabilizing force of the entire free world. Truman spoke haltingly, in monotone, appearing at first as a cautious, unsophisticated Midwesterner with "down-home, farm-boy" inflections, replacing the towering figure of Franklin Roosevelt. But the confidence of the nation was vested in its institutions and in its impending success in the war. While the country grieved its loss, the new President honed his administrative and leadership skills, quickly mustering his self-confidence to shoulder the responsibility thrust upon him. The responsibility for the nation during almost eight more years would rest in the hands of a man whom the country barely knew, a man it certainly had not selected as its President.

Truman, on the other hand, slipped rather quickly into harness. He studied every aspect of the challenges handed him. He gathered capable allies and advisors; he gathered Roosevelt's best confidants to help him understand Stalin and Churchill and the war and what the peace might bring. He understood that at the base of the Yalta plan for Russian hegemony in eastern Europe lay the need for Russia to declare war on Japan to help bring that bloody war to an end at the earliest possible moment. Distinguished diplomats were dispatched to review with Churchill and with Stalin the fast moving events of the world. The Germans surrendered unconditionally on May 9, followed in June by the successful completion of the United Nations Charter in San Francisco, which was approved by the Senate 89 to 2 in July. In the same month, Truman attended the meeting in Potsdam, Germany, bringing him together with Stalin and Churchill. It was a frustrating endeavor which failed to settle the future of Germany or the liberation of Eastern Europe.

Truman approved the testing of the atom bomb and gathered a blue ribbon committee of scientists and educators to determine whether the bomb should be employed to end the war. The decision to drop the atom bomb on Hiroshima and Nagasaki was reached soon after the bomb was successfully tested and the special committee on its use reported its findings that the bomb should be employed. It had been estimated that no less than half a million Americans and possibility a similar number for the Japanese would be saved by a quick end of the war. Further, the war would have taken no less than eighteen more months. The alternatives were clear to the decisive President who firmly believed he had done his homework. On August 14, 1945, the war ended with Japan, with a surrender that Truman demanded be unconditional, except for the right of the Japanese people to keep the Emperor, subject to a final vote of approval on the Emperor by the Japanese people. It was a minor compromise which many believed expedited the return to normality in Japan.

The end of the war brought fears of the kind of severe recession which followed the demobilization after the First World War, a collapse which caused Truman's own business to fail. And this concern brought out the politician and New Dealer in Harry Truman within days after V.J. Day. He prepared an extraordinary lengthy and encompassing program for social legislation that would rival any submitted by Wilson or F.D.R. The legislation would have provided for both full and fair employment, expanded unemployment compensation, a housing program, expansion of the T.V.A. concept and veteran benefits. The President was establishing his command of the job as well as his deeply entrenched dedication to the working man. His proposals reflected his distrust of the ability of very big businesses to fulfill the economic needs of the nation. Truman believed in the philosophy of the redistribution of wealth in an economic environment of scarcity. He was carrying on the tradition of aiding the common man to "go ahead," with the government taking the active role promulgated by F.D.R.

Neither Congress nor the nation were ready for so much liberal legislation. Truman salvaged little more of his program than the G.I. Bill of Rights for veterans and the Council of Economic Advisors to assist the President in his overview of the economy. The nation had had enough of war and of government, the economy was functioning well as the war ended, and there was no interest in any more New Deal, or Fair Deal, as Truman called his program. Universal military training was rejected, demobilization was stepped up, and the unfulfilled wants and needs dating back to the 1930's became the principal concern of the world's only major nation not physically damaged by the war. Now comfortable in office, Truman began his tough, aggressive and sometimes belligerent political confrontation with the Congress and the voters, which became his trademark. Although his foreign policy would be given bipartisan support, getting tough with Congress on liberal policies did not work.

Upheaval reined as 1946 began. Rarely in American history has a president been faced with so many challenges while a country was at peace and free from depression. It was a strike filled period with as many as one million workers walking off their jobs. War time controls were ending, and workers were hoping to improve their share of the economic pie. Appearing anti-union, the government sought to draft the railroad workers to prevent a strike. The coal mines were taken over and operated by the government. But shortly thereafter, Truman vetoed the Taft-Hartley Act, limiting the power of the unions, totally confounding all who tried to understand the strong-willed, independent President. Congress overrode his veto. The impatient nation did not respond well in the November elections, voting in the first

Republican Congress since Herbert Hoover's days. And festering in the background was China, torn by civil strife resulting from the revolution of Mao's Communists against that weak nation's government forces led by Chiang Kai-Shek. The United States could shoulder only so much responsibility in an unstable world. However, Truman sent George C. Marshall, the retired Chief of Staff of the Army and the military helmsman for all allied strategy in the war, to China to try to understand and resolve the issues there and to prepare a policy which the nation might follow.

Britain, weakened by the war effort, pulled away from its long standing defense of the Eastern Mediterranean, particularly Greece and Turkey, as 1947 began. The United States shipped food to England and Europe, now struggling to survive, and it enacted legislation which would sustain Greece and Turkey from any onslaught from Russia, now apparently expanding to absorb all nations along its borders, converting them to friendly Communist satellites. The Truman Doctrine for Greece and Turkey began a long process of containing Communism and protecting democratically elected states that would end with the lifting of the Iron Curtain some forty years later.

During the days when Britain and France ruled the world, the balance of power was vested with economic coloration. When America began to assert world authority under Harry S. Truman, a kind of Monroe Doctrine for democratic, or, more accurately, non-Communist, governments would prevail. It would not be South American nations, nor would it be England, France and Spain that might be interlopers; but it would be Communism, either Russian or Chinese, that would be warned away from or forced to retreat from any non-Communist nation in the world. Economic gain might accrue to the United States, but it seems incontestable that far more than economics was at stake for the United States as it confronted the totalitarian Russia and, later, China. World peace and democracy were imperiled.

The Congress was not inclined to follow the President in domestic matters, but it took two months to pass the aid bill for Greece and Turkey. The bipartisan foreign policy took root, with the containment of Communism holding sway over any isolationist sentiment. It was a conservative sentiment, actually, in the wake of a failure to stop Hitler in time to prevent World War II. It was equally conservative to oppose strong unionism and the expansion of the New Deal. But Truman remained undaunted, trying to maintain good relations with Congress, while continuing to be an active and surprisingly innovative President, who gathered about him men of skill, talent and experience. The armed forces were unified, creating the Defense Department and the Joint Chief of Staff. But the situation in Great Britain, France and Italy worsened as those countries failed to restore their economies or lead their citizens. Washington was concerned that a Communist or tyrannical government might take over any of these nations.

George C. Marshall, now Secretary of State and the spokesman of the administration, proposed a massive plan to aid and rehabilitate Europe in June of 1947. By November, Congress was considering his proposal for a $17 billion aid package for Western Europe over four years, at a time when the federal budget was $36 billion. Congress resisted the "outlandish" proposal at first. Select committees were formed by Truman to define the need and describe how it could be met with fiscal responsibility. Czechoslovakia fell to the Communists in February 1948. Congressmen traveled to Europe to discern for themselves how truly fragile were the democratic governments of Europe. The Russians stepped up their efforts to win domination in Italy and France. By April, Congress approved $5 billion of the $6.8 billion Truman had requested as the first installment on what became known as the Marshall Plan. Bipartisanship prevailed. An internationalist view overtook the more isolationist Congress.

As world crises ensued, Truman traveled to Mexico and to Brazil to extend the hand of friendship and the "good neighbor" policy to these South American nations, returning with expanded joint defense agreements with each. While these relations within the hemisphere were improving, turmoil expanded elsewhere. Nationalist China was losing its battle with the Communists, and in April of 1948, the Russians closed the roadway access to Berlin from allied zones to the west, a near war-like act that might have brought on troop confrontation but for the insightful resolution reached by the administration. Food and fuel were air lifted daily to Berlin by 130 planes. By June, the Senate passed a resolution approving the concept of a unified European defense with American participation. It was the first step toward the North Atlantic Treaty Organization (N.A.T.O.).

* * * * *

IV.

1948 was filled with an array of foreign tensions that would easily rival those faced by any U.S. President, but it was also an election year, and as tensions and pressures upon the American people expanded, so did inflation and the general discomfiture. Truman suffered a popularity rating of only 36%, according to a Gallup Poll about the same time that the air lift to Berlin was begun. By 1948, the war was past, new conflicts confronted the nation abroad, and at home, labor continued to disrupt the domestic scene. America was administered by a President who, although respected, could not inspire enthusiasm for his style of leadership or for his courageous stance on so many issues.

While Truman easily won the Democratic nomination for President, defeating several challengers, it seemed a foregone conclusion that Thomas E. Dewey, the Republican nominee, would complete the Republican take over of the executive as well as the legislative branch of government in November. The Democratic campaign was plagued with a severe shortage of funds, barely meeting the cost of stamps for the mailings needed to solicit contributions. The left and right deserted the party as Henry Wallace, a strong advocate of appeasement to Russia, formed a party of his own, as did Senator Strom Thurmond, a southern Democrat who gathered about him all those who opposed Truman for his civil rights proposals.

The press tended to like the President who spoke frankly and frequently with them, always giving complete and knowledgeable replies or clearly stating "no comment." His relationship with the 80th Congress was another matter, however, despite the cooperation he received on foreign affairs. Truman used the Congress and its reluctance to pass his liberal domestic policy as a whipping post in the election. He called them back into special session after the nominating conventions, demanding that they enact legislation to provide for national health insurance, an expansion of social security and rural electrification and an increase in the minimum wage. Of course, the Congress failed to respond to his demand.

As the polls produced more certain evidence that the President could not be elected, Truman set out on a "whistle stop" back-of-the-train speech-making tour of the nation to communicate with the electorate. His relaxed self-confidence about winning the election set him apart from everyone in his administration and in the party. He damned the "do nothing" 80th Congress and spoke intimately and extemporaneously to each small and large group that gathered to hear him. The crowd readily joined in with the spirit of the plain spoken candidate with such encouraging shouts as "Give 'em hell, Harry!" He traveled over 30,000 miles, giving an average of ten speeches a day to upwards of fifteen million people. It was a testament to his political savvy and also to his remarkable endurance and strength and to that of his wife and daughter who accompanied him on the tour.

Despite the failure of all but one pollster to predict a Truman victory, he won the election, with Dewey receiving only 45% of the votes, sweeping in a Democratic Congress with him. The victory was attributed to Truman's campaign, but it was also due to a favorable farm economy that produced unexpected Midwest Democratic votes.

Further, the slight economic downturn in the fall caused a turnout of the workers who rallied behind the President who had vetoed that hated Taft-Hartley Act. Jewish support was in response to his recognition of the State of Israel. Blacks voted for him because he had banned discrimination in the armed services and in the Civil Service. Truman would now be a President elected to office, out of the shadow of F.D.R., his own man.

* * * * *

V.

The joy of victory was there for Truman as much or more than it had been for any President elected to a second term because he had so miraculously plucked success from the jaws of failure. He had none of the spirit of destiny that had been present in the minds of some who had won their second-term elections. The unpresuming Truman understood history and his role in it well enough to know that he must run for the office and that he must fight for it, but it was not a battle endowed with self and ego, as it certainly was for Teddy Roosevelt, Wilson and F.D.R., leaders who were also innovative and courageous. Truman was essentially an affable person, frequently smiling and generally cheerful in a folksy sort of way. He was customarily unflappable in the face of crisis, and he depended greatly on the highly qualified men who filled positions of power around him to counsel him so as to fulfill his meticulous style of planning and leadership.

In his Inaugural Address he stressed his vision for a new world order through his foreign policy, promoting support for the United Nations, the recovery of Europe through the Marshall Plan, military aid to the nations of the free world and, finally, assistance to the underdeveloped nations through the transfer of knowledge in science and industry.

Congress continued its bipartisan support of foreign policy, approving N.A.T.O. in April of 1949. A military draft had been reinstituted the previous year. Europe apparently absorbed much of the attention the nation could muster, as the Nationalist Chinese acknowledged defeat in 1949 and retired to Taiwan. The United States had contributed more than $2 billion to that cause, but the administration finally concluded it could save China from Communism only by sending in American troops. The Nationalist Chinese were suffering from weak and corrupt leadership, unable to maintain morale and esprit among their own forces.

The fall of China would have serious repercussions for Truman and the nation. It brought forth a group of China supporters whose vehemence over what they called a treasonable loss of a free nation opened a Pandora's box of investigations into Communists in the Truman administration that wreaked havoc in the nation for the remaining term of the President. There is little evidence that Nationalist China could have been saved, short of sending in troops for what conceivably would have been a Vietnam-style tragedy. Truman's policy probably took well into account both the military and the political reality that the American people would not tolerate a long and indecisive war. This was demonstrated to George Washington, and it would be again to Johnson and Nixon and to Truman himself. Lincoln certainly grasped the point well.

While the affairs of Europe and China festered, a political sectionalism overcame domestic America. Truman would not be given any leeway to expand civil rights or social legislation with a Democratic legislature that was dominated by Southern and Western conservatives. But such domestic matters did not dominate his second term. Although the Berlin blockade ended, the power of Russia expanded as it exploded its own atomic bomb, encouraging Congress and the nation to back the President on his initiatives to aid Europe. America became blanketed with a fear of Russia and Communist expansion, which, though realistically founded, had some of the intensity of paranoia.

The United States perfected the H-bomb to assure military superiority. A bipartisanship to stop Communist expansion evolved, leading to competition between the President and Congress over the seat of greater anti-Communist leadership and control. An organization known as the China-First lobby became the outspoken Communist fighter, attacking the administration for the loss of Nationalist China. Yet military troop build-up at home was not a part of the equation for either the administration or Congress. The Marshall Plan was beginning to revive Europe, the line was being successfully drawn for Soviet expansion, trade with Europe was fostering American economic growth. In the face of expanded foreign aid, the armed forces became the sacrificial lamb to the desire for a peacetime economy with a balanced budget. The military dropped from twelve million men in 1945 to 1.5 million in 1947. It was one of several compromises that Truman would make early in his second term. He feared federal deficits and he understood that limits existed to the responsibility which the United States might take and that prioritization was necessary. The turmoil of the 1940s and early 1950s were relatively uncharted seas for America and the world, although the lessons of World War I and II illustrated the danger of not standing up to totalitarian expansion in its early stages.

The fall of China in 1949 set off a wave of anti-administration salvos that unnerved the public and the President. The most notorious player in a display of anti-communist investigations was a Senator from Wisconsin, Joseph McCarthy. The British had discovered Communist agents in its government, and Truman had initiated his own housecleaning of disloyal Americans early in his second administration. The Soviets made no secret of their drive to infiltrate and take power wherever they could. The United States and its administrative departments would have no reason to be exempt. Yet, Truman became defensive and testy over inquiries, dredging forth his most political and petty side in positing a Republican plot, unrelated to any possible factual basis for investigation. Defensiveness pervaded the administration and nastiness pervaded those probing Communism in government.

Truman had carried Roosevelt's mantle in his first term, serving as the unelected caretaker of the office he inherited, protecting his political flanks, observing a level of protocol with the Republican opposition which he loosened in his second term. He attacked Republicans as being incapable of any act that would not serve special interests. He accused Republicans of seeing a Communist in every closet; he saw Republican chicanery in their every inquiry into Communist infiltration. Truman defended federal employees who were investigated in the manner of a machine politician protecting his fold. The public showed its distaste for the loss of China, the investigations and Truman's response to them through the polls that gave him a favorable rating of only 37% in 1950.

Richard Nixon had made a name for himself in 1948, exposing Alger Hiss as a Communist employee of the state department. But in 1950, Joseph McCarthy established a pattern for reckless, unsubstantiated charges against the administration for harboring Communists. He lied, was a demagogue, fiercely attacking the state department and the Truman administration and particularly George Marshall for the loss of China, implying a conspiracy to aid Communism. The public listened as they felt the pain of China's loss to the enemy, possibly through the deliberate acts of members of the state department. The American public, always impatient with failure, honed in on the loss of the nations of Eastern Europe and China to Communism. The nation that had so gloriously won the war could not tolerate the anxiety of a Soviet power which had occupied and retained territory in that war or a China lost because the administration avoided providing troops to sustain the forces of Nationalist China. Public sentiment, some bad judgment and the weight of world crises combined to sour the second administration of Harry Truman, when the war in Korea would dominate the world scene.

In January of 1950, Truman agreed to a defense and aid agreement with Korea, which Congress refused to fund. Secretary of State, Dean Acheson, did not include Korea in the primary Asian defense perimeter of the United States in January. In June, the North Koreans invaded their southern neighbor, setting off a war that neither the administration nor the American people wanted. But United States involvement seemed the logical step in meeting every Communist force with force in the defense of non-Communist frontiers. Truman's response was instantaneous. Whether Russia was party to the attack was unknown, but there was no time to find out, as the North Koreans marched South, threatening the survival not only of that ally but also of Japan and the very presence of the United States in Asia. The invasion might have been the start of similar attacks in Eastern Europe and the middle east. The line would be drawn where it was broken, in Korea. Truman and Acheson called on the Security Council of the United Nations to intervene militarily to halt the incursion. Russia had boycotted the U.N. over its failure to seat Communist China, allowing the United States to petition successfully that international body to defend South Korea. The move strengthened the U.N. by the leadership role thrust upon it, as American and free world opinion supported the concept of the world body as peace keeper. The consequences for America became complex, for Truman did not go to Congress to declare war, placing the legislative branch in a subservient role to that of the U.N. in the expanding conflict.

Naval forces were the first to be employed, as the South Korean forces were almost immediately overwhelmed by the army from the North. By the end of June, Truman supported General Douglas MacArthur's suggestion that American troops be deployed to save the

Korean Peninsula. Congress was asked to approve a $10 billion appropriation to expand the military to defend both Asia and Europe. The funds were approved, but Congress, particularly the Republicans, contended that they should have been kept informed of the administration's position on the conflict, a mistake which Truman might not have made in his first term.

The American forces, under the command of MacArthur, proved no greater match for the North Koreans than did the South Korean army, as the combined defending forces found themselves pocketed at the south boot of Korea in August, about to be pushed into the sea. In September 1950, MacArthur maneuvered as brilliantly as he had at any time in his career, invading the western shores of Korea near Seoul at Inchon, successfully driving a wedge into the heart of North Korean troops, winning back all the territory that had been lost. Truman, following MacArthur's advice, ordered that the U.S. forces move north of the 38th parallel, the border between North and South Korea, but not cross the border into China with either troops or planes. In retrospect, that decision to move north of the 38th parallel and to limit the war both incited the Chinese Communists and protected them from air attacks. In late October, hordes of Chinese troops swarmed across the border. By late November, the U.N. forces were in disarray and in full retreat. MacArthur had wanted to bomb the bridges crossing the Yalu River between China and North Korea, but Truman refused, fearing this might expand the war by bringing in the Soviet Union. It was probably a mistake.

The midterm election brought surprising strength to the Democrats, defusing some of the criticism of Truman's handling of the war. But by December, the President was forced to declare a state of emergency; wage and price controls were instituted, taxes were raised, the National Guard was called up, the draft was extended, the army expanded. The military budget first rose to $22 billion and then to $50 billion by 1953. The failure of the nation to prepare itself for military conflagration was being turned around. The failure to declare war, however, dampened public allegiance to a "police action" that dragged on for the remaining two years of the Truman administration.

By January 1951, Seoul was lost again, but by March it was re-captured and the 38th parallel held. The U.N. began peace negotiations with the Chinese, but it also declared them aggressors. Douglas MacArthur pursued an independent course and demanded that the U.N. carry the war north of the Yalu River into China, against the express orders of Truman who was diligently attempting to reach a compromise truce with the Chinese that would allow them to save face. MacArthur's attacks on the Chinese and his demand for their total defeat led to Truman's decision to fire the popular general. It was a courageous and decisive move by the President, but hardly one that would enhance his popularity with either the general public, now tired of the war, or with the conservative elements in Congress.

Truman initiated the idea of a limited war which would set the standard for the Vietnam War. Although the Korean War was one that could be maintained at the 38th parallel, it was not without damage to the popularity of the President. June of 1951 brought an announcement at the U.N. from both the Russians and the Chinese that truce negotiations might begin. Meanwhile, Senator McCarthy used the unpopularity of the administration to make his attacks on George Marshall, manipulating the American public to join him in charging those he blamed for failures and weakness in combating Communism. Truman remained steadfast in defending Marshall and in fighting the war. An armistice could have been consummated in late 1951 or early 1952 if Truman had allowed the forced return of all Chinese and North Korean prisoners, regardless of the expressed desire of some to remain in the South. Truman refused forced repatriation for all the prisoners, prolonging the war. And while the war was now contained in Korea, Truman expanded United States forces attached to N.A.T.O. in defense of Europe. He defended George Marshall as a great patriot and attacked the investigative tactics of McCarthy. In one of his few domestic actions in his second term, he asked for legislation to take over the steel mills in the face of an impending strike which he believed would impair the war effort; but he failed to receive congressional support.

The 1952 election pitted General Dwight D. Eisenhower against Governor Adlai Stevenson of Illinois, who would not permit his name to be associated with Harry S. Truman in his nomination or in the campaign. The Eisenhower victory was attributable to the adulation with which he was held by the American public, but it was also an expression of dissatisfaction with Harry Truman.

★ ★ ★ ★ ★

VI.

Presidents who lean against the wind and propose a course which is not already firmly entrenched in the American psyche will endure unpopularity. Washington, Jefferson, Lincoln and F.D.R. knew this. It is a courageous President who will lead and spend his political popularity in causes he believes to be in the best interest of the nation and the free world. Truman was not gifted with urbane rhetoric; his leadership had to rest with his ideas and his acts. Grant, for one, was a President who feared to risk. Jefferson acted, but did not try to bring either the American public or Congress with him. Truman, on the other hand, was a driving force for change who lacked the innate skills to rally a wide constituency to him. He undoubtedly benefited from the clear-cut lessons of World War I and II that the aggressor is best stopped early.

Truman and the high quality personnel he gathered around him produced innovative solutions in a wide array of both domestic and foreign crises. He developed the containment policy which would be followed for forty years, eventually bringing the Communist world into the council of nations.

He was, however, a man who gave no joy to the country in his leadership. He contrasted totally with F.D.R. and his style. Truman was so plain and so unceremonial, yet reasonable and appropriate, that the ingestion of his policies was taken by the American public almost as a dose of castor oil. He would initiate a dramatic new policy and implement it with diligence and intelligence and dispatch, yet he could be intemperate and petty, displaying such characteristics in explosive episodes which Americans found distasteful.

Truman's first term was exemplary for its innovative risk taking forays into uncharted leadership. He had vision for world peace and domestic achievement which he communicated adequately to both Congress and the nation. His second term, however, focused only on what he and the nation believed to be the defense of the anti-Communist and democratic way of life. Although it limited the scope of that term, it clearly followed the vision he had set for the nation and the world.

In retrospect, popularity and style do not function well as a measure of a President. These may represent pandering to public sentiment, following the polls, playing it safe, postponing solutions, avoiding confrontation and conflict. Truman did none of that. He was a compromiser, but he was also contentious, sometimes in excess. He led America and the anti-Communist world through seven years, leaving the nation and the world far stronger and safer and enduring.

Reader's Score of Harry S. Truman

Defense: _____

Economic: _____

Vision: _____

Communication: _____

Lead Congress: _____

Lead without Popularity: _____

Invincibility: _____

Consistency: _____

Self-Confidence: _____

Strengthen Nation: _____

TOTAL POINTS: _____

Dwight Eisenhower

Dwight D. Eisenhower

Momentous events permit gifted leaders to rise to greatness. World War II offered Dwight David Eisenhower one of these rare opportunities for success, and he seized the day with a singular mixture of intelligence, intuition and character. The presidency would not offer an equal opportunity.

Eisenhower was one of six sons raised in Abilene, Kansas, by religiously devout Pennsylvania Dutch parents who preached and practiced morality, the work ethic and pacifism. Despite their strict heritage, the boys were given sufficient freedom for Ike to become a popular and competitive member of the "gang." Although his interest was more with athletics than with books, he had pleased his mother by reading the Bible from cover to cover as a young boy. Achievement, commitment, humility, fulfillment of duty and hard work were all inculcated into the Eisenhower boys. Throughout his professional career, Eisenhower conveyed some hint of repressed rebelliousness to this burden of service thrust upon him. The most obvious indication of this was the rage he would express at unexpected moments. His fierce temper, which would expend itself quickly, was legendary. His vacillation on accepting the nomination for President and his occasional reluctance to confront may also have reflected this hidden resentment.

His military prowess was clearly revealed in 1926, when he graduated first in his class in the Army's Command and General Staff School. His many years as aide to General MacArthur in Washington and in the Philippines gave him insight into the military as well as national and international politics. Pearl Harbor brought him into a close working relationship with General George C. Marshall, Chief of Staff of the Army, for whom he prepared a briefing on the military and political implications of the Japanese attack. Eisenhower, cogent, direct, concise, and both militarily and politically astute, quickly became head of planning for the Army, and by June of 1942, little more than six months after Pearl Harbor, he was named Commanding General, European Theater of Operations. It was a tribute to Eisenhower, but also to the judgment of Marshall, Roosevelt and Churchill.

The Second World War was the first in history to employ military forces of several nations under the command of one of the participants. Eisenhower met the challenge with uncommon military and political acumen, always falling back to evaluate the nature of the challenge, sidestepping personalities and tucking his own ego and even his rank into the background to bring together disputing factions to reach the objective. He never failed to delegate, to staff fully, nor did he shirk direct responsibility and decisiveness. He personally gave the order for the D-Day invasion. He developed strong personal friendship with or knowledge of Churchill and the other leaders of the Western World.

Eisenhower was a man who elicited deep respect from those around him, no matter the rank. He conveyed an aura of strength. He was a man of great ambition and striving, camouflaging that drive with apparent equanimity and forbearance. His self-confidence would rival that of any President, yet he carried it with a reserve and dignity shared only by George Washington. His intelligence would surprise the casual observer, for he generally displayed his amiable, cooperative, leadership qualities, concealing the intellectual insights that underlay his achievements. His administrative and organizational skills were driven less by his rigid military training and discipline than by an imaginative and masterful understanding of the individual, his abilities and how to motivate him. Eisenhower had the rare ability to identify those who were in control or might control a situation, and he was diplomat enough to manage diverse rivals and calamitous events with profound success.

The end of the war brought hero status to the general. The American people loved him for his triumphs, and also for his humility and his broad smile that warmed the nation and brought the allied commander to their hearts. He served as Army Chief of Staff after the war, assisting in the unification of the military. In 1949, he became President of Columbia University; and in 1952, he returned to government as the first commander of the North Atlantic Treaty Organization (N.A.T.O.), establishing Eisenhower's commitment to collective security through the alliance of the West.

★ ★ ★ ★ ★

Both political parties wanted to nominate Ike for President as early as 1948. But it was the Republican party which he selected as his party for the nomination as President in 1952. Earlier, he had conveyed disdain for politics and had waffled, even in entries in his diary, as to whether he wanted to be President. He never doubted that he could do the job, but he doubted his desire to bear the responsibilities that the office would thrust upon him. Had he not already served enough? He hinted that he felt sated and craved no more power or authority. But if so, the mood was soon set aside.

Eisenhower played so hard-to-get that the convention almost nominated Robert Taft, the powerful "Mr. Republican" Senator from Ohio.

But Eisenhower's staunch supporters and his last minute campaigning turned the tide. He was nominated on the second ballot.

The campaign was noteworthy for three of Eisenhower's speeches. One outlined the Communist threat to the world and the necessity for a long term commitment by the American people to stand up to Communist expansion. Another failed to defend his close friend and mentor, George C. Marshall from attacks by Senator Joe McCarthy. The silence, apparently for political benefit to himself, was a measure of Eisenhower's inner drive to win the White House. Finally, the speech which probably won him the election hands down was the one in which Ike said that, if elected, he would go to Korea. That war seemed endless, and the triumphant general was offering to bring it to a close. Eisenhower and his Vice President, Richard Nixon, won 55% of the popular vote, defeating the intellectually stimulating Adlai Stevenson. It was no landslide, for the Democrats retained some of the old loyalties from the days of F.D.R. But the Republicans won the presidency and both houses of Congress, though not by overwhelming numbers.

★ ★ ★ ★ ★

Eisenhower won because he was the popular, beloved commander who had defeated the Nazis. But he won also because Americans were ready for a change after twenty years of Democratic rule, two wars and unresolved domestic and foreign tensions. Some of the electorate voted for Eisenhower to restore a two-party system, and still others to bring the isolationist Republican party under the guidance of a leader who had demonstrated a world view. His first term would satisfy those who wanted America to join in the council of nations, but it would not gratify those who sought to alter the Republican party, for, first, Eisenhower was as conservative as any of the party stalwarts, and, second, he chose, as a matter of leadership strategy and personal style, to sidestep customary party politics. His objective was to retain leadership through personal popularity, which would take precedence over the popularity of the party.

Eisenhower, according to one historian, seemed to manipulate his world through the use of apparent contradictions in his personality, particularly the contrast that existed between his public and private persona. Publicly he would appear to stumble, to be uninformed on issues, to depend on his appointees in all matters, to be unskilled in ordinary grammar and sentence structure, to play golf more than he worked and to be without either political knowledge or aptitude. Privately, he did his homework, writing clearly and cogently the policy which his staff was to follow and explaining why the policy had been evolved. He worked long days, and evenings, if necessary, to be informed and prepared. His working relationship with the leaders of both parties in the Senate and House would rarely be equaled in history. Yet, he projected the image of an unperturbed, lovable, frequently politically innocent, highly dignified Chief of State who could do no wrong. This method of operation confounded his critics and provided insulation for the President that assured his popularity, while permitting his behind the scenes freedom to maneuver.

Eisenhower was a true conservative in domestic matters and an internationalist in foreign affairs. He had great administrative skills, he had patience and a long term view of the world and its trends, and he was a man driven, as were Grant, Wilson and F.D.R., to maintain his popularity. Eisenhower seemed to know instinctively how to harness his need for popularity by using it as a means to advance his leadership, not to support his ego. As with Jefferson and Grant, he avoided confrontation, and his popularity and behind-the-scenes management became shields against confrontation. As President, he sacrificed gratification that might arise from a more open and overt route to achievement. This administrative methodology would deny him personal credit for some of his successes; it would result in diminished achievement, on occasion, but it was, nonetheless, the route that Eisenhower would follow during most of his tenure as President.

* * * * *

Eisenhower was deliberate and expeditious in his assault on the office of the Presidency. In the administrative sector, he set about, prior to his Inauguration, to establish an executive line of command that would bring order to what he believed to be a chaotic scene. He created a chief of staff, filling that position with Sherman Adams, a hard working task master, obedient to the wishes of the President and a stern authority figure. He appointed a liaison person to work with Congress and a head of the Bureau of the Budget. His cabinet was a collegial assembly, geared to implement and criticize Eisenhower's various programs. He frequently used his cabinet as lightening rods, allowing them to shoulder blame for unpopular acts of the President, shielding his own popularity. He established the National Security Council to coordinate the conduct of foreign affairs. Eisenhower was a tireless worker, beginning at 7:30 a.m., reading several newspapers and preparing for his agenda each day. He was always prepared for his meetings and visitors, having fully completed his homework.

Although a fiscal conservative, Eisenhower understood the electorate well enough to know that the New Deal must stay intact. In fact, during his first term, he expanded Social Security; he initiated the Interstate Highway Program, the largest public works project in American history; and he brought about passage of the St. Lawrence Seaway. He cut defense spending, he sponsored a tax cut. The Department of Health, Education and Welfare was established. He vetoed increased price support for farmers. The economy of the nation was growing at a rapid rate, and unemployment was low for all but a few periods in the Eisenhower years. While the gross national product expanded, inflation was no more than 1.4% annually. Eisenhower, the conservative, believed that a policy of planned alternatives to aggressive New Deal expansion was the most effective tool to preserve minimal government.

The domestic scene, however, was anything but tranquil. Senator Joseph McCarthy had made life quite miserable for Truman and had threatened to do the same for Eisenhower. It was a time when the failure to win in Korea, coupled with the expansionist success of both Soviet and Chinese Communism and the growing concern about the security of the nation, all came together to bolster the demagogic tactics of all those playing on such tensions to gain power and an audience. None was more skilled than Joe McCarthy, as he attacked the seat of government for its "softness" on Communism, for its "traitorous" weakness in the face of Communist growth and for its retention of employees, particularly in the Department of State, whom he alleged were secretly Communist.

It was Eisenhower's strategy to avoid personal confrontation with any opponent, and, particularly, with a demagogue such as McCarthy. He would not get into the mud with him. From January of 1953 through December of 1954, the fear of McCarthy's threats influenced administrative policy, both domestic and foreign. Programs for foreign cooperation with both allies and neutrals, confrontations with China, policy toward Russia, plans on military budgets or appointments of ambassadors—all came under the microscopic scrutiny of Senator McCarthy and the test of anti-Communist discipline as he defined it. It was a distraction from the administration's programs. The attention of the entire nation was diverted.

Eisenhower would not confront the man or his tactics until very near the moment of McCarthy's impending censure by the Senate in 1954. He worked deliberately behind the scenes to encourage Senators to oppose McCarthy, and he proposed a massive cleanup of government to forestall investigation by McCarthy. McCarthy was finally trapped as he attacked the U.S. Army for weakness on Communism at the very time that the Senator used undue influence to gain favors for a former aide.

The President succeeded in isolating himself from the assaults of McCarthy, while he worked behind the scenes to defuse his power. But the stress on the nation, on his own programs and on the employees of the federal government might have been lessened and the time for rebuff shortened had Eisenhower gone to the American people with his opposition to McCarthy. It was a trying time in American history, and Eisenhower was parsimonious about the expenditure of his goodwill and popular support. He did not spend it willingly nor, to his mind, needlessly. The matter was resolved in due course, which conformed with Eisenhower's understanding of the man and of the problem. Eisenhower was a relatively patient man, able to endure delay to maintain his method of leadership.

Despite Ike's growing popularity, the 1954 midterm election saw the Democrats take hold of both the Senate and the House. It was a loss to the Republicans; but it was not necessarily a great loss to Eisenhower, who found the old guard Republican leadership almost more difficult and uncompromising than the Democrats. For example, the Bricker Amendment, though defeated after a long battle, was a Republican effort to limit the treaty authority of the President. Republicans voted against a measure supported by the President, censuring McCarthy; they blocked his proposals to send funds to neutral nations; they demanded a cut back in New Deal programs and pushed for more stalwart attacks on Communists. These actions occurred while the President spent hours in personal dialogue with leaders of both parties in each House, in behalf of his own programs. He actually found the Democratic leadership more receptive than were the Republicans to his international and domestic legislative agenda, depending on them to carry his programs to success. Eisenhower was considered a weak advocate by his critics, but in most matters he found an oblique, indirect route to the seat of power and struggled with that power to compromise and persuade until he achieved an acceptable measure of success.

* * * * *

His first term was highlighted by major foreign policy initiatives. The armistice in the Korean War in July of 1953 was engineered through secret negotiations with China through third party nations, with Eisenhower hinting that failure to end the war might bring on nuclear destruction. The Russians detonated a hydrogen bomb in 1953, setting the stage for a nuclear standoff with the U. S. The pro-Communist governments of Iran and Guatemala were overturned through C.I.A. engineered coups. The collective security doctrine was expanded in Europe, in Southeast Asia and in the middle East.

It was a highly activist time in foreign affairs which was publicly led by the State Department under the ardent guidance of John Foster Dulles who conveyed a strident and bellicose anti-Communist face to the world. Under his tutelage, America was the grand player of the game of brinksmanship, laying massive retaliation at the door step of Russia and China as a response to Communist expansion. One major component of this strategy was for the nation to depend on the threat of the use of the nuclear bomb as an alternative to a large and costly military, permitting Eisenhower to achieve his goal of a non-deficit economy. The game was played through on several fronts, some with greater success than others.

A clear and successful example of Eisenhower's command of foreign affairs was the relatively peaceful defense of the island of Formosa, the homeland of Nationalist China, now known as Taiwan. Formosa was effectively protected, despite the fact that the near-shore islands of Quemoy and Matsu, under nationalist China's control, were bombarded for many years by the Chinese Communists, injecting fear of an attack on Formosa. But a strategy cleverly thought-out by Eisenhower warded off a Communist takeover of the Islands and of Formosa, while keeping American forces out of conflict. It was the implied threat of war which proved an adequate deterrent, a far better resolution than the actual use of nuclear arms suggested by leading conservative Republican defenders of Nationalist China.

Vietnam first entered the American vocabulary in 1954 as the French were losing in their defense of that nation to a Chinese Communist supported regime. The Americans and British were invited to assist the French to fight off that Communist inroad, but the British declined. Eisenhower also declined, asserting that the best interests of the United States would not be served by being bogged down in jungle warfare that would end in local, probably Communist, domination when American forces would finally be withdrawn. He advanced his view that the United States cannot serve its best interest by resisting each and every Communist aggression. Eisenhower believed that in the long run, the confrontation with Communism would end successfully. Taking the long view, he wished to select each battleground with full flexibility of choice, analyzing the risks and the opportunities, the potential results and the benefits for the nation on a case by case basis.

The foreign policy of the administration had two faces during Eisenhower's first term. Dulles was bellicose, the spokesman for rigid, uncompromising "brinksmanship" anti-Communism. He refused to meet Chou En-lai, premier of China, when Chou asked for a dialogue. Dulles frequently suggested that there be a rollback of Communism in Eastern Europe. In contrast, Eisenhower expressed his conviction that America did not have such absolute power. Eisenhower, who took final responsibility for foreign policy, shared Dulles' view of the Soviet and Chinese threat, but he publicly and privately reiterated his passionate belief that nuclear war was unthinkable and that a peaceful accommodation of adversaries was essential. This was the underpinning of Eisenhower's foreign policy, although the assertive tones of Dulles was the one most heard in his time as President.

Eisenhower sought peaceful coexistence with Russia briefly when Stalin died in 1953. Again in late 1953, Eisenhower pursued a peace offensive with his proposal, made before the United Nations, that the

United States and the Soviet Union contribute atomic material and know-how to the entire world for peaceful purposes. World opinion was tumultuous in its praise of the proposal. At first, the Soviets' response was favorable but soon became protective and uncooperative. Eisenhower's major objective was not fulfilled, and the disappointment was great, although nations did cooperate in atomic research which included the study of nuclear fusion as an energy source. However, at that time the arms race was in its infancy; the old guard in Russia and in the United States were wary of cooperation and were protective of their defenses.

In 1954 and in 1955, the Soviets, under the new leadership of Nikolai Bulganin and Nikita Kruschev, announced a peace offensive of their own, liberating Austria and proposing disarmament and an international inspection of nuclear and conventional weapon plants. The United States was embarrassed by the offensive and refused, fearing that the American technological superiority in weaponry would be compromised by such inspections. At a Big Four Summit in Geneva in 1955, Eisenhower countered the Soviets by proposing an "open skies" concept for reducing world tensions, allowing the Soviets and the United States to fly over each other's territory to inspect military encampments. Although it was a popular proposal, it earned little more than propaganda benefit for the United States, although it did that very well.

World events heated as Eisenhower's first term drew to a close. An uprising in Hungary seemed to bring promise of the rollback of Communism that Dulles had sought, but Eisenhower made it known that the United States was in no position to give military assistance to this isolated Eastern European nation.

Very late in his first term, Eisenhower's decisiveness gave way to vacillation to bring about an unfortunate application of strategy. Gamil Abdul Nasser had ended British colonial influence in Egypt, as King Farouk was deposed as the head of that nation. Nasser played the United States against the Soviet Union to obtain the support of each nation for his economic expansion. The United States came close to funding the Aswan High Dam, a major Nile reclamation project. But the cautious administration demurred, backing away from support. Shortly thereafter, Egypt nationalized the Suez Canal, taking possession from the French and the British. It was an anti-colonial move which generally conformed well with American foreign policy, but it placed great stress upon America's relationship with its major allies and opened the door to Soviet adventurism. The United States appeared to stand back as events unfolded. The Israelis, the British and the French planned to retake the Canal. The U.S., along with the United Nations, effected a brief delay of the invasion. The invasion took place, with the United States siding with Nasser and the Soviets in forcing the retreat of the British and the French from the Suez and from the entire middle east, causing those countries to become second class nations in the eyes of the rest of the world. Eisenhower and Dulles apparently played the game with Nasser at their most cautious and frugal level. In retrospect, the failure did not open the middle east to Communism; but at the time, the success of anti-colonialism seemed badly tainted by vacillation and the embarrassment of America's allies. It was a less than auspicious conclusion for America's foreign policy in Eisenhower's first term.

In September of 1955, Eisenhower suffered a heart attack. His political future lay in doubt, though his health seemed relatively stable. It left the Republican party leadership for the '56 election in turmoil, along with the future of the Republican party. But the President rebounded, finding his recuperation an unacceptably boring time. Despite his own early questions, he agreed to run for a second term. The 1956 election brought together the same candidates, with Nixon continuing as the Vice-Presidential nominee, despite Eisenhower's open dissatisfaction with him. Once again, he would not confront an issue directly. Eisenhower defeated Adlai Stevenson again, but by a greater margin than in 1952. The Republican party did not fare as well, however, as the Democrats increased their lead in both houses of

Congress. Eisenhower received 58% of the popular vote. It was a measure of his personal popularity.

★ ★ ★ ★ ★

A President who is elected to a second term expects to do no less than continue in the path he followed in the first. To Eisenhower, this meant enhancing a conservative domestic policy and collective security and containment of Communist expansion abroad, a reduction in world tensions where possible and a retention of his popularity and leadership. He wrote in his diary that he thought his second term might be easier than the first, with so many lessons already learned. But it was not to be. It seemed that enthusiasm for the office may have diminished for Eisenhower in his second term. He did not shirk the burdens of responsibility, but they appeared to rest heavily on his shoulders as he fulfilled his final years of public service.

Eisenhower's second Inaugural Address, which was to set the tone for the second term, was filled with a vivid profile of America, no longer a fortress unto itself, dedicated to the flourishing of freedom in small nations and committed to peace between the super powers. The President sought to entice Americans to win over third-world nations, a program which came to be known as the Eisenhower Doctrine. The keystone of that program was the appropriation for foreign aid, which the previous Congress had cut, with its staunchest opponents being the Republican leadership.

It was 1957, and Eisenhower would have three very challenging, and frustrating events overtake his stewardship during that first year of his second term. The first was the budget process itself, the second involved civil rights, and the third was the Soviet success in lifting a satellite into orbit.

The budget, as the embodiment of the administration's program, included expanded welfare, school construction funds and foreign aid. It was to be the enactment of the theme of his Inaugural Address; it was the expansion of the policies of his first term. However, the process became troubled from the start, as his own Treasury Secretary, George Humphrey, came out in favor of cuts in the President's budget. The President, surprisingly, supported his secretary, stating that the Congress should pare where it believed cuts might be made. Confusing almost everyone, Ike then went over the heads of Congress, speaking to the American people in support of his program. But the Congress finally cut $4 billion from the $72 billion dollars originally proposed. Foreign aid was cut from $3.86 billion to $2.86 billion. Eisenhower's critics, and some within his own administration, looked upon the debate, the opposition of his own party and the final appropriation as a major defeat for the President. But Eisenhower himself supported the reevaluation of the budget, indicating that he was ever the fiscal conservative who believed in his programs, but he also prized fiscal caution and the independence of Congress from executive influence. His fear of an unbalanced budget, which might threaten the future of the nation as much as would any foreign invader, was a basic thread through all of Eisenhower's strategy and planning. He was ready to compromise, so long as the essence of his long range goals was served. Yet it must be said that the President vacillated in the management of his budget proceedings. His public statements on the matter gave mixed signals, hinting at a lack of conviction within Eisenhower on the merits of the programs he promoted.

The Supreme Court had ruled in 1954 in the case of Brown vs. Board of Education that school segregation was unconstitutional. Eisenhower had privately expressed his dissatisfaction with the ruling, expressing his conviction that cultural practices, such as racial integration, take a great deal of time to change and cannot be hurried. By the fall of 1957, the significance of the Supreme Court ruling became clear to all when black students attempting to attend high school in racially segregated Little Rock, Arkansas, were physically restrained from doing so by the National Guard, called out by Governor Orval

Faubus. After several weeks of delay and a failure on the part of the President to persuade the governor to abide by the Supreme Court ruling, Eisenhower nationalized the Guard and brought in soldiers from the 101st Airborne Division to restore order and enforce the right of the Negro students to attend classes. Eisenhower set aside his own conservative views to support and defend the Supreme Court's interpretation of the Constitution, despite his own exasperation over the events and their resolution. It was an unsettling time in domestic relations, with Eisenhower's decisive, though belated, action to enforce the law becoming a calming force. But such social issues as civil rights were of minimal interest to him or his administration.

October of 1957 brought home to the entire world that the Soviets were moving briskly and innovatively to expand their military and technological capability by lifting its "Sputnik" satellite into space. Shortly thereafter, a satellite lifted a dog into orbit. The nation was jarred into a competitive spirit, feeling the sting of a "backward" Communist nation achieving scientific success that had apparently eluded America's space program. The administration was defensive, citing its almost $1.5 billion missile program. There is no question that the Russians appeared to be beating the United States in space, with serious military implications. Defense against attack from space came into question. The nation became frightened. The space program was soon expanded, scientific education was promoted, and the United States sent its own crafts into space, although utilizing rockets less powerful than those used by the Soviets.

Congress, under the guidance of Senate majority leader Lyndon B. Johnson, took charge of the legislation that quickly implemented a radical expansion of the country's space program. Eisenhower was satisfied to allow Johnson and Congress to lead the way. The apparent fiasco was a product of the administration's conservative and frugal military program. In the long view of history, the failure was insignificant. It was, however, the motivation for the intensive expansion of scientific and engineering study that followed the Soviet success. It was, indeed, the reason for the significant expansion of the space program. It spearheaded advances that would occur in science and technology, but it also greatly intensified the sense of urgency for a marked expansion of the military. Finally, it was probably the basis for the moon exploration of the Kennedy/Johnson era, designed to reinstate lost American prestige.

In September of 1957, Congress enacted its first Civil Rights' Bill since the days of Reconstruction. The administration, although not a strong advocate of the bill, facilitated its enactment and aided in eliminating some of what Eisenhower believed to be its more destructive amendments. It was Lyndon Johnson, however, who was given the greatest recognition for the passage of the legislation which was considered momentous, despite its limitations. Eisenhower's role in the new law was overshadowed by the dynamic Johnson.

The ebulient popularity which Eisenhower had worked so diligently to preserve began to fade as 1957 drew to a close. Although high by many standards, his popularity dropped to 57% as the nation responded to Sputnik, budget fights, civil strife and what appeared to be indecisive leadership by the President. And, in November, to make matters worse, he suffered a slight stroke impairing his speech, but causing no other damage. The effects of the stroke were short lived as his vigor was rather quickly restored. But as unemployment rose, the sense of malaise remained. The problems facing the nation and the world were not subject to ready resolution or dramatic moves. NASA was established to improve the missile and space program but, it was not enough to buoy America's self-confidence. U.S. troops were sent into Lebanon to defend a coup that was said to have Communist support. The show of strength enhanced Eisenhower's image and gave notice that Communist incursions would be resisted. But the nation was not heartened, as the worst recession since the '30s Depression sent almost 5.5 million into the ranks of the unemployed. Eisenhower tenaciously resisted all calls for spending increases or tax cuts, fearing inflation and budget deficits, allowing the economic crisis to resolve itself.

The President's problems intensified as he suffered a telling blow to his administrative cohesion. His Chief of Staff, Sherman Adams, the stern force through whom all policies and programs seemed to flow, was accused of using his influence to assist a business friend in his dealings with the government. At first, Eisenhower defended his right hand; but as political pressures grew, Adams resigned, adding to the intensifying burden of the second term. Fidel Castro's success in Cuba, establishing the first Communist state in the Americas did not add to the President's comfort as 1957 drew to a close, and 1958 and 1959 brought little respite in bad news. The 1958 election saw the Republicans troubled at all levels, as they lost seats in the Congress and in the governorships. John Foster Dulles, who had been fighting cancer for several years, died in the spring of 1959, thrusting foreign policy fully into the hands of the President.

Eisenhower responded with surprising resiliency to the wave of events that might have swamped his administration. He invited the Soviet leader, Nikita Kruschev, to visit the United States to improve relations between the nations and to lessen world tensions. It was a successful visit, with a clear opening of communication between the two nations. Eisenhower made a tour of major countries in Europe, Africa and India, inspiring the people of those parts of the world to see him as a champion of peace and good will. His popularity at home and abroad was restored to its greatest height.

The Kruschev trip to the United States was followed by a four power summit in Paris in May of 1960, which was to move the major powers toward a still greater spirit of cooperation and a reduction in confrontation and world tension. It was to be followed by an Eisenhower trip to Moscow. Unfortunately for the conference and its grand plan, the administration had determined that surveillance of the Soviet Union was essential for American defense. When the "Open

Skies" proposal had been rejected by the Soviets in 1956, the United States implemented photographic missions over the Soviet Union in a high-flying U2 airplane, not accessible to Russian attack. It was not accessible until just prior to the Paris Summit meeting, when the Russians succeeded in shooting down a U2, capturing its pilot and parading him for all the world to see. The Soviets had known of the flights but had made no protests against them, as this would have demonstrated that the Soviets had no means to defend against such overflights.

Kruschev stated early on that he assumed that the President was uninformed of the flights and sought to ameliorate their impact on the relationship between the nations. The administration waffled in its reply to the charge of spying over Soviet territory, lying at first about the plane's existence and purpose. But when Eisenhower finally acknowledged that he was aware of the flights, Kruschev demanded an apology from Eisenhower, who refused. The summit was doomed to failure. Eisenhower sat quietly at the summit meeting, as Kruschev ranted through his tirades against the President and the United States. The planned trip to Moscow was canceled.

The nation and the world were embarrassed and saddened by the dramatic demise of the summit. In retrospect, the U2 flights might have been called off prior to the meeting, but the flights were considered both necessary and secure, with the additional safeguard that the pilot was to destroy the plane and commit suicide if the plane were hit. Eisenhower's peace endeavor was to end ignominiously, but he accepted the outcome with his customary poise, taking the long view once again that this was only one skirmish in the battle for peaceful coexistence.

As his public career drew to a close, Eisenhower traveled to South America to further enhance his and America's image abroad; but he was not well received, with anti-American sentiment at an all time high. Compounding his problems, he was forced to cancel a trip to

Japan in the face of equally strong negative sentiment there. But despite the failed summit conference and the unfavorable impact of the response to America in South America and in Tokyo, Eisenhower could easily have won a third term as President had he wished the office again and had the twenty-second amendment not prohibited it.

The 1960 election set Richard Nixon against John Kennedy. Despite a halting and uninspiring campaign by Nixon, and the failure of Eisenhower to support him openly until just prior to the election, the electorate came very close to continuing the Republicans in office. Kennedy's modest victory ended that hope, playing on the theme that Kennedy would "get the country moving" again.

* * * * *

Eisenhower's great caution in spending his popularity and in revealing the manner in which he managed his administration has diminished the appearance of success during his administration. He failed to win votes in Congress for the complete fulfillment of his domestic and foreign programs. His wary and guarded view of the Soviet and Chinese Communist expansionism preserved a world from confrontation between the nations. He might have begun his entrees to Kruschev earlier, and dialogue with Chou en Lai of China might have proved fruitful. However, Kruschev was a suspicious man, untutored in western customs, surrounded by hard liners who opposed cooperation with the West and who demanded a full military buildup. There is no evidence Eisenhower could have effectively brought the Soviets into the council of nations in the 1950s. His efforts to do so were heralded at the time and certainly became part of the great underpinning of the long struggle to end American-Soviet confrontation.

Eisenhower's stalwart conservatism was stamped indelibly in all of his programs. He "preserved the New Deal," but expanded it no more than he deemed necessary to forestall more aggressive spending and government services. He accepted civil rights legislation and enforcement only to the extent that the Congress and the Supreme Court dictated. The nation was at the cusp of change, and there was unrest building in society for resolution of problems for which Eisenhower may have been ill-suited.

During his two administrations, the gross national product expanded by 20%, the county was left without a federal deficit, inflation remained at 1.4% and the nation was at peace for eight years. Because of Eisenhower's calm, warmly comforting demeanor, much of the nation felt tranquil during his tenure. His second term, however, was full of missteps and unforeseen barriers which made those four years seem unproductive. This opened the door to John Kennedy who protested that the nation demanded more from their government and that the administration had been too cautious in its military preparedness. Kennedy successfully proposed to "get America moving again," both productively and militarily. As the civil rights movement gained momentum, the conservative Eisenhower would have been forced to change his views or be left behind. He had, in fact, rarely led the nation in the resolution of the social unrest that lay beneath the surface of job creation and prosperity.

His final address to Congress warned of the dangers of the industrial-military complex and its potential for undue influence over foreign and domestic policy. A military man himself, he resisted military adverturism. He resisted excessive expenditure on military hardware, utilizing the threat of nuclear weaponry as a deterrent, without the massive buildup that some proposed and that was in fact implemented later on. He supported America's missile program, but paced its advance to maintain budgetary constraint. When the Russians accelerated their missile and military buildup, Eisenhower appeared to have misjudged. History has proven, however, that there was time. There were ample opportunities for him to send in troops to areas of conflict, embroiling the nation in wars in Vietnam, with Communist China over Formosa, and with Russia over Hungary. Eisenhower, endowed with great ego, yet dedicated to the service of the nation and the long term good of America, disciplined and subordinated himself to his intuitive judgment of what was militarily possible and what was best for America's future.

His tenure would be a contrast to what was to follow. As did Washington, he felt the need for the nation to be protected from excessive involvement with foreign affairs. For Washington, it was an infant nation to be allowed to develop unfettered by participating in European wars. For Eisenhower, it was a mature nation, deeply imbedded in international affairs which must be given as cloistered an environment as possible in which to flourish as a nation. Only a President can give such leadership. Remarkably, he left the nation in at least as good a state as he found it. He fulfilled that childhood dictum to serve.

Reader's Score of Dwight D. Eisenhower

Defense: _____

Economic: _____

Vision: _____

Communication: _____

Lead Congress: _____

Lead without Popularity: _____

Invincibility: _____

Consistency: _____

Self-Confidence: _____

Strengthen Nation: _____

TOTAL POINTS: _____

Lyndon Johnson

16

Lyndon Baines Johnson

"**H**ey, hey L.B.J.—how many kids have you killed today?" Few Presidents have experienced such blatant taunts as those echoing along the boulevards of Washington, D.C. and on college campuses across the country in late 1967 and 1968. Lyndon Johnson was being attacked by the right-wing conservatives and by his potential opponent in the next election, Richard Nixon, for not "winning" the war. Those opposing the war paraded and jeered, making headlines. As the Vietnam War raged, Lyndon Johnson hoped to preserve his Great Society programs while paying for a costly war. The odds against success for any of his causes were diminishing as the embattled President secluded himself in the White House to shield himself from an evermore hostile public.

Lyndon Baines Johnson, strangely, seemed to act out the programs and the times of several of the two-term presidents who preceded him. He frequently attempted to usurp their qualities, their character, their goals, hoping somehow to integrate these with his own intense and driven nature to achieve his own goals and success. It would bring him finally to devastating failure. He personified the power that the office of the presidency can instill in one man and also how fleeting this power can be. His time in office illustrates, profoundly, how very personal is the office and its execution. His denial of any disparity between the ends he sought and the means he used confounds his supporters and critics and demands that history not stray from an analysis of Lyndon Johnson in his driving, relentless, single minded, pursuit of power.

He, as so many who preceded him, utilized his great power to fulfill a voracious need for adulation; but for Johnson, this power became overweening, a need to grasp public acclaim, to hold and control it himself, to be its master. His brilliance in political strategy and chicanery won him the fulcrum of power. He had a great sense of what motivates people and a keen perception of where authority lay and how he might align himself with it. He then carefully took on that power himself, most frequently without losing the friendship of those whose power he usurped, making a career in politics for L.B.J. that few would rival, despite his failures.

* * * * *

Lyndon Johnson was the product of the strivings of an intelligent, educated mother determined to have her son succeed, as her husband had not. She was a mother who wished her son to possess the fantasized luster of her own father and achieve as she had not. She granted and withheld her love to lead him toward goals she set, but she never relented in her demands upon her boy. It would inject an abiding insecurity into Johnson's nature.

The Johnsons were never poor, but neither were they prosperous in their rural Texas community. His father and his father's father were men whom he both admired and feared, and whose successes and failures he exaggerated to fulfill his fantasies and to augment his storytelling. Johnson's father was a farmer of modest proportions who traded in cattle and real estate. He had shown promise in politics, being elected to the state legislature. He was a stark contrast to his intellectual, moralistic wife, with his hard-drinking and rough language. It is not surprising that the younger Johnson took little comfort in the contentious home life of his childhood.

Johnson was a precocious child, learning from his mother to read and recite poetry early; yet, as he grew to adolescence, he adapted his father's rough language, personal style and his penchant for conversation. Johnson was able to talk freely and persuasively, a quality he would utilize fully through the years. He was not inclined to confront a difficult situation, yet he would not tolerant weakness or a hint of failure in himself or others. His art of non-confrontational, reasoning persuasion in a one-on-one relationship, filled with charming talk and exhortation, became a valuable tool in his drive for power and his mastery over the elements of power. He avoided situations which did not accommodate to his needs and his methodology of manipulation and control. Manliness, macho strength, preserving self-esteem played a part in his campaign to lead, and not to be led, to enhance his self-esteem, to deny his insecurity.

He had enough of classrooms, of study, of books, of ideas. After high school, Johnson ran off to California for two years before returning to Texas where he entered a teachers' college near his home. It was the turning point in his career, where the anti-intellectual who believed not in ideas, but in work, set his path toward success, utilizing his significant brain, his boundless energy, his power to negotiate and control. He became a student leader, an honor student and editor of the paper.

Johnson had been raised by both his parents in the tradition of populism and progressivism. His mother, in particular, preached the lesson of serving mankind, the downtrodden and the underprivileged. In college, as he would thereafter, Johnson harnessed his great ambition for himself to the lessons of his childhood, as his leadership in college testified. His method, which he would use again and again, was to ingratiate himself with men of power. He became a favorite of the president of the school and then mustered a group of students in support of his power thrust to make some needed changes in the school program. He combined use of power with good works, a mixture he would follow throughout his public life.

* * * * *

After graduating from college in 1930, Johnson taught high school in Houston for fifteen months, before being called upon by the Congressman from his district to come to Washington to serve as his legislative secretary. It was a job which was offered him because of a rousing political speech he had given the previous year. His career in Washington was launched, and Johnson took full advantage of the opportunity despite his total lack of experience in the world beyond rural Texas. He quickly absorbed the lessons to be learned in Washington about power, with whom it lay, how it was utilized and how he might master it. He worked harder than any other legislative secretary. He took on more tasks within the Congress, becoming a leader among the secretaries, asserting his own force and power and influence and recognition and control over others. He achieved his inroads into authority by seizing opportunities others missed, by understanding people, by better organization and by combining these together to bring authority unto himself.

Johnson left Washington in 1935, sensing that the true power there lay in the hands of the elected officials. F.D.R. established the National Youth Administration to create jobs for the mass of unemployed young people in the nation. Johnson used the influence he accrued from his years in Washington to gain the directorship of the Texas N.Y.A. The job became a stepping stone to his return to Washington. Johnson was innovative and energetic, receiving strong statewide and national recognition for his stewardship. He put people to work, gave them jobs and money, and in return he expected and received the praise and support he craved and would need to achieve higher office. It was the perfect match. There was no confrontation, only a creative opportunity to manipulate money and people under his complete control, fulfilling a true need of the recipients, but bringing them evermore under his spell and dominance. The people whom he served looked to him as their benefactor, and he bathed in the pleasure of his power.

★ ★ ★ ★ ★

Opportunity struck for Johnson again, when the Congressman of his district died in office. He lost no time in declaring his candidacy, drawing in the support of powerful political friends and utilizing his boundless energy. He campaigned in the name of Roosevelt and his programs and with the promise to bring electricity to the meager farm region he would represent. He was elected and, at the age of twenty-nine, returned to Washington to expand his world of power and authority. It was 1937.

His years in Washington gave vent to Johnson's populist and paternalistic spirit. He delivered electricity to his farmers. In the cities, W.P.A. built new housing projects and post offices. It was the beneficence he had bestowed and would bestow that made his career in Congress bearable, despite the tedium that set in for the stridently ambitious freshman in that tradition-bound, seniority-ruled House.

Once again, circumstances provided his chance for advancement with the death of a Texas senator in 1941. Johnson ran for the office in a special election, narrowly losing to the very popular governor of the state. The close race taught a bitter lesson he would remember well in his next Senatorial race.

Johnson returned to his House seat, to become the first Congressman to enlist in the military when Pearl Harbor was attacked. During his twelve months in service, he secured a questionable Silver

Star for duty on a mission that probably was not heroic. Yet, his war experience was an exhilarating one which set his conviction that one must stand up to the bully. With the spirit of Teddy Roosevelt, he would try to bring American principles of democracy to other nations, to forestall the encroachment of nation upon nation, all with Lyndon Johnson's own interpretation of what the world is like.

The restless, manipulative, power-hungry Johnson used his years in the House to promote his own business interests and wealth through the acquisition of radio stations which he advanced through the assistance of the Federal Communications Commission. With the capable involvement of his wife, "Lady Bird," he expanded his wealth over time to include TV stations, real estate and other investments, allowing him to join the ranks of Texan millionaires he had cautiously refrained from attacking when he promoted his New Deal programs during campaigns for the House.

* * * * *

1948 became another year of opportunity for Johnson when the junior Senator from Texas decided not to run for reelection. Would he dare risk the loss of his House seat to run for an office which had escaped his grasp seven years before? The ever anxious, striving Johnson, knowing that he would be out of public office if he failed, reluctantly accepted the challenge. But once he made up his mind, he pursued the campaign with utmost zeal. Invoking an "I will not be defeated" posture, he worked himself to exhaustion, making flamboyant helicopter flights into every corner of the state, spending vast sums for media advertising. Responding to the conservative Texan mood, he avoided New Deal rhetoric. But his strenuous efforts for victory were nearly frustrated, as Johnson won what became a notorious election by only 87 votes. His opponent charged that Johnson supporters had stuffed ballot boxes and that the election was illegally won, a charge which was carried to the U.S. Supreme Court, where Johnson lawyers successfully argued that the Court had no jurisdiction. He had won the coveted Senate seat.

Whom would he conquer and whom would he maneuver to achieve power in the Senate? Johnson proceeded cautiously, but diligently, to establish himself within the echelons of the upper house. He set aside flamboyance to accommodate to the sedate body with quiet mood, conservative, guarded tone and deliberate alliances. The Senate was controlled by a combination of Southern Democrats and conservative Republicans dedicated to minimal government in social programs and civil rights. If Johnson were to gain the power and control he sought, he reasoned that this group must adopt him. To achieve his goal, Johnson soon became the undisputed protégé of the leader of the conservatives, Richard Russell of Georgia, befriending and entertaining the austere bachelor. But he shrewdly steered a path of accommodation and independence with the conservatives, for he did not want his name associated with only one point of view in the Senate. He sought to influence the entire body.

He sidestepped joining the Southern caucus, a group dedicated to stifling civil rights' legislation, yet he frequently voted with it. His strategy and tactics to achieve his objective were flawless. He was elected party whip in 1951 and Democratic minority leader in 1953, just four short years after entering the chamber, posts historically reserved for its most senior members. When the Democrats won control of the Senate in 1954, Johnson became the all-powerful majority leader, implementing much of the legislative agenda of the Republican President Eisenhower. He harnessed his cunning and frequently ruthless political savvy to round up votes for the Republican administration.

★ ★ ★ ★ ★

Lyndon Johnson wanted to be President in 1960, but his nature could not take him there. He had become the undisputed leader of the Senate by jawboning with senators in the cloak room, negotiating stoutly and vote-trading one-on-one. These were techniques which tied together his ambition and power, assuring Johnson's Senate authority. But such talents did not fit the political world that election year. John F. Kennedy stumped the states, winning primaries which delivered him the nomination on the first ballot. Johnson shrewdly did not enter the primaries where he could not control, where he felt his being a Southerner would be a handicap, where his discomfort with speaking before large audiences put him at a disadvantage. On the other hand, the powerful leader of the Senate could deliver the Texas delegation to Kennedy, so Johnson was selected to be the Vice-Presidential running mate of the popular, debonair Kennedy. Johnson was ready to move on, detecting that a President less passive than Eisenhower would not allow so much power to rest in the majority leader. And there was the chance that the Vice Presidency might be the kind of stepping stone he had found before.

Johnson suffered through his years in that barren office of the Vice President, exercising no authority over legislative matters, where he obviously had considerable ability, but which Kennedy did not utilize. He worked on civil rights and space matters. He traveled abroad extensively, but there he remained the cloistered parochial observer, seeing all people as being like himself, with needs and wants identical to those of Americans. It was a desolate, frustrating, unproductive period for Johnson.

★ ★ ★ ★ ★

The assassination of John Kennedy in November of 1963 brought swift restoration of power and control to Lyndon Johnson, only now in a proportion far exceeding any he had known. The nation had experienced more than the loss of a President; it had lost a symbol of itself, an image of youth, a wholesome American spirit of self-confidence and vigor that had moved the hearts of many Americans, even though Kennedy had not inspired great legislative change. Johnson handled the passage of authority with artful skill and uncommon good judgment. If he had shown talent in comprehending the inner desires of his Senate colleagues, he most assuredly understood the mood of the nation seeking reconciliation, deliverance from its grief, someone strong and quiet to hold onto. Johnson offered all of this and more. He retained Kennedy men in positions of authority. This served two purposes. The continuation of Kennedy policies would be assured, preserving and utilizing the clout of the name and his programs, while it would also send a message that government would continue in an uninterrupted flow. Further, it had the effect of putting the popular Kennedy mantle around the shoulders of the insecure, unelected, relatively unknown Lyndon Johnson. As he had done when he first entered the Senate, Johnson posed as the compliant, respectful, minister to the Kennedy program. He would be its wet nurse, its protector. Kennedy would be the progenitor; Johnson, the good and true servant. He carried on the Kennedy program, but soon the legend would carry the Johnson brand. It all worked wonderfully well during the fourteen months left for Johnson in the Kennedy presidency.

His boundless energy, his intense and comprehending mind and his judgment of people blended to cause the subtle, yet very real, movement of the authority of Johnson from that of caretaker to that of President. Johnson turned Kennedy programs into crusades. Projects conservatively evaluated by his predecessor were given an aura of urgency and moment. The Congress and the nation paid tribute to Kennedy by allowing the powerful and swift movement to legislation of plans that the Kennedy administration contemplated. For example, a series of programs to help the poor became a "War on Poverty." A crusade indeed! The Economic Opportunities Act was passed containing almost a billion dollars in programs to enhance the poor. The economy was thriving; the memory of the dead President was keen, so that business and labor alike supported the legislation that would later become part of Johnson's newly proclaimed "Great Society."

By June, a new and powerful civil rights bill had passed, overcoming an extended filibuster. The anti-poverty legislation and the tax bill required legislative skill and maneuvering, but it was the Civil Rights Bill that became the imposing challenge to the determined Johnson. He utilized all of his wily, cajoling ways, only now his wheeling and dealing would carry the image of the President without having to confront legislation directly. He gathered both the liberal Democrats and Republicans to defeat the Southern Democrats and the conservative Republicans to win the vote for the Civil Rights Bill about the time the Republican Convention was assembling to nominate its candidate for the 1964 Presidential election. Senator Barry Goldwater from Arizona, the Republican nominee, proposed that the United States use strong military action against Communist expansion and hinted at the use of the bomb, if needed, to contain Communist aggression in Vietnam.

Johnson reveled in the impact of his domestic programs on the voters and the opportunities it offered for the adulation and approval he needed. He found success in bringing to fruition the legislation of John Kennedy. Interestingly, his programs expanded the role of government in fighting poverty beyond those proposed by his predecessor and, except for civil rights, exceeded the demands reflected by any underlying discontent, turmoil or displacement in the body politic. Except for civil rights discontent, it was a time of relative tranquillity and prosperity for the nation. Lyndon Johnson was the paternalistic patron of the poor, the downtrodden, the masses. Johnson was determined to use his popularity to improve the lot of voters who were not generally in the streets demanding change. It was not, except in civil rights issues, a time of the level of unrest which led to the innovations implemented by Theodore Roosevelt, Wilson or F.D.R. Johnson led the nation toward causes which Franklin Roosevelt and Truman had promoted and were the causes supported by labor; but it was not, generally, a time of crisis or festering discontent toward which the programs of Johnson were directed. Johnson created the whirlwind, not necessarily listening to those toward whom his beneficence was directed.

The programs he pursued in those final months of the Kennedy administration were Kennedy's, except that he expanded the war on poverty beyond the scope of Kennedy's plan. They were expansions of proposals by Truman, concepts created by F.D.R. Now there was prosperity and a Congress that was harnessed to the thrust of Lyndon Johnson, and legislation would flow.

Vietnam had been a relatively minor issue during the Kennedy administration, absorbing attention as the frail, allegedly corrupt government of South Vietnam struggled with incursions from the internal rebel Viet Cong and the neighboring hostile North Vietnamese. Eisenhower had refrained from entangling the United States in the conflict. Kennedy and his advisors had taken the tack in his campaign for the Presidency that his administration would be more assertive than the passive Eisenhower in resisting Communist expansion. The Democrats were competing with the conservative China lobby for the title of "Communist fighter." There was a common fear in America that Communism might spread throughout all of the Far East if it were not stopped at any point of expansionism. The fear was that the flood gates might open, that nation after nation would all fall to "wars of liberation." It was stated over and over that this would resemble dominos falling. There was, of course, also the preservation of a macho image for the Kennedys, the party and the nation. Further, there was that unselfish feeling of Americans that democracy must be expanded and protected—a philosophy going back to the Monroe Doctrine.

By 1964, Nikita Krushchev had been deposed as the Soviet leader, sparking new concerns about the Soviet Union. And yet a Nuclear Test Ban treaty had signaled a warming of relations with Russia. Johnson would spend his efforts on domestic affairs prior to the election of 1964, but he did respond firmly to an event in August of 1964 which would have far more impact on the nation than was contemplated by the administration or the Congress at the time. American naval vessels were allegedly attacked by the North Vietnamese in the Gulf of Tonkin. The President ordered a reprisal raid against the North Vietnamese and immediately thereafter asked Congress to allow the President to take any measures necessary to repel armed attack and to prevent further aggression. The "Tonkin Gulf" Resolution passed the Senate with only two dissenting votes and the House unanimously, virtually giving the President authority to wage war in Vietnam. It defined the security of South Vietnam as being vital to the United States and to world peace. The national sentiment strongly supported an aggressive stature against Communist expansion, and it supported an independent Vietnam. There were few dissenters at this time.

Johnson now had the image he needed to meet the campaign rhetoric of Goldwater. He had been both assertive and yet restrained in fighting Communism. He had built a consensus with his war on poverty. His civil rights legislation would lose him votes in the South, but he would receive powerful support among the working and middle classes of the rest of the nation.

The August Democratic Convention was in Johnson's palm. He refused to accept the popular Robert Kennedy as his running mate, a man whom he feared politically, selecting instead the liberal Senator from Minnesota, Hubert Humphrey. The old Johnson was now willing to show himself. He campaigned tirelessly, jetting across the country, piling up vote upon vote in an election that was his by virtue not only of the popularity of Kennedy but also of his own. The selection by the Republicans of the unpopular Goldwater helped Johnson as well. The election of 1964 might have followed the same path were John Kennedy to have lived, but it was truly Johnson's consensus victory, gleaning for him 61% of the votes and rivaling F.D.R.'s victory in 1936. Johnson would now serve as President of the United States in his own right.

The opportunity to achieve greater social good than had Wilson, F.D.R. or Truman was in his grasp. Johnson now had the opportunity to bring great pride to the nation through its influence throughout the world as was dreamed of by Theodore Roosevelt. He had the opportunity to bring economic and political equality to the masses and law and order to the world as dreamed of by Woodrow Wilson and Franklin Roosevelt. The challenge to contain Communism met by Truman and Eisenhower would now be placed in his hands. But Johnson saw more in the presidencies he would emulate than their goals and successes. He understood from their experiences, but also from his own keen sense of his own life, that adulation, popularity, success are all transitory and fragile and that he must act with dispatch before his power might fade away.

Yet at no time in the history of the nation had the country been so momentously poised for peaceful change, without great unrest or crisis—even though there was evidence of underlying social turmoil in the Civil Rights movement. Success reigned for a consensus President whose inner drive for power and voracious need for approval wed perfectly with his public plans. He intended to become the most powerful and popular President ever elected.

★ ★ ★ ★ ★

Johnson said that he liked doers, not thinkers. He tended to distrust ideas; he trusted action, particularly his own action. There can be little doubt, however, that his Great Society, which took root at the end of his first term and came to fruition in the first two years of his second administration, were filled with a vision. He was imbued, with a philosophy about society and people and travail and about how fear might be eliminated and how even discomfort might be reduced. Good health, medical care, a quality environment, education, the elevation of the poor were all to be part of his plan. It was not to be a redistribution of wealth, for there was plenty, but there would be the creation of more wealth. Values would be adjusted to conform to the new society. This was to be a quantum leap from the "go ahead" spirit as interpreted in Andrew Jackson's days and actually carried right through to the New Deal. The role of government in the welfare of everyone's daily life was to experience a sea change. Care and concern by people for each other and by government for everyone were to bring happiness, not just economic success. But Johnson was in a great hurry to achieve all of this. Power and popularity are fleeting, affection can be turned off as quickly as it is turned on, so Johnson moved along with his reforms with profound speed, if not haste.

Study teams were established to evaluate programs and to propose areas of legislation. Johnson met with leaders of labor, of industry, of education, of civil rights groups, with Congress, with his staff. He ran it all and he ran it hard. He returned to his former self as the relentless, frequently ruthless, cunning, manipulative tyrant who would have his way.

During some of the Kennedy years and during Johnson's first administration, civil unrest and alienation had been the hallmark of riots in cities in the North and South. The Civil Rights movement had taken on a spirit of its own, yet the legislation passed by Congress had attempted to keep pace with the changing mood of Americans. But many of the youth of the nation, accustomed to prosperity, joined civil rights protests in the evolution of a free spirit and anti-establishment mood that demanded much of government by way of reform. They sought improvement of their economic life, but they also demanded political equality and recognition. The civil rights advocates wanted it their way, and, as time wore on, they began to seek more militant leadership such as that provided by Martin Luther King, Jr. Legislation alone was not enough. The movement demanded a compassionate and personally accessible leader. Johnson passed effective legislation, but he could not inspire confidence among the blacks that he was their spokesman.

A John Kennedy or Robert Kennedy might have effectively responded to that evolving vocal minority, but Lyndon Johnson was not tuned in to them. He was in step with the kind of change that was taking place in society, and, in social legislation, he was far ahead of it. But he was not suited by temperament or sentiment to accept the anti-establishment uprisings; therefore he could not communicate with the large minority that came to oppose him. It was a time of transition with civil unrest in this country, with America's prowess challenged by the Soviets, with nation after nation pulling away from American influence toward independence or Communist domination. Blacks demanded equality now! Yet the nation was at peace, and prosperity abounded. It was in this environment that Lyndon Johnson would lead.

Two of Johnson's legislative measures passed very quickly in 1965. One was a far reaching aid to education bill, the other was Medicare for those under Social Security. The Economic Development Administration was established to disburse funds for programs in underdeveloped regions of the nation. A public housing bill was passed. With Johnson's political and legislative prowess, these legislations passed both Houses by April. An elementary and secondary school education bill was signed that month as well. The voting rights legislation, assuring blacks the vote they were being denied, was signed in August, an Immigration act in October. Over five hundred programs were enacted within the Johnson Great Society. It was Roosevelt and the Hundred Days all over again, but now there was no Great Depression to spur on the Congress, there was only Lyndon Johnson.

All was far from tranquil on the domestic scene during those months of victory in Congress for the programs of the Great Society, however. The Civil Rights movement was reaching its moment of critical mass as Martin Luther King, Jr. led his march from Selma to Montgomery, Alabama, in support of voter registration in March of 1965. It was a part of a bloody episode that drew national attention to the plight of the black voter in the South, leading to the enactment of the voter rights legislation. Johnson publicly supported the pro-testers and fought for and won the legislation. Unfortunately for Johnson, the movement into the street by civil rights activists signaled a form of civil disobedience and public protest which he found diffi-cult to accept. It was only the beginning of unrest, however, for there would be other forms of civil disobedience as the anti-Vietnam War demonstrations would soon fill the campuses and streets of the nation's schools and cities.

* * * * *

In 1963, under Kennedy, there were 11,000 American advisors in Vietnam. By late 1966, the North Vietnamese were threatening the South's major air field, causing the military to ask for more troops. Johnson complied with an unannounced increase in 1965 to 42,000, then to over 60,000, then to 75,000 and then to 125,000. A high of 550,000 troops was reached in 1968. Intensive strategic bombings were conducted against the Viet Cong and North Vietnamese, with all of the targets selected personally by the President.

The lesson learned in World War I and II was that the aggressor must be stopped before he becomes uncontrollably dangerous. Men of Johnson's generation had been raised to understand this lesson. It was a lesson applied to the North Vietnamese invasion of the South. Johnson would pick up on this part of the lesson of the two world wars; but, confounding one branch of his critics, he would not wage an all out-war as the Allies did in each of the two major wars. Instead, he added to the lessons of the 1930s the lesson of the Korean conflict, where hordes of Chinese joined the war to prolong it. He applied the lesson of the Cuban missile crisis where the threat, not the implementation, of massive confrontation caused the Soviets to back down. The lessons of Korea and the Cuban missile crisis must be combined with Johnson's fear that the conservative anti-Communists in America might destroy him if he "lost Vietnam" to the Communists, as they had attempted to do to Truman for "losing" China.

Compounding the situation was Johnson's long standing fear of confrontation and his need to seem the all-powerful macho leader. Add further the fact that he had no intuitive sense of how an oriental mind and culture functioned. Complicating the matter still further was the fact that the North Vietnamese looked upon the conflict as a civil war. Aggravating the perplexity of the situation, Johnson saw the danger that the war might bring to his "Great Society" and to his fulfillment of public adulation. All of this provides the makings of a Greek Tragedy for the President, for the nation and for the more than 50,000 Americans who would die in Vietnam.

Eisenhower had the self-confidence, the broad military and political savvy and the perception of diverse cultures and of America's self interest to stay out of Vietnam. John Kennedy did not significantly expand America's involvement. Whether either would have stayed the course in 1965 and 1966, no one knows. But Johnson did not! He fought a limited war to save a corrupt South Vietnam for democracy and to save it from the aggressive, enveloping designs of its Communist neighbor which believed it was fighting a civil war. The recipe for failure was ready for mixing.

The nation supported Johnson in the war until 1968 when the Tet offensive of the Communists temporarily overran vast areas of the South, including much of Saigon, apparently exposing the fragile hold the vast American forces had on the territory they were pledged to defend. Although that offensive was not as successful as first believed, the negative impact on public opinion in America was resounding. By 1968 Johnson had tried every way his instincts would allow to dislodge America from the war. He offered the North Vietnamese a T.V.A.-type project for the Mekong Delta, hardly an attraction to a devout Communist nation. At times, he halted the heavy strategic bombing raids to induce the North to negotiate without demanding any compromise in return. He refrained from bombing the North's capitol of Hanoi, from bombing dikes to flood that city, from mining Haiphong harbor. These moves were designed both to forestall Chinese intervention into the war but also to induce the North Vietnamese to negotiate for peace. But Johnson's moves were seen by the North Vietnamese as evidence of a lack of determination to win, as, of course, they were.

North and South Vietnam were nations created in the 1950s by an accord in Geneva, supervised by the United Nations, in which America did not participate. The North, opposing the split, was waging a civil war to reunite the nation. But Americans failed to understand this, fearing that the move was part of a world Communist plan for world domination, to be followed potentially by the fall of Thailand, Indo-China and possibly the Philippines and Japan. The United States, it turned out, was defending a totalitarian dictator in the South whose primary objective was to maintain the war effort to bolster his power, authority and wealth. There is no evidence that the conflict would have spread Communism to the neighboring countries.

Fearing that his Great Society would not survive the war, Johnson concealed the build-up of troops and postponed telling Congress and the people what the war was costing. The truth about the rising expense of the war and its casualties filtered through to the people, sparking escalating protests and demonstrations against the war. Meanwhile, Congress resisted Johnson's costly domestic programs. Suddenly some of his own staff were turning against the war. He protested that a wealthy nation could afford both the war and the "good life" for all, finally supporting new taxes, late in his term, to meet the rising cost of the war. Inflation crept into the language of economists. In January of 1968, the Tet offensive brought the truth home to all Americans and to Johnson in particular, that the North Vietnamese were unfazed by his limiting the war. He had failed. Students through-out the nation protested against the war; and, although they were a minority, L.B.J., hearing the message of the anti-war movement, felt rejected, misunderstood, a failed President, unloved. He announced on March 31, 1968, that he would not run for reelection.

His days of grandeur would end, his broad vision for the nation and for himself bogged down in the same thickets of war as were the American troops. In that same speech he announced a cessation of all bombing of North Vietnam to bring that nation to the peace table for the first time, but it would be almost four years before the tragic war would end. It is not clear that an all-out war against North Vietnam was winnable. Certainly the war, once waged and not won, caused great hardship for the defeated South Vietnamese. Was it the time and place for the United States to fight for protection of democracy or for the containment of Communism? Lyndon Johnson did not take the time nor did he have the temperament for such an analysis.

★ ★ ★ ★ ★

According to Lyndon Johnson, everyone had his price. But a price for what? Generally, it was what he wanted, when he wanted it and how he wanted it. He may have had the potential for a broad, non-provincial view of the world and its inhabitants. But he did not achieve that breadth. He would brilliantly and fiercely achieve success and applause for himself under the banner of helping broad sectors of the population. He may have been sincere in wishing to aid the downtrodden; but Johnson was so tyrannical and domineering in his style and his means, that his ends became somewhat tarnished, particularly when so much personal gain was joined to the ends he sought. His programs were sometimes wide of the mark—failing to achieve their defined goals. Their implementation was hasty. There is the belief that many of his programs induced a spirit of excessive dependence on the federal government.

The Vietnam War would not respond to Johnson's learned responses designed to control his world. He could not cajole, persuade, reason or threaten Vietnam to do his bidding.

Lyndon Johnson, in his second term, proved how difficult it is to administer the Presidency, how transitory is its power and how broad must be the mind, the intuitions and skills of that President who would survive when change thrusts great challenge upon the Chief of State.

Reader's Score of Lyndon Baines Johnson

Defense: _____

Economic: _____

Vision: _____

Communication: _____

Lead Congress: _____

Lead without Popularity: _____

Invincibility: _____

Consistency: _____

Self-Confidence: _____

Strengthen Nation: _____

TOTAL POINTS: _____

Richard Nixon

Richard Nixon

By the time Richard Nixon resigned the Presidency on August 9, 1974, almost a year and a half into his second term, he had visited more embarrassment upon the American people than had any other President. America's pride in the presidency had been severely bruised, while many Americans felt disgraced and humiliated.

In its fullest sense, the Watergate affair, its extended investigation and Nixon's resignation must be viewed in the context of the Cold War and as the culmination of a long interweaving nightmare that overtly began with the death of John F. Kennedy in November 1963. The nation was in a period of transition that was coupled with a climate that bordered on a war-time mentality. That time of widespread social unrest, of upheaval, of discontent in American history is comparable only with the events preceding and during the Civil War and to the Great Depression.

The 1960s and early 1970s were a time of radical change in several very compelling respects. The search for self-realization and civil rights among blacks led them to vent their frustrations through protests, street violence, and the burning of sections of such cities as Los Angeles, Detroit and Washington, D.C. The Vietnam War became immensely unpopular with college students in the mid-60s. Protesters against the war became commonplace on college campuses, with students demonstrating against the war, the President and, seemingly, the very cultural and moral roots of the nation. Young people were rebelling against so many traditions related to sex, lifestyles and dress that some thought a revolution was at hand. Moreover, it was a time of military and civilian preparedness against such Communist aggression as the invasion of South Korea and the Berlin Blockade. Americans had built bomb shelters in the 1950's; they endured the Cuban Missile Crisis. Although war had not been declared against North Vietnam, the nation was surely at war.

President Nixon's resignation following the Watergate debacle must be evaluated and can be comprehended only in the context of these traumatic times in American history. Nixon, his personality, his character and his leadership style interplayed dramatically with the jarring occurrences of that time to induce the Watergate fiasco. In a broader sense, however, the scourge of Watergate cannot be allowed to hide the enduring impact the presidency of Richard Nixon had upon the social, economic and diplomatic fabric of the nation.

★ ★ ★ ★ ★

Richard Nixon was raised in a struggling, frugal household in the southern California communities of Yorba Linda and, later, Whittier where the family operated a grocery store. As a child, Nixon spent all of his time working in the business, when he was not studying or reading.

Richard, one of three sons, was a studious, bright child, with an excellent memory. He was knowledgeable about politics from the age of six. His mother, a staunch Quaker, expressed her intense devotion and discipline in a quiet and unemotional manner that enveloped Richard Nixon. He, like his mother, avoided confrontation. His father, on the other hand, was grossly outspoken and opinionated, especially when it came to politics.

Although the Nixons worked long hours, wore hand-me-down clothes, never took a vacation nor ate out, they were a self-respecting, close-knit family, surrounded by devotion and trust. Richard's mother's family lived nearby in Whittier, extending the reach and source of this sense of well-being. Yet Richard was reserved, a bookish child who felt snubbed by his peers, always struggling to find recognition. He had no friends to speak of.

Although he had to study hard for his grades, Nixon did well in high school. He excelled in debate and dramatics and joined clubs, while continuing to work long hours at the family store. He was a shy young man, apparently lacking in self-confidence. Although he seemed to accept the world as he found it, he apparently was filled with resentment over perceived slights and rejections.

Nixon attended Whittier College in his home town, staying at home to save money, passing up a scholarship to Harvard because the family could not afford the extra expense. His parents were heavily burdened with the care of one of Richard's brothers who was suffering with and later died from tuberculosis. Nixon would not acknowledge the disappointment he must have experienced, denying that Whittier was any less enticing than Harvard. He was a young man who would be troubled frequently by the intense emotions that crisis or failure might produce.

At college he once again excelled in academics as well as in debate and dramatics. Although he was only a second string member of the football team, he found that sport suited his competitive spirit. Upon graduation from college in 1934, he received a scholarship to the newly established law school at Duke University bringing him East for the first time. He once again became a top student and was politically shrewd enough to be elected president of the Student Bar Association.

The East was not hospitable to Nixon after graduation. He was rejected in his bid to join New York law firms, returning to Whittier to become a small town lawyer, where he practiced uneventfully until the war. After a brief stint as an attorney for the Office of Price Administration in Washington, he entered the Navy's Officer Candidate School. His naval service brought him to the edge of conflict in the South Pacific, yet it is his rather significant success at poker that became one of his notable feats while in the navy.

Fortuitously, the war's end brought immediate public life to Richard Nixon. While still in military service, a group of Whittier business men asked Nixon to run for Congress against a five-term Democrat, Jerry Voorhis, whom they considered to be pro labor and anti business. Nixon readily accepted, waging a hard fought battle against the popular Congressman.

Nixon's defeat of Voorhis in that 1946 campaign would presage much of the reputation Richard Nixon accrued over his political life. At a time when fear of the Soviet Union was only beginning, Nixon effectively charged that his opponent was under the influence of the Communist-dominated Political Action Committee of Congress of Industrial Organization. Voorhis, who actually had developed somewhat of a national reputation for his anti-Communist stand in Congress, unsuccessfully protested that the allegation was false. The election became tainted with smears and unsubstantiated accusations. His strident campaign aside, Nixon won because he was a returning war veteran who had appealed to the voters as an aggressive candidate who would protect the nation from un-American influences, while promoting family values and a work ethic. The defeat of Voorhis gave Nixon national attention for defeating the popular Congressman in a hard fought political battle. However, much of the national press and all of the liberal Democrats marked Nixon as someone to be watched, if not scorned. In this, his first entry to public life, he displayed a determined and sometimes defiant posture that characterized his political career.

Nixon rose quickly to super-star status in the House, as he seized the role of chief investigator in what became known as the Chambers-Hiss affair. Nixon, a member of the House Un-American Activities Committee, became its most prominent member as he doggedly pursued this case. Whitaker Chambers, a senior editor of *Time* magazine, voluntarily testified before the committee that in the 1930s he had been a member of the Communist party. He stated that during the period, he had received secret papers from Alger Hiss, then a high-level employee of the State Department who had been an advisor to Franklin Roosevelt at Yalta. Chambers then passed on the documents to Soviet agents. The case, the first to establish clearly that Communists had infiltrated the government, became headline news. Richard Nixon became synonymous with the fight against the Soviet threat to American security. It was a time of fear, even hysteria, among Americans, fear of a Soviet Union that threatened to expand its power, potentially to take over all of Europe, spreading the Communist way of life. Nixon's career rode this wave of anxiety. In an aura of high drama, Nixon relentlessly pursued Hiss, who was later convicted of having perjured himself before the committee.

Although Nixon's two terms in Congress were marked most notably by his success as an anti-Communist fighter in the Alger Hiss case, he also strongly supported the plan to help Greece and Turkey fend off a Communist takeover; and he later supported the Marshall Plan. His home district had overwhelmingly opposed this foreign aid, but Nixon, determined that the containment of Communism was essential, stood his ground as an internationalist.

The Chambers-Hiss affair catapulted Richard Nixon on a career that would lead to a second term in the House, a term in the Senate, the Vice Presidency and, finally, the presidency. The time was ripe for a serious anti-Communist fighter with intelligence, cunning, political savvy, debating skill and an opportunistic genius.

Nixon easily continued on the path that led him to Congress and to his success there as he sought the vacated Senate seat from California in 1950. His fight against Voorhis had earned him the enmity of liberals, in general, and liberal journalists, in particular, who believed he utilized unfair means to defeat a Congressman who was one of theirs. The Voorhis campaign paled, however, when compared with Nixon's Senatorial race against a popular liberal Congresswoman, Helen Gahagan Douglas. By 1950, fear of the Soviet Union and the goal of worldwide expansion of Communism had become entrenched in the minds of many Americans. Nixon charged Douglas with Red-leaning sympathies, in part because of her vote against aid to Greece and Turkey. The battle line was clearly drawn. Nixon alluded to Douglas' leftist voting record as he stumped through the state as the leader of the anti-Communist thrust in politics, alleging that Douglas and the entire administration were "soft" on Communism. Nixon soundly defeated Douglas, moving him on to the Senate, clearly identified as a ruthless campaigner by those who opposed and feared him. The name "Tricky Dick" became the watchword of his enemies.

★　★　★　★　★

Only two years later, Nixon, still popular because of his role in the Chambers-Hiss affair, was selected as Dwight Eisenhower's running mate in the 1952 Presidential election. The most memorable part of this entire campaign was Nixon's famous "Checkers speech." The Democrats had accused Nixon of having a secret campaign fund, a charge which tainted his and Eisenhower's integrity. In a last minute effort to save his place on the ballot, Nixon went on television for a half hour defense of his character. He defended his integrity, pleading his modest resources by pointing out that his wife Pat owned only an "honest" Republican cloth coat. Finally, he referred to the only gift he had received, a little dog, Checkers, which he said he would keep for the sake of the children. The TV audience, responding to his request for support, gave him overwhelming affirmation. But the episode colored the image of Nixon in the eyes of both his supporters and enemies. His performance seemed contrived to those who hated him and an unfortunate, almost embarrassing, event for the party, instilling a general feeling of discomfort in his friends and distrust in his enemies. Eisenhower never got over the feeling.

There is considerable evidence that Eisenhower would have preferred someone other than Nixon as Vice President during his second term. But, failing to decisively remove Nixon, Ike retained him as his running mate in 1956.

Although Nixon's tenure during two terms as Vice President was relatively uneventful, a memorable highlight was his assignment, given by Eisenhower, to open an American exhibit in Moscow in 1959. Nixon met Soviet leader Nikita Krushchev in two successive confrontations in which Nixon stood up for America's strengths in civilian product development and spoke assertively for greater respect of each country's military strengths, while reducing threats and tension. Public response to the Krushchev meetings was favorable and became one of the many factors that assured Richard Nixon the Republican nomination for President in 1960.

The campaign pitted Nixon, the candidate from a family of modest means, with a small town heritage, against the urbane, sophisticated, Harvard educated, wealthy John F. Kennedy. It was a hard fought campaign, highlighted by the first of four television debates, in which Nixon appeared tired and nervous and far less dashing than did the debonair, glib Kennedy. Despite all the predictions in the media that Kennedy would win easily, it was an extremely close race, with Kennedy winning by only 113,000 popular votes out of 68,800,000 votes cast. Nixon had received 49.6 percent of the total vote. The electoral ballot was more decisive, however, with Kennedy winning 303 to 219. Nixon's anti-Communist stance, his determined and effective campaign which appealed to the conservative mood of the average American and the coattails of the Eisenhower administration nearly won him the election in 1960. It was a far greater show of popularity for Nixon than is customarily remembered when he is viewed in the shadow of Watergate.

Nixon did not challenge the vote count of the extremely close race, appearing to be magnanimous in his plea for national unity. He was, however, deeply hurt by the loss, believing that Kennedy had unfairly won by false balloting in Illinois and Texas. There is no question, however, that Kennedy had won over the media, giving the Democratic candidate somewhat of an edge; and, further, Eisenhower had failed to give Nixon the enthusiastic support that might have made a difference. Nixon's sense of having been cheated out of the election became an abiding and brooding motif for him.

After the defeat, Nixon moved to California, becoming a partner in a law firm to make money and to build a political base in that state. Unfortunately, he chose to return to office by running against Governor Edmund G. Brown, who had an excellent record and was well-liked. Nixon's campaign in that 1962 election leaned heavily on his experience in national and international matters, conveying little knowledge of such state problems as water and education. Brown's defeat of Nixon was a humiliating blow to the former Vice President and presidential candidate. His so-called farewell interview to the press is the most remembered quote from the debacle: "You won't have Nixon to kick around anymore . . . " It appeared to many that his political career was ended.

Never daunted, Nixon picked up the pieces of his life and moved to New York in 1963, joining a prominent law firm which became the base for his return to the national political scene. John Kennedy was assassinated Lyndon Johnson overwhelmingly defeated the Republican candidate, Barry Goldwater in 1964, to become President. The

Vietnam conflict heated to riveting intensity, dulling the impact of Johnson's Great Society programs. The nation entered a period of civil rights unrest and rioting, anti-war demonstrations and general social upheaval. Lyndon Johnson withdrew as a candidate for the presidency early in 1968. Robert Kennedy was assassinated.

The events were made to order for the return of Richard Nixon to national prominence and to the fulfillment of his quest for the presidency. Johnson's overwhelming defeat of Goldwater in the election of 1964 had left a void in Republican party leadership that Nixon readily filled. He campaigned for local candidates throughout the nation during this hiatus, building a strong political base. His criticisms of Johnson and his handling of the war became headline news. He traveled to world capitals on behalf of his legal clients, enhancing his own image as an informed international figure. Nixon became the Republican party spokesman, especially after Johnson's withdrawal. He fanned the fires of discontent among the white middle class, later dubbed the "silent majority," which had become fearful and troubled by the riotous proportions of civil disobedience that filled the streets and campuses with all forms of protesters—some peaceful, some violent. Crime and violence escalated dramatically.

The party coalesced behind Nixon as most competing candidates fell away and Eisenhower lent his support. He won the Republican party nomination for the Presidency on the first ballot with 692 votes, but not without a threat from competitors such as Ronald Reagan.

As the campaign began, the Republicans urged voters to examine a "new Nixon," who appeared to be freed from the slick, aggressive image of the past. In truth, he was now more comfortable with himself, older, financially more secure, an experienced politician who attempted to wear the mantle of the statesman returned to duty.

The campaign between Nixon and Hubert Humphrey, Johnson's Vice President, was primarily fought on such domestic issues as crime, violence and civil disobedience, despite the fact that the Vietnam War had escalated to a point where over 550,000 American troops were in the conflict. Although the candidates chose to avoid the war as an issue, the American public placed it high on its agenda. As the election neared, with Nixon well ahead in the polls, the Johnson administration proposed turning over most of the fighting to the South Vietnamese, and Johnson intensified his efforts toward a peace conference with the North Vietnamese by offering a halt to the bombing in the North.

The impact of impending peace was resounding, as Nixon's lead dwindled to a dead heat with his rival. But it was not enough to deny him the election. He won 43.4 percent of the popular vote; Humphrey received 42.7 percent, and a third party candidate, Southern Democrat, George Wallace, gained most of the balance of the vote. Nixon won the election, but he had failed to secure the vote of confidence he sought.

★ ★ ★ ★ ★

Richard Nixon came to the office of the presidency in 1969 as well prepared for that office as any of his predecessors. He was a naval officer in World War II, served two terms in Congress, had been a Senator and was Vice President for eight years. He had been a participant in foreign and domestic affairs and knew and was respected by many world leaders.

Despite the blot that Watergate spread upon the administrations of Richard Nixon, he must be counted among the most powerful of U. S. Presidents. He readily took risks in both his foreign and domestic programs, scoring notable achievements in each. But unlike other strong Presidents, such as Jackson, Lincoln, Wilson and both Roosevelts, Nixon is the only one who continuously faced a Congress of the opposing party. Yet, in the mold of all strong Presidents, he was determined to control the entire political, economic and social spectrum. His leadership would be at times defiant and secretive, leading him to utilize extra-legal measures in what he considered to be a war-time environment.

Nixon's knowledge of government and world affairs became the underpinning of a vision for his administration and for America's future that would be rare in the annals of presidential history. The Cold War had taken the nation through the crises of the dropping of an iron curtain around the edge of the Soviet bloc nations, Western protection of Greece and Turkey, the Marshall Plan to save Europe, the Korean war, the Berlin blockage and continued threats against that bastion, the Cuban Missile Crisis and the Vietnam War itself. Anti-Communist fervor, with its fear of Soviet and Chinese aggression, epitomized a war between good and evil.

Nixon was determined to diminish the confrontation and reduce tension through détente. His plan would include a dialogue with the Soviets and opening the door to China. This grand plan for world geo-politics was to secure peace or, at least, a reduction in the threat of world destruction. But it was also to lead the way to a cessation of the Vietnam War without the humiliation of a formal American defeat. He hoped that a more peaceful Soviet Union, spurred on by a China now in dialogue with the West, might influence its client state, Vietnam, to end the war on terms acceptable to the United States.

Nixon also had plans for the domestic front. To the dismay of his conservative supporters, Nixon would propose legislation that would rival the programs of Lyndon Johnson in his attempt to aid the poor and the struggling middle class.

Although his reputation in foreign matters is considered his hallmark, Nixon's administration engineered legislation in the mold of the New Deal and Johnson's War on Poverty as he expanded the role of government in the daily lives of ordinary citizens. During his first term, legislation was passed creating such programs as OSHA, to protect worker safety and CETA for job training. Social Security was indexed, giving annual cost-of-living increases to the elderly. To help pay for his programs Nixon, incorporated Social Security tax payments into the general fund in calculating the amount of Federal deficit. Various environmental laws were passed, including one creating the Environmental Protection Agency and one promoting clean water. On the civil rights front, Nixon advanced the desegregation of schools in the South by ordering, for the first time, the Justice Department to bring suit against schools to force desegregation.

He implemented a program to reorganize government following business principles. Block grants were approved, giving the state and local communities moneys for all categories of local improvement without their having to follow any of the rigors for such grants dating to the days of The New Deal. In one grand effort, his "New Federalism" removed authority from the federal bureaucracy and from Congress, dispensing authority to local governmental units, without touching the power of the President. The legislation reflected Nixon's contempt for Congress as well as his intent to decentralize government. Surprisingly, during his first term, Nixon spent more money on civil rights activities than did L.B.J. He implemented more affirmative action regulations to benefit women and minorities than did Kennedy or Johnson. Although he impounded funds for some programs he opposed, Nixon expanded government spending for his domestic agenda. A Democratic Congress approved much, though not all, of his domestic proposals, for Democrats were loathe to reject initiatives that so obviously benefited the poor and improved the environment. Congress rejected his plan for a massive welfare overhaul which incorporated income maintenance through a negative income tax. And Congress failed to enact a National Health Insurance Partnership that would have given health benefits to the poor. Interestingly, Nixon's beneficence was relatively ignored by the news media, although it did not go unnoticed in the election of 1972.

Nixon, however, is primarily remembered for his risk-taking and innovative forays in foreign affairs, including his handling of the Vietnam War. Nixon wanted an honorable peace in that war; he did not want to be the first President to lose a war. He believed that America's allies must be able to count on this country in the event of aggression. Although he steadily reduced America's troop strength in that conflict, he would not end the war in his first term. He summoned the "silent majority" of the nation to support him in his battle against the Communist threat from the North Vietnamese. But he also pursued the cooperation of the Soviets in his quest for an end to the war. Peace negotiations begun in Paris by Lyndon Johnson were carried on by Henry Kissinger, the National Security Advisor, a skilled and talented negotiator who followed Nixon's directives in his dealings in Paris. The North Vietnamese were intransigent. Nixon had somehow hoped that he could pull off in Vietnam what Eisenhower had achieved in ending the Korean War. But the war continued through the four years of Nixon's first term. He tried every means at his disposal, short of a major escalation of the war by invading the North, to persuade the North Vietnamese of his intent to win an honorable peace.

Ever distrustful by nature, brooding in spirit and suspicious, Nixon drew a cloak of secrecy around his maneuvering both to continue fighting and to end the war. He believed the campus anti-war uprisings were Communist-inspired and a deterrence to North Vietnam compromise. He responded to these demonstrations by developing his own small force of investigators to counter the negative impact of unrest. As the Paris peace talks became stalled, Nixon secretly planned the bombing and, then, invasion of Cambodia which was believed to be the staging area for North Vietnamese troops. This escalation of the war and the secrecy with which it was implemented infuriated the growing throngs of anti-war Americans. A firestorm of protests burst forth after four student anti-war demonstrators at Kent State University in Ohio were killed by National Guardsmen. Nixon appeared more intent than ever to fight the war and to deter the impact of the opposition. He, remarkably, did succeed in somewhat temporarily reducing opposition to the war by ending the draft in 1971 and by steadily withdrawing American forces from Vietnam. By the end of 1972, with South Vietnam carrying the burden of supplying most of the troops, only 25,000 Americans were in this combat. Despite the war and the intense opposition to it, Nixon maintained his popularity because he eliminated the draft, almost totally withdrew U.S. troop involvement and appeared to be totally in charge of both foreign and domestic affairs.

Yet an intense feeling of insecurity, suspicion and distrust overwhelmed the administration. Secret Defense Department documents, the Pentagon Papers which revealed past deceptions in fighting the war, were stolen by a former administrative employee and published in the *New York Times*. The administration's secret investigating force illegally broke into the office of a psychiatrist to obtain evidence against one of his patients, the man who had given the papers to the *Times*. Nixon began taping all the conversations in his office to know exactly when any of his aides disagreed with his policies or leaked inside information to the press. As the war dragged on and the demonstrations and the press became more hostile, secrecy became the administration's mode of operation. The White House seemed to be in a state of siege as buses surrounded the executive mansion providing barricades against protesters.

Early in 1972, during his fourth year in office, Nixon strode to the very height of international diplomacy. After almost a year of highly secret negotiations, Richard Nixon became the first American President to set foot on Chinese soil, an honored guest of Mao Tse Tsung, the all-powerful leader of that Communist country. It was a political coup of historical proportions.

That spring, the North Vietnamese launched a massive offensive which overwhelmed the Southern forces, forcing Nixon to escalate the war by bombing Hanoi and mining its harbor. Nevertheless, pursuing peace, in May of 1972 he became the first American President to enter the Kremlin, implementing a dialogue with the Soviets and negotiating a slowing of the arms race. Nixon's efforts would not result in an improvement in relations with the Soviet Union, but this initiative was possibly a precursor to the break-up of the Soviet state and the end of the Cold War.

Yet it was not these brilliant foreign policy ventures for peace nor was it his show of force in fighting the enemy in Vietnam for which 1972 is frequently most remembered today in the Nixon saga. On June 17, 1972, five men were caught breaking into the headquarters of the National Democratic Committee in the Watergate Building in Washington. Apparently, the group known as the Plumbers that had been formed in 1969 to provide investigative services directly for the White House, had disbanded; but several of its members continued their extra-legal surveillance services as employees of the Committee to Reelect the President. The break-in was designed to "bug" Democratic Headquarters. To cover up the connection between the break-in and the White House, apparently Richard Nixon personally approved that the F.B.I. be removed from this investigation, asserting that it was a C.I.A. operation.

Meanwhile, Nixon was renominated for President. His opponent was Senator George McGovern, a man who alienated many moderate Democrats with his anti-war and liberal views. He was no match for the skillful campaigner who, with vast sums of money, stumped the country as the powerful defender of middle class values and the world leader who sought peace while preserving America's role as the defender of liberty. Although Nixon won the electoral votes of every state except Massachusetts, providing him an overwhelming landslide victory, the Democrats retained control of both Houses of Congress. The Watergate break-in had no impact on voter sentiment, for it was not a front page story at that time.

When Franklin Roosevelt was defeated in his court-packing scheme, he retreated into himself; he became withdrawn. For Richard Nixon, it was victory which sent him into withdrawal. It was as though success was less manageable, less able to bring out his strengths and spirit than were stress and crisis. He asked his entire Cabinet to resign, alleging that he wished to start his second term with a clean slate. He did, however, intensify the bombing of North Vietnam, which may well have caused the North Vietnamese to agree to a cease fire on January 27, 1973, on terms which were all too similar to those of-fered in 1969. The war in Vietnam was finally over for the United States. Sixty days later, all prisoners of war were released and all Ameri-can forces were withdrawn from Vietnam. It would appear that Rich-ard Nixon was at the dawn of a triumphant second term, but it was not to be.

★　★　★　★　★

During his remaining approximately one and a half years in office, Nixon was consumed with very little other than his defense of the Watergate charges. The Senate opened an intensive investigation of the Watergate break-in, while the Justice Department employed a spe-cial investigator to pursue the evidence. The public was forced to endure endless testimony during 1973 that finally produced incon-trovertible evidence that White House personnel had obstructed jus-tice in the initial investigation by demanding that the F.B.I. not pur-sue the case. Further, John Dean, the President's counsel, became a star witness against his client, testifying that there had been a number of illegal break-ins by the same group involved in the Watergate break-in. More disastrous for the President, he testified that Nixon had offered to provide large sums of "hush" money to pay those caught in the break-in to remain silent concerning White House involvement. It became Dean's word against the President's concerning Nixon's personal involvement in the crime. Had Nixon approved the removal of the F.B.I. from the case, had he been involved in the cover-up? But then another White House aide dropped a bombshell by disclosing the existence of tapes of all the President's conversations within the Oval Office.

There ensued a tug-of-war between the President and the special prosecutor as well as the Senate Investigating Committee to obtain the tapes. Nixon's offer to provide excerpts was rejected. Nixon, conveying a spirit of Presidential invincibility, refused to destroy the tapes in the belief that executive privilege would protect their privacy. Further, he stated that he wanted them saved for their historical relevance. It was a fatal mistake, for the tapes would convict him. Through it all, Nixon seemed adrift, with events of the Watergate Investigation overwhelming him. In great matters of foreign intrigue, he was clear-thinking, masterful in his deliberations. In a personal struggle touching him so intimately, he seemed devoid of the insight needed for self-preservation. Despite his landslide election victory, the impending Watergate exposés seemed to cast a pall of morbidity over Nixon, which prevailed as the investigation proceeded. He appeared to fixate on the belief that the power of the office of the presidency would save him, while he avoided the one sure way to safety which was to destroy the tapes.

In the meantime, Spiro Agnew, Nixon's Vice-President, was forced to resign for taking bribes. He was replaced by Gerald Ford, a man more favored by Congress than by Nixon.

In the fall of 1973, world affairs diverted Nixon's attention momentarily, as the October war against Israel, instituted by Syria and Egypt, threatened havoc in the Middle East. Nixon acted swiftly, supplying arms to the embattled Israelis, allowing them to regain the initiative. The President briefly returned to his former self as he intervened with the parties to end their hostilities.

Unfortunately, his decision to help Israel led to the economically debilitating oil embargo by major Arab oil producing states. Nixon diligently attempted to diminish the impact of the embargo by such measures as reducing highway speeds and cutting the use of electric power. The challenge of world events momentarily restored Nixon to a position of authority.

But it was the Watergate affair that absorbed Nixon's mind and spirit. The special prosecutor demanded the tapes, and Nixon, in what became known as the "Saturday Night Massacre" responded by demanding that he be fired. Thereupon, the attorney general resigned, and his deputy was fired. Nixon's show of power did him no good; seven of Nixon's closest aides in the White House were indicted by the Watergate grand jury. Nixon appealed to the Supreme Court to retain the tapes, but the Court ruled against him in 1974, ordering him to turn them over to the investigators. On July 27, 1974, the House Judiciary committee voted three articles of impeachment against the President, charging him with obstruction of justice, abuse of power and contempt of Congress.

Weeks before, Nixon had made a trip to the Middle East and to Moscow, hoping to recoup some measure of power, reliving his former triumph. It was to no avail. On August 8, 1974, Richard Nixon resigned the office of the Presidency.

* * * * *

If Nixon had ended the Vietnam War early in his first term, his need for secrecy and illegal intelligence gathering might have seemed less necessary and there might not have been a Watergate break-in. Nixon, however, believed that he was obliged to pursue his goal of an "honorable peace." Further, if Nixon had not chosen to represent himself as counsel in the early days of Watergate in evaluating the entire break-in affair, he might have been given advice to separate himself immediately from any form of cover up. But even this opportunity was probably not open to him, for the break-in preceded the election. Nixon feared that revelations would have brought into the open the very real connection to the White House of this and other secret extra-legal surveillance that had been performed by and for the administration.

In retrospect, Richard Nixon demonstrates how relevant are character and temperament in the effectiveness of a president. For Richard Nixon, it seems that his breadth of insight into and vision for foreign and domestic affairs brought about the precursors of the end of the Cold War and the fulfillment of programs which were at least designed to improve the environment and the lot of the poor. Yet it is apparent, indeed, that Nixon's downfall came because of his brooding, secretive, untrusting and suspicious nature. He displayed a defiant nature, a controlling spirit and a belief in his own invincibility. It almost seems Watergate became a reality because all of these qualities were present at a time when there was an unpopular war and civil unrest all of which led Nixon to extend his authority, utilizing extra-legal measures to deter opposition to the war.

Other strong Presidents have confronted Congress or even the courts and survived. Andrew Jackson successfully ignored the rule of the Supreme Court when he removed Native Americans. Most of the strong Presidents have experienced defeat at the hands of Congress at some point in their terms in office, but none as disastrously as did Richard Nixon. Congress almost succeeded in blocking Jackson's elimination of the U.S. Bank. Theodore Roosevelt faced a Congress that terminated his plans for conservation. Wilson suffered the defeat of his plans for peace and the League of Nations. FDR faced the defeat of his court packing scheme and Jefferson endured the rejection of his embargo. Richard Nixon was not alone in facing a hostile Congress united to end his power.

Nixon differs from his presidential peers in his misjudgment of the extra legal use of power, however. He believed that the Vietnam War and the Cold War allowed him to take license with the law as Presidents such as Lincoln, Wilson and Franklin Roosevelt had done during times of war. But first, the country was not truly at war; second, he lacked the support of his own party in power in the Congress to protect him; third, he had accumulated enemies who were all too ready to believe he had broken the law; and finally, Nixon had provided the "smoking gun" evidence of his guilt with his tapes.

The administrations of Richard Nixon illustrate in graphic ways the measures for an effective President set out in the Introduction to this book. In his first term, Nixon remarkably fulfilled many of these tests. He generally maintained his leadership of Congress and his popularity with the electorate. He had a vision which he communicated to the nation. He protected America from foreign threat, ending the hated Vietnam War. He brought on economic prosperity and spread its beneficence broadly through the economy. His second term failed more than any other in the history of the presidency, however, because of his spirit of invincibility and the violation of the moral code of the nation. Richard Nixon's defiant nature, his proclivity for secrecy, his spirit of distrust and his drive to control overwhelmed him.

Reader's Score of Richard Nixon

Defense: _____

Economic: _____

Vision: _____

Communication: _____

Lead Congress: _____

Lead without Popularity: _____

Invincibility: _____

Consistency: _____

Self-Confidence: _____

Strengthen Nation: _____

TOTAL POINTS: _____

Ronald Reagan

Ronald Reagan

Ronald Reagan was rare among the Presidents elected to a second term for his temperament and character. Like so many, he sought the applause and love and adulation that come with the office. But unlike Grant, Wilson and Johnson, for whom the need for public praise became overwhelming, Reagan quietly and with unusual self-confidence played upon the public support that was awarded him, without distress, with grace and with acumen. In his second term, the Iran Contra Affair threatened this source of sustenance, briefly diminishing the capacity of the man; but he persevered and survived an ordeal that might have destroyed the effectiveness of others. During his terms in office, and more particularly in his second term, he was willing to spend that popularity for the fulfillment of his visions for disarmament. He conveyed a self-confidence about the support he had with the public to stand firm for his program. He presumed he knew best. As with Eisenhower, Teddy Roosevelt, Franklin Roosevelt and Andrew Jackson, he believed he was the best man for the job. He, at least overtly, did not pander to the masses to maintain his popularity. He was a leader who fought for what he believed with an inner self-confidence and vision that placed him among the most self-assured of those who achieved a second term. To what effect was his self-assurance and vision and what was the measure of his presidency?

Ronald Reagan, following the tradition only of his most stalwart predecessors, came through the ordeals of his second term relatively unscathed. Many of the two-term Presidents did battle with events during their second terms which were of their own making, some were beyond their control. For some, the events were overwhelming, for others victory and popularity prevailed. What qualities of character and temperament allow a President to be the master of his destiny despite adversity? To what extent has the office of the presidency changed? How has television, the growth of staff and the movement of America into predominance in the world scene altered the presidency? The terms of Ronald Reagan serve well to answer these questions.

★ ★ ★ ★ ★

II.

The modest Middle West upbringing, marked by financial and emotional struggle, left their mark on the 40th President. Throughout his life he retained a humility and near modesty that was instilled by his spartan upbringing. It was a quality that brought him to the endearment of many. His communicative skills allowed him to project these qualities to the masses. Yet he was aloof and almost defensive in his resistance to personal and close relationships, except with his wife. His father was an alcoholic, and it is frequently stated that Reagan's aloof behavior stemmed from his relationship with a father with whom he could not stay in touch. He judged the world around him by how it might sustain him and give him pleasure and security and applause. But he also saw it in terms of a need of people for self-reliance, for independence and for the kind of self-confidence he himself knew. Once fulfilling his own needs, he looked beyond, to what he believed people needed, whether they were the average man in the street in

America, the nation as a whole or the entire world. He did not philosophize, but he knew which direction he wanted the nation to go.

He completed a degree in economics at Eureka College in Illinois in the early 1930s and went on to be that successful radio sports announcer he spoke of so often as President. His interest in sports and drama far outweighed his preoccupation with studies at college. He was an average student. He was imbued with an instinct for self-fulfillment that led him to Hollywood in the middle of the 1930s where he achieved almost instant success, although never super-star status. His interest in matters worldly led him into leadership in the Screen Actors Guild, the actors trade union, becoming its president in 1947, a position he held for five years. Reagan had consistently maintained a vital interest in politics and world affairs throughout his tenure in Hollywood, keeping himself fully informed of events, frequently overwhelming the less informed of his fellow actors with his opinions on all matters of politics and economics. He took his union leadership seriously, defending actors in moments of change and turmoil in Hollywood following World War II, rebuking Communist infiltration into both the union and the movie industry. It was at this time that he switched from his staunch loyalty to the Democratic party, and especially Franklin Roosevelt, to become a Communist fighting, conservative Republican.

Reagan had always been well liked, affable, physically attractive, and charming. People warmed to him readily. He was always ambitious, yet able to couch this drive in an unassuming, non-threatening and gracious nature that served him well. People, both individually and in groups, were comfortable with him. He had the makings of a successful politician from his earliest days.

He retained and expanded his notoriety through his stint as host of the G.E. television show for eight years. He spent those years visiting and lecturing to G.E. employees throughout the country. All of this led to his rather preemptive campaign for governor of California in 1966. He won the office readily, although it took several years for him to accommodate to the demands of office, failing at first to master the most elementary demands of administration and leadership. He came into office without any legislative program nor any knowledge of how to work with the legislature. Reagan would be known throughout his political career for his pragmatic resolution of conflict in search of goals. He learned this tactic as governor of California. He learned it gradually, over time to effect the conservative agenda he pursued. But Reagan would be known in politics as one who delegated responsibilities for governing, lightening the burden he carried on his shoulders. Some looked upon the Reagan style as lackadaisical, almost lazy. He would be among the very few Presidents to follow the edict that the "man must rest as he may." Reagan set this pattern for himself as governor for eight years and would follow it as President.

Although he sought the Republican presidential nomination in 1976, it was not until 1980 that he and the nation were ready for each other. Big government had been losing favor. It forced busing, it did not solve crime, many of the social programs of Lyndon Johnson and Richard Nixon appeared to have faltered in bureaucratic excess. Reagan campaigned throughout the country proclaiming that government had grown too large, too unresponsive, too uncaring, too wasteful and bureaucratic. The experiments of Roosevelt, Johnson, Carter and even Nixon were the targets of a man determined to weaken the hold of the federal government. Inflation was in double digits, interest rates approached 20 percent. The nation seemed to be drifting, if not sinking, toward trouble on all fronts. The Iranians held the American Embassy staff hostage. The self-image of Americans had been diminished by the defeat in Vietnam, by Watergate and Nixon's resignation. The populace felt leaderless. The government seemed unable to grapple effectively with events at home or abroad. Ronald Reagan and his running mate, George Bush, won the election against the incumbent Jimmy Carter with 51 percent of the vote, and the Republicans won control of the Senate for the first time since 1952.

Reagan came into office with more of a plan, more of a vision statement, than had almost any President in the history of the nation. Possibly only Woodrow Wilson, Lyndon Johnson and Theodore Roosevelt would compare. He proposed to reduce the size and influence of government, increase the military preparedness of the nation and alter the relationship—although he could not guess how—with the Soviet Union. His preeminent drive in regard to the impact of government was to cut income taxes. A corollary of that was a reduction in the federal budget, which was intended at first to match the reduction in taxes.

It was a time when legend had it that the federal government was unmanageable, that Congress was unresponsive to any President, that parties could no longer implement legislation, that the bureaucracy could undo the wishes of any chief executive. Yet Reagan, the man who struggled for at least two years to understand how to be governor of California, sailed almost effortlessly through enactment of the first phase of his agenda. By July of 1981, less than seven short months after being sworn into office, legislation was signed into law reducing taxes from as high as 70% to 37.5%. The federal budget was cut, but not to the levels that Reagan wanted nor to the extent that his budget director, David Stockman, believed to be necessary to balance the budget. Senate conservatives, fearing the rapid growth of the federal deficit, proposed a smaller tax cut which would be tied to the cut in spending, but Reagan would not hear of it. Cutting taxes was an unalterable goal, not necessarily paired to the budget cuts. It was a historically momentous victory in a time frame that rivaled F.D.R.'s 100 days. It had a vision that Franklin Roosevelt's program did not possess. It was passed far more quickly than was Johnson's Great Society. It must be acknowledged, however, that the scope and breath of Reagan's legislative package did not compare to either F.D.R.'s or

Johnson's. The impact of his tax program on the economy was impressive none-the-less, some would be for good, some would not be so beneficial.

The President, worked effectively and efficiently, utilizing every ounce of his nature, his talent and his effort to win the needed legislative support. He traveled to Congress to visit and win over its members. He was casual, warm, friendly, relaxed, full of persuasive good humor and charm. He compromised, he was flexible, he telephoned even from his hospital bed where he was recuperating from an assassins bullet which nearly fatally injured the President. He gave up only five percentage points of the tax reduction he sought, but he traded favor after favor to special interest groups seeking tax relief to achieve his goal. He did not fight equally hard, however, for budget cuts. Although the breadth of legislative success would not compare with that of either FDR, Wilson or Lyndon Johnson, the image of the restoration of authority and leadership of the President was certainly spectacular. The effect of the tax cut on the financial well-being of the majority of Americans would be enormous, at least over his terms in office.

Before his first term ended, almost half of the reduction in taxes was restored, partially to protect the Social Security Trust Fund; other increases were to help cut the deficit, others to promote highway construction. Reluctantly, Reagan cooperated with the congressional effort to increase taxes. It was a time of unusual cooperation between the executive and legislative branches of government and between the Democrats and the Republicans.

Despite the protestations of his budget director and the increase in taxes a year later, the federal deficit ballooned to a $100 billion in 1982, then $200 billion, with larger deficits forecast for the future. But Reagan would not consider either raising taxes to resolve the deficit, or doing battle with the Congress to further cut the budget. He had expended all the energy on that he intended. The deficits would remain for another generation to resolve. Although Congress readily passed the Tax Reduction Act, they were not as prepared to cut programs and government spending. Ronald Reagan would not again display the intensity of drive and application of energy to enact legislation that he did in his first six months in office.

★ ★ ★ ★ ★

Early in his first term, Reagan told his Secretary of Defense, Casper Weinberger, that he had a blank check to expand America's military arsenal, and Congress willingly funded the plan. It would be part of Ronald Reagan's strategy in foreign affairs, which was to end, if possible, the Soviet and Communist threat. His reference to the Soviet Union as the "Evil Empire" sent chills along the backs of the N.A.T.O. Allies, who feared that Reagan was a shoot-from-the-hip cowboy who would thrust the world into war. A nuclear freeze and arms control agreements were being proposed, but Ronald Reagan was building the forces of the military in all categories.

By the end of his first term, the economy, which had suffered a severe downturn in 1981 and 1982 rebounded robustly, creating millions of jobs and expanding the gross national product, although it was not expanding enough to impact the $200 billion deficits facing the nation.

As his first term came to an end, Ronald Reagan remained in tune with the American people who did not want government solving each and every problem. They liked the tax cut and the image, if not the reality, of less government. Reagan had sent troops to Lebanon to counter an Israeli incursion into that country and hopefully diminish the general unrest in that embattled country. But it was a failed mission, with 241 American Marines killed in an Arab attack on their barracks. Unflinching, Reagan sent troops to Granada just two days later to wrest that Caribbean island from Communist control. Reagan had a way of rising above every situation, allowing him and America to come out the winner. It was like the class "B" movies in which he had once starred.

★ ★ ★ ★ ★

Reagan won his second term defeating Walter Mondale convincingly, but not by a landslide, taking 59% of the vote. The Republicans retained control of the Senate. He had run a campaign steeped in American historical tradition and pride for the nation. He received worldwide publicity for his speech at Normandy commemorating D-Day and at the Olympics where America ran away with the medals because the Soviet Union had refused to attend. It was a patriotic nation that Reagan reflected and one that rallied around him in the election. The vote was less for the agenda that he certainly had for the nation—which included less government, lower taxes, more defense and reduction of the Communist threat—than it was for the man who inspired confidence and a feeling of achievement and self-worth within the citizenry. The public felt delivered from the failures of America in Vietnam, in Iran, in competition with the Soviets and Communists generally. The economy began to surge in late 1982, increasing employment and income, while inflation diminished to below 5%. It was a boon to the reelection of Reagan. The nation was prospering and it was at peace. The ingredients were there for a popular President to have a picture-perfect second term. It would be a time when Ronald Reagan might pursue the pleasure of the office of the presidency. He did his homework, but sparingly, delegating to others the principle task of administering the office. Reagan reserved for himself the major policy decision, expending only that energy necessary to carry out the part he selected to play.

Domestic legislation would not receive very much of Reagan's attention in his second term. One exception stands out. A tax reform of startling proportions was proposed by Reagan in 1984. As with the tax reduction bill, Republicans and Democrats in the Congress worked in tandem to hammer out a tax simplification bill which eliminated tax brackets and tax preferences to produce a remarkable alternation in the way taxes would be assessed, introducing greater fairness into the system. It was Congress, not Reagan, which seemed more concerned about limiting the deficit.

There was an unexpected consequence to the tax reform act, however. It included a provision which eliminated passive income losses, to be written off against ordinary income. This provision drastically reduced the value of recently developed office buildings, apartments, and shopping centers. Many of these had been built to achieve the benefits under the earlier tax code. Depreciation schedules had favored development. Savings and Loans were encouraged to lend heavily in these projects under relaxed rules enacted in Reagan's first term guiding their practices. The combination of a less supervised S & L industry and defaults in commercial real estate caused by the 1986 tax reform led to the Savings and Loan debacle. A half a trillion dollar bail-out of their industry occurred after Reagan left office.

During his second term, Congress passed an emigration bill providing for a more realistic handling of illegal immigrants from Mexico and an improved free trade agreement with Canada. Neither the President nor any group of lobbyists in the nation petitioned for that initiative, a rarity in government and certainly indicative of the paucity of domestic leadership provided by the President. The result was not necessarily detrimental to democracy, however, for the legislative branch of government became more responsible than it might have under a more controlling Chief Executive. Neither branch, however, would firmly and directly confront the issue of the ballooning federal deficit.

Reagan, as President, was frequently a stubborn man, not given to great curiosity, without sentiment for individuals loyal to him. He pursued a few ideas that seemed right to him, compromising where necessary to achieve his main goal. He had set a course in his first term which might almost have allowed him to float effortlessly through his second term. But a combination of his own initiatives and the flow of events in the Soviet Union, in Central America and in the Middle East would not allow such a scenario.

Mid-term elections in 1986 brought the Democrats control of the Senate, despite the thriving economy and the popularity of Reagan. November of 1986 was also the occasion when a potential fiasco for Reagan exploded in the news media. The administration had been selling arms to Iran in an effort to induce the Iranians to release American hostages held in Lebanon by pro-Iranian terrorists. Americans were dismayed that the President, who had lashed out so fiercely at Carter for not achieving the return of fifty American hostages held by Iran, would himself deal covertly and suspiciously with this terrorist nation. To make matters much worse, it was revealed that the proceeds of arms sale were diverted to support the anti-Communist fighters in Nicaragua, known as the Contras. Reagan had pursued Congress to support the Contras, fighting as hard as he did for any legislation in his second term. Congress, fearful of another Vietnam with American troops being somehow committed and then bogged down in an anti-Communist war in Central America, kept a short leash on the support given the Contras. The funds for military supplies were drastically limited and Reagan felt deeply frustrated in his drive to eliminate what he believed to be the only Communist threat in all of Latin America other than in Cuba.

The Iran arms deal quickly became known as the Iran-Contra Affair. Reagan admitted the sale but remained silent on the issue of diversion of the proceeds to the Contras, a move which was clearly against a law which Congress had passed concerning aid to the Contras. It had all the makings of another Watergate, and the nation responded with trepidation. The Democrats, who had cooperated with a President at once friendly and yet in true control of the tenor of legislation they passed, possibly found the lever to flip control freely from the

President to themselves. The arms sale, which was no more than an embarrassment, lost center stage to the scandal of illegal diversion of funds to the Contras.

At a news conference in November of 1986, the President seemed vague and out of touch, unable to instill the confidence in his leadership that the country had become so accustomed to expect. The President might be about to lose his base of power, his popularity. It was more than the tool of power; it was part of the underpinning of his self-esteem that he had known throughout his public life.

The diversion of funds had been under the direct supervision of Lieutenant Colonel Oliver North who reported to Vice Admiral John Poindexter, Reagan's National Security Advisor. The President appointed a committee to investigate the affair, but, more importantly, the Senate initiated its own investigation which threatened to rival the Watergate hearings. Throughout 1987 and into 1988 Ronald Reagan appeared an embattled President, denied the popular public platform he and the nation had so long enjoyed.

It was not to be Watergate again, however, as Oliver North turned his testimony into a pulpit for him to preach for all to support the Nicaraguan freedom fighters. 1987 brought discontent for the nation as American flags were placed on Kuwaiti tankers in the gulf to protect them from Iranian attack. A Reagan nominee for the Supreme Court was rejected, and the stock market crashed in October.

Reagan regained his composure and his popularity, however. The Iran-Contra hearings produced evidence against North and Poindexter, but it could not place any responsibility for the illegal use of funds in the hands of either President Reagan or Vice President Bush. Unlike Richard Nixon or U.S. Grant, Ronald Reagan felt no inner drive to save subordinates who had been loyal to his program. The President was to come through this year of potential ordeal unscathed. The economy did not sink into economic chaos after the October dip, but actually began to show strength; and the Reagan military buildup and foreign policy initiatives began to bear fruit in unpredictable proportion.

Ronald Reagan was an eloquent public speaker, and he used this skill to engender an era of good feeling and self-confidence among the populace. Only when he promoted his tax cut in his first six months of his first administration did he go over the head of Congress to sell the American people on a specific program he wanted passed. He was generally a consensus builder who avoided confrontation. Possibly his greatest success as President, however, was in his direct confrontation with Communism, particularly Soviet Communist. He achieved this without the use of his most noteworthy attribute: his ability to sway the mass of Americans.

Reagan had encouraged the rapid build up of all aspects of militarily weaponry. One of these, Reagan's own Strategic Defense Initiative or Star Wars concept, became particularly prominent. This project, which apparently frightened the Soviets as much as any plan of the American military buildup, was to devise a system of high technology weaponry that could destroy incoming missiles. The purpose was to defend America, but in the eyes of the Soviets, it would eliminate deterrence as a defense. There was no evidence at the time that "Star Wars" had any potential for success, but that did not deter Ronald Reagan from developing the weapon nor lessen the concern of the Soviets. The U.S.S.R. could conceivably be attacked by the United States but could not retaliate. But Star Wars, or S.D.I. as it was known, was only one element in a constellation of negotiation resulting in a foreign policy metamorphosis that would occur in the cold war and the relationship of the United States and the N.A.T.O. nations with the Soviet Union and the Warsaw Pact.

Michail Gorbachev came to power in the USSR in the spring of 1985. He followed the frail tenure of Brezhnev in his final years and the brief tenures of Andropov and Chernenko. The United States had prospered and grew strong militarily, while the Soviets struggled with a military industry straddled with a third-world domestic economy that was showing strains of potential collapse. The world powers were no longer on an equal footing except for nuclear destructive might. Gorbachev seemed determined to confront his nations economic problem directly and openly. Meanwhile, Ronald Reagan, the conservative infighting anti-Communist, had from the first moments of his first administration pursued simple solutions to the Communist problem. He disliked the nuclear confrontation that America faced, and he suggested that the bombs be eliminated. This thought contrasted with the prevailing view which held that the expansion of nuclear arsenals must be limited in size and number. No one of political prominence, however, seriously suggested reducing the number of nuclear weapons; no one, that is, except Ronald Reagan. His discerning attention to the nuclear threat had led him to encourage the Star Wars solution in 1983. That solution was funded slowly and haltingly; but it was early in his second term that Reagan began a series of maneuvers—with the encouragement of his wife, Nancy, and of the Secretary of State, George Schulz, to open a dialogue with the leaders of the U.S.S.R. He had written personal letters to Brezhnev, but his naive style did not stir recognition in the Soviet leadership. Reagan's bellicose tone intimidated the Soviets.

Reagan opened a dialogue at first with the Soviet foreign minister shortly after his second term began, and, by the time Gorbachev settled into office, diplomacy between the two super powers began a political sea change that would alter history. In the short run, Gorbachev grasped the spotlight from the American President, but drama was staged from both capitals. In a series of summit meetings, the two leaders exchanged one-upmanship in declaring their willingness to eliminate nuclear weapons. Reagan had proposed a plan years before to have each of the powers cut out intermediate range missiles, but it was Gorbachev who stole center stage with the concept. At one point, in a failed conference, Reagan and Gorbachev had apparently agreed at a brief Summit in Iceland to the absolute elimination of all nuclear weapons, which frightened the U.S. military leaders and the leaders of the N.A.T.O. allies. Many in the United States were at first pleased with the prospect, but then more cautious minds began to wonder if the Iran Contra scandal had impaired Reagan's thinking. They misjudged the President. He was not a complicated thinker. He knew what he knew. He simply wanted to free the nation of the threat of nuclear extinction.

As his last year in office drew near, intermediate missiles were removed from Europe, and on-site inspection—an unheard of concept—was instituted. But no more would be accomplished during Reagan's tenure to reduce the strategic or long range nuclear force.

The world traveled a path less hostile, however, as reduction in conventional arms became the new objective. The Warsaw pact would crumble, the Soviet block would be no more. Germany would reunite.

★ ★ ★ ★ ★

What did Ronald Reagan have to do with all of this? Was he simply the man in the White House at the moment that the Soviets were ready to improve their storehouse of civilian plant and equipment and know-how so as to survive in the real world? What can be said is that Reagan reached the Soviet leadership with his jibes and cajoling. He called them the "Evil Empire." He demanded that they tear down the Berlin Wall. He personally caused the military build up and the S.D.I. program in such breadth and scope and tone as to force the Soviets to examine very closely their ability to stay as equals with the United States in all but nuclear weaponry. Further, Ronald Reagan, the leader of the more successful of the two super-powers, was no less ready nor less inspired to lead toward nuclear disarmament than were the Soviets. Finally, no one could accuse Reagan of being soft on Communism in his disarmament proposals. He was a very popular leader, despite the Iran-Contra fiasco. Many experts in military strategy believed him to be naive and untutored—or even untutorable—but he knew the direction he wanted to take the nation and the world. He led the way toward a less confrontational world. He stood by, undisturbed, as Gorbachev appeared to absorb more of the applause the world would give for the change occurring in the world. It was all rather clear testimony of a Reagan of unusual self-confidence, of a President who thought broadly in a rather narrow list of terribly important issues, alligning determination with large credibility, to grasp success quietly. Interestingly, he achieved this success on the world stage, avoiding what had been thought to be his greatest talent in the eyes of many, his ability to sway a large audience.

Despite the Iran-Contra affair, Reagan generally avoided controversy as President. In fact, he thrived on popular accolade throughout his presidency. He fantasized much about the world in which he lived, seeing reality in the dream of Star Wars defense, for example. He refrained from committing long hours or careful strategic planning to his stewardship. In his first term, he worked diligently to cut taxes and to advance substantially America's military buildup. To the disappointment of many of his supporters, he did not utilize the mantle of authority given him in his second term to cut the budget or to reduce the size of government. Employment, income and production all flourished; but there was a cost. In his second term, particularly, he set a pattern for diminished governmental activity in the regulation and supervision of the Savings and Loan industry leading, in part to the catastrophe that swept the industry. Further, despite Reagan's clear intent to limit its future growth, the outreach of the welfare state was not measurably reduced. Avoiding confrontation, he fought only sparingly in his second term to achieve those goals involving a rollback in government or reduced spending.

His greatest successes during his second term were in foreign policy, where the customarily public Reagan utilized quiet, behind-the-scenes diplomacy to achieve disarmament and help end the Cold War. This success will forever be matched against a presidency which produced rapid economic growth, yet burdened the nation with a Savings and Loan debacle, widespread stresses from private financial greed and excess, and a federal deficit of unmanageable proportions. The character and temperament of Ronald Reagan were such that only a select few endeavors absorbed his time and attention, particularly during his second term. The balance of his goals were allowed to languish. The objectives which absorbed Reagan, together with those he neglected, will distill into a legacy which only time can measure.

Reader's Score of Ronald Reagan

Defense: _____   Lead without Popularity: _____

Economic: _____   Invincibility: _____

Vision: _____   Consistency: _____

Communication: _____   Self-Confidence: _____

Lead Congress: _____   Strengthen Nation: _____

TOTAL POINTS: _____

Conclusion

Three conclusions can be drawn from a study of the second term. First, the responsibility and challenge of the presidency has not changed over time, despite the growth of government. The measures for success apply today as much as they did in George Washington's day. Second, effectiveness in office is directly related to the ability of a President to work with Congress. Finally, although all Presidents elected to a second term look upon their reelection as a mandate for their special agenda, their objectives and their successes differ widely.

Expanding on the first conclusion, the focus on the saga of the two-term Presidents confirms, among other things, that the presidency and the ten measures for success in the presidency have not radically changed, despite the metamorphoses that have occurred in the nation since 1789. The effectiveness of Presidents in their second terms makes this clear. Ronald Reagan had all the success of Andrew Jackson and, surprisingly, with some similar policies. The office and the prerequisites that make a President successful have remained constant over time.

As America's role in the world scene has altered over the course of history, protecting the security of the nation, a basic need for Americans, has taken on new meaning and placed new demands upon the President. Yet concern with national security dates back to the days of Washington and Jefferson. Fear of presidential prerogative overwhelming the authority of Congress has always been a concern. The Jeffersonians feared the big government of Hamilton. Lincoln and Wilson ruled more rigidly during wartime than did Franklin Roosevelt during the Second World War. Jefferson and Madison sent warships to destroy the Barbary pirates without Congressional approval. Jefferson bought Louisiana without a vote of Congress, a shocking expansion of presidential prerogative for his day or any day. All of these are examples of how the presidency has not changed.

An "Imperial Presidency!" Essentially the office has always had the potential to be an "Imperial Presidency." For this reason, the American people want a Congress on its guard against excess use of power and the violation of authority and morality. They demand that their President succeed, but the leeway of the President is limited. He must prove constantly that he is meeting the tests of a successful President.

The measures for a successful President listed in the Introduction, which are derived from a focus on second terms, may be utilized to allow a voter to compare candidates and to evaluate how their character and temperament might function in office and how an incumbent President might fare in a second term. But also intriguing is the lesson to be found in applying the ten measures for success to evaluate the Presidents who have been elected to a second term. The measures require that the President provide for defense and economic opportunity. He must communicate his vision effectively with both the nation and Congress and occasionally lead in directions which are not popular. He must have retained both public confidence and self confidence and leave office with the nation as strong and as secure as when he became President.

Applying the ten measures for success, interestingly, not one second-term President was found wanting for a failure to defend the nation. Two Presidents, Johnson and Truman, experienced diminished popularity and would not have been reelected because they pursued wars that lost favor. Jefferson was criticized by his enemies for failing to build an adequate defense against the British. However, despite the importance that must be assigned to defense, this measure has not led to failure for two-term Presidents, for they clearly understood its importance, substantially satisfying the issue.

Moreover, economic crises have not been a major cause of difficulty for two-term Presidents. Of those elected to a second term, financial panic damaged the careers of only Cleveland and Grant. Jackson was not blamed for the depression in his second term because of his popularity, but the crisis may have been one cause of the failure of Martin Van Buren, his chosen successor, to be reelected. And certainly, the Great Depression destroyed the presidency of Herbert Hoover. On the other hand, when economic opportunity and civil liberties were expanded during the terms of action oriented Presidents, their innovations frequently became the norm and were then defended as the status quo.

How then do the remaining measures for success apply? As stated in the second conclusion, Presidents who experienced diminished effectiveness or failure were those who lost control over Congress in the essential management of the affairs of state. Most often this was accompanied by a loss of popular support, although Jefferson, Grant, F.D.R. and Wilson maintained their popularity during adversity. Furthermore, a spirit of invincibility and hubris, leading to misjudgment of presidential authority, has been a significant cause of deteriorated relations with Congress for a number of Presidents elected to a second term. Although excessive self-confidence diminished but did not destroy the effectiveness of Franklin Roosevelt, it compounded the plights of Richard Nixon and Lyndon Johnson. The revelations of Watergate lost Richard Nixon the trust of the nation. He had a vision, the economy thrived, the war was over, the nation was relatively secure; prior to Watergate he communicated with the public at large and, to a great measure, with Congress. These were not enough. He was forced to resign because of his hubris and his consequent misjudgment of what represented honesty and integrity and the authority of the presidency.

Lyndon Johnson also lost control over Congress and the trust of and influence over the populace because he led the nation into a war that Americans would no longer support. Ironically, he believed he was defending America and the free world in Vietnam, but he was wrong. His temperament, which led to a rigid adherence to his Vietnam policies for most of his second term, would not allow him the flexibility to understand and then respond to the unique aspects of that war. Eisenhower, on the other hand, maintained his authority with Congress and the nation by using military power parsimoniously. He avoided sending troops into combat, carefully evaluating what truly was in the vital interest of the nation.

Grant could not control Congress because of his failure to overcome the misdeeds of his associates and his unwillingness to grasp firmly the reins of authority implicit in the office. Congress overwhelmed Monroe as he became a pawn in a political game being played by those running for the Presidency. Unfortunately, Jefferson failed to confront Congress directly to acquire Florida, and he misjudged his ability to implement his Embargo, as Congress turned against the policy. Wilson mastered public support for his vision of world peace, but that was inadequate in his fight with Congress. He believed, incorrectly, that he need not compromise with Congress over the League of Nations.

Ronald Reagan departed office with popularity, but his standing in history is impacted by the economic consequences of potentially devastating budget deficits engendered during his administration. He was unwilling to persuade Congress that spending cuts were as essential to his plan as were tax cuts. Interestingly, Jackson overcame what might have been insurmountable opposition from Congress in his fight against the Bank of the United States.

Those Presidents who were most accomplished, such as Lincoln, Washington, Theodore Roosevelt, Jackson, Eisenhower, Truman, Wilson, (except for the League) and Franklin Roosevelt in all but his second term, maintained sufficient influence over Congress to achieve their major goals. They did this by substantially fulfilling the remaining measures for a successful presidency. They communicated their vision for the nation, retaining their self-confidence and authority as President, based on the underlying support and confidences of the electorate.

★ ★ ★ ★ ★

Amplifying the final conclusion, a striking aspect of the second term is how Presidents seized their vote of confidence to implement their special vision for America to place their emblem clearly in the annals of history. While those customarily ranked as the most popular Presidents were those who wished to expand the power of the presidency, approximately forty percent of those used their mandate to limit its scope. Among these were Washington, Jefferson, Madison, Grant, Coolidge and Reagan. Although Eisenhower was a relatively assertive President in foreign affairs, he favored only modest domestic change, generally opposing the expansion of the role of the federal government. He did effectively implement his vision for America which was to assure the security of the nation and preserve its economic vitality.

Throughout the history of the nation, there has always been an ebb and flow in the amount of federal power deemed appropriate for the nation to function and preserve itself.

Those Presidents who set out to expand the power of the presidency were Jackson, Lincoln, Cleveland, Theodore Roosevelt, Wilson, Franklin Roosevelt, Truman, Johnson and Nixon. Interestingly, impacting the number of expansion-minded Presidents is the fact that Theodore Roosevelt became President only because of the death of McKinley, and, further, he delivered the election to Wilson by splitting the Republican vote in 1912. Lyndon Johnson came into office with the assassination of John Kennedy. Finally, Lincoln won the presidency because of a split in the Democratic party ticket. *Moreover, it is apparent that except for Lyndon Johnson, two term Presidents who sought and received Congressional approval to expand the authority of the presidency and the federal government served at times of crises or moments of significant transition. Further, they were all men who used their strength of personality and will to pursue change aggressively.*

★ ★ ★ ★ ★

In conclusion, to fulfill a vision for America, whether it be for more or less government, a President must be able to cope with Congress, to communicate with the electorate, to sidestep the pitfalls of being a lame duck or the pernicious effects of unethical or extra legal acts. He must withstand the potentially destructive impact of unforeseen events, and he must avoid a spirit of invincibility and hubris to establish a legacy for himself. The ten guidelines for success in the presidency have not changed from Washington to today, forming a pattern for judging a President. There is no escaping the interplay of these measures with the character and temperament of a President.

★ ★ ★ ★ ★

The relative effectiveness of seventeen Presidents elected to second terms is compared in the following chart, utilizing the measures for success in the presidency. The chart evaluates each of seventeen Presidents elected to a second term. This is based on the ten criteria for success which are assigned a value based on the effectiveness of each, with ten being the most effective and one being least accomplished. The values are then totaled for each chief executive, allowing a rank ordering of these Presidents.

The reader is encouraged to complete a blank chart, copy it and return it for tabulation and a report of the results. The reader may also predict the effectiveness of candidates running for office.

RATING THE PRESIDENTS

	Defense	Economic	Vision	Communication	Lead Congress	Lead Without Popularity	Invincibility	Consistency	Self-Confidence	Strengthen Nation	TOTAL
Washington	10	10	10	7	10	10	10	8	8	10	93
Jefferson	5	5	10	6	6	6	7	7	7	6	65
Madison	6	8	7	5	5	7	8	7	7	8	65
Monroe	8	6	6	5	6	5	8	5	8	6	60
Jackson	7	10	10	8	10	9	9	7	7	7	85
Lincoln	10	10	10	8	10	8	10	10	8	10	94
Grant	8	3	3	3	3	3	5	3	5	3	39
Cleveland	5	4	6	4	7	3	4	5	6	4	48
T. Roosevelt	9	10	10	9	7	8	8	7	9	8	85
Wilson	10	8	10	7	6	5	4	7	7	7	71
Coolidge	4	6	4	7	7	5	7	1	6	1	48
F. Roosevelt	8	8	9	10	9	8	6	9	10	9	86
Truman	8	6	9	6	9	8	8	6	9	9	73
Eisenhower	6	8	8	7	9	7	8	6	8	8	79
Johnson	9	5	9	6	6	5	5	5	4	5	62
Nixon	7	6	8	5	4	3	1	3	3	5	50
Reagan	8	8	8	6	8	6	8	5	8	5	70

RANKING BY TOTAL SCORE

1.	Lincoln	94	10.	Jefferson	65
2.	Washington	93	11.	Madison	65
3.	FDR	86	12.	LBJ	62
4.	T. Roosevelt	85	13.	Monroe	60
5.	Jackson	85	14.	Nixon	50
6.	Eisenhower	79	15.	Cleveland	48
7.	Truman	73	16.	Coolidge	48
8.	Wilson	71	17.	Grant	39
9.	Reagan	70			

READER'S RATING OF THE PRESIDENTS

	Defense	Economic	Vision	Communication	Lead Congress	Lead W/O Popularity	Invincibility	Consistency	Self-Confidence	Strengthen Nation	TOTAL
Washington											
Jefferson											
Madison											
Monroe											
Jackson											
Lincoln											
Grant											
Cleveland											
T. Roosevelt											
Wilson											
Coolidge											
F. Roosevelt											
Truman											
Eisenhower											
Johnson											
Nixon											
Reagan											

Candidates:

RANKING BY TOTAL SCORE

1. _____   8. _____   15. _____
2. _____   9. _____   16. _____
3. _____   10. _____   17. _____
4. _____   11. _____   18. _____
5. _____   12. _____   19. _____
6. _____   13. _____   20. _____
7. _____   14. _____

To forward your rankings copy this page and mail to: Presidential Press, 444 E. Main St., #203, Fort Wayne, IN 46802 or fax to:(219) 422-9301 or send to E Mail: stzacher@aol.com or 102164.153@compuserve.com
To receive a report of the results: provide your fax number, your E-Mail number or send a self-addressed stamped envelope.

THE SUCCESS OF SECOND-TERM PRESIDENTS
UTILIZING THE TEN MEASURES
SET OUT IN THE INTRODUCTION

	Successful Second Terms	Troubled Second Terms	Failed Second Terms	Special Situations
1.	Washington			
2.		Jefferson		
3.	Madison			
4.		Monroe		
5.	Jackson			
6.				Lincoln*
7.			Grant	
8.			Cleveland	
9.	T. Roosevelt			
10.		Wilson		
11.				Coolidge**
12.		F. Roosevelt		
13.		Truman		
14.	Eisenhower			
15.			Johnson	
16.			Nixon	
17.	Reagan			

* Though Lincoln was successful in his brief second term, it is inappropriate to include him with those serving four years.

** Coolidge was highly popular during his second term, yet history judges him to have been a failed President.

★ APPENDIX ★

PRESIDENTS OF THE UNITED STATES

President	Party Affiliation	Years in Office	Birthplace	Born	Died	Age Took Office
1. George Washington	Federalist	1789-1797	Virginia	1732	1799	57
2. John Adams	Federalist	1797-1801	Massachusetts	1735	1826	61
3. Thomas Jefferson	Democrat-Republican	1801-1809	Virginia	1743	1826	57
4. James Madison	Democrat-Republican	1809-1817	Virginia	1751	1836	57
5. James Monroe	Democrat-Republican	1817-1825	Virginia	1758	1831	58
6. John Quincy Adams	Democrat-Republican	1825-1829	Massachusetts	1767	1848	57
7. Andrew Jackson	Democrat	1829-1837	South Carolina	1767	1845	61
8. Martin Van Buren	Democrat	1837-1841	New York	1782	1862	54
9. William Henry Harrison	Whig	1841	Virginia	1773	1841	68
10. John Tyler	Whig	1841-1845	Virginia	1790	1862	51
11. James K. Polk	Democrat	1845-1849	North Carolina	1795	1849	49
12. Zachary Taylor	Whig	1849-1850	Virginia	1784	1850	64
13. Millard Fillmore	Whig	1850-1853	New York	1800	1874	50
14. Franklin Pierce	Democrat	1853-1857	New Hampshire	1804	1869	48
15. James Buchanan	Democrat	1857-1861	Pennsylvania	1791	1868	65
16. Abraham Lincoln	Republican	1861-1865	Kentucky	1809	1865	52
17. Andrew Johnson	Republican	1865-1869	North Carolina	1808	1875	56
18. Ulysses S. Grant	Republican	1869-1877	Ohio	1822	1885	46

President	Party Affiliation	Years in Office	Birthplace	Born	Died	Age Took Office
19. Rutherford Hayes	Republican	1877-1881	Ohio	1822	1893	54
20. James A. Garfield	Republican	1881	Ohio	1831	1881	49
21. Chester A. Arthur	Republican	1881-1885	Vermont	1830	1886	50
22. Grover Cleveland	Democrat	1885-1889	New Jersey	1837	1908	55
23. Benjamin Harrison	Republican	1889-1893	Ohio	1833	1901	55
24. Grover Cleveland	Democrat	1893-1897	New Jersey	1837	1908	55
25. William McKinley	Republican	1897-1901	Ohio	1843	1901	54
26. Theodore Roosevelt	Republican	1901-1909	New York	1858	1919	43
27. William H. Taft	Republican	1909-1913	Ohio	1857	1930	51
28. Woodrow Wilson	Democrat	1913-1921	Virginia	1856	1924	56
29. Warren Harding	Republican	1921-1923	Ohio	1865	1923	51
30. Calvin Coolidge	Republican	1923-1929	Vermont	1872	1933	51
31. Herbert Hoover	Republican	1929-1933	Iowa	1874	1964	54
32. Franklin D. Roosevelt	Democrat	1933-1945	New York	1882	1945	51
33. Harry S. Truman	Democrat	1945-1953	Missouri	1884	1972	60
34. Dwight D. Eisenhower	Republican	1953-1961	Texas	1890	1969	62
35. John F. Kennedy	Democrat	1961-1963	Massachusetts	1917	1963	43
36. Lyndon Johnson	Democrat	1963-1969	Texas	1908	1973	55
37. Richard M. Nixon	Republican	1969-1974	California	1913	1994	56
38. Gerald R. Ford	Republican	1974-1977	Nebraska	1913		61
39. James Earl Carter	Democrat	1977-1981	Georgia	1924		53
40. Ronald Reagan	Republican	1981-1989	Illinois	1911		70
41. George Bush	Republican	1989-1993	Massachusetts	1924		65
42. William J. Clinton	Democrat	1993-	Arkansas	1946		46

★ BIBLIOGRAPHY ★

Chapter 1–Succeeding in the Second Term

Barber, James David. *The Presidential Character, Predicting Performance in the White House.* Englewood Cliffs, NJ: Prentice Hall, 1972.

Barone, Michael. *Our Country, The Shaping of America from Roosevelt to Reagan.* New York: The Free Press, 1990.

Bechloss, Michael. *Seven Ways to Win Friends,* The New Yorker, January 30, 1995, Vol. 70, N. 47, pg. 51.

Corwin, Edward S. and Louis W. Koening. *The Presidency Today,* New York: New York University Press, 1956.

Cronin, Thomas E., editor. *Inventing the American Presidency.* Lawrence, KS: The University Press of Kansas, 1989.

deToequeville, Alexis. Edited by J. P. Mayer, Translated by George Lawrence, *Democracy in America,* New York: Harper & Row, 1966.

Donovan, Hedley. *Roosevelt to Reagan, A Report Encounters with Nine Presidents.* New York: Harper & Row, 1985.

Hofstatter, Richard. *The American Political Tradition and the Men Who Made It.* New York: Alfred A. Knopf, 1948.

Hughes, Emmet John. *The Living Presidency, The Resources and Dilemnas of the American Presidential Office.* Baltimore: Penguin Books, 1974.

Kammen, Michael. *Mystic Chords of Memory.* New York: Alfred A. Knopf, 1991.

Lott, Newton Davis. *The President Speaks: The Inaugural Addresses of the American Presidents, From Washington to Clinton.* New York: Henry Holt, 1994.

Milkis, Sidney M. and Michael Nelson. *The American Presidency, Origins and Development 1776-1990.* Washington, DC: C. Q. Press, 1990.

Neustadt, Richard. *Presidential Power.* New York: John Wiley, 1960.

Schlesinger, Arthur M., Jr. *The Imperial Presidency,* Boston: Houghton Mifflin Co., 1973.

Skowronek, Stephen. *The Politics Presidents Make, Leadership from John Adams to George Bush,* Cambridge, MA: The Belknap Press of Harvard University Press, 1993.

Tulius, Jeffrey K. *The Rhetorical Presidency,* Princeton: Princeton University Press, 1987.

White, Theodore H. *America in Search of Itself.* New York: Warner Books, 1982.

Wood, Gordon S. *The Radicalism of the American Revolution.* New York: Alfred A. Knopf, 199.

Notes

Pg. 1, Bechless, pg. 51.

The ten measures for success of a President are influenced by Guy E. Swanson, who as professor of social psychology at the University of Michigan, taught a course which included a "filter theory" of social action and behavior.

Chapter 2–George Washington

Callahan, North. *Thanks, Mr. President, The Trail-Blazing Second Term of George Washington*, New York, Cornwall Books, 1991.

Flexner, James Thomas. *George Washington in the American Revolution 1775-1783*, Boston, Little Brown & Co., 1967.

—. *George Washington and the New Nation 1783-1793*, Boston: Little Brown, 1970.

—. *George Washington Anguish and Farewell (1793-1799)*, Boston: Little Brown, 1972.

—. *Washington The Indispensible Man.* Signet, 1969.

Morgan, Edmund Sea. *The Genius of George Washington*, Washington, DC: Society of the Cincinnati, 1980.

Washington, George. *The Diary of George Washington from 1789 to 1791*; Freeport, NY: Books for Libraries Press, 1972.

Wills, Garry. *Cincinnatus: George Washington and the Enlightenment.* Garden City, NY: Doubleday, 1984.

Notes

Pg. 7 - Lott. *The Presidents Speak*, pg 6 & 7.

Chapter 3–Thomas Jefferson

Adam, Henry. *History of the United States of America During the Administration of Thomas Jefferson.* New York: Library of America, 1986.

Commager, Henry Steele. *Jefferson, Nationalism and the Enlightenment.* New York: Braziller, 1975.

Cunningham, Noble E., Jr. *In Pursuit of Reason, The Life of Thomas Jefferson*, Baton Rouge: Louisiana State University Press.

Jefferson, Thomas. *Writings.* New York: Literary Classics of the U. S., c. 1984.

Malone, Dumas. *Jefferson and His Time*, Vol. 1, Jefferson the Virginian. Boston: Little Brown and Co., 1948.

—. *Jefferson and His Time*, Vol. 2, Jefferson and the Rights of Man, Boston: Little Brown & Co., 1951.

—. *Jefferson and His Time*, Vol. 3, Jefferson and the Ordeal of Liberty, Boston: Little Brown & Co., 1962.

—. *Jefferson and His Time*, Vol. 6, The Age of Monticello, Boston: Little Brown & Co., 1977.

—. *Jefferson and His Time*, Vol. 4, Jefferson the President, First Term 1801-1805, Boston: Little Brown & Co., 1970.

—. *Jefferson and His Time*, Vol. 5, Jefferson the President Second Term, 1805-1809, Boston: Little Brown & Co., 1974.

Chapter 4–James Madison

Adams, Henry. *History of the United States of America During the Administration of James Madison*, New York: Library of America, 1986.

Cappon, Lester. *The Adams-Jefferson Letters.* Vol. 2. Chapel Hill, N.C. University of North Carolina Press, 1959.

Hamilton, Alexander; Madison, James; Jay, John. *The Federalist.* with an Introduction by Edward Gayland Bourne, Ph. D., Vol. 1 of 2. Washington and London: M. Waltes Dunne, 1901.

Ketcham, Ralph Louis. *James Madison; a biography,* New York: Macmillan, 1971.

Madison, James. *James Madison, 1751-1836; chronology, documents, bibliographic aids.* Dobbs Ferry, NY: Oceana Publications, 1969.

McCoy, Drew R. *The Last of the Fathers, James Madison and the Republican Legacy,* Cambridge: Cambridge University Press, 1989.

Rakove, Jack N. *James Madison and the Creation of the American Republic.* New York: Harper Collins, 1990.

Rutland, Robert A.. *James Madison, The Founding Father,* New York, Macmillan, 1987.

—. *The Presidency of James Madison.* Laurence, KS: University Press of Kansas, 1990.

Rutland, Robert A. *James Madison The Founding Father.* New York: Macmillan, 1987.

Notes

Pg. 52 Rutland, Robert A. *James Madison The Founding Father.* New York: Macmillan, 1987, pg. 225.

Pg. 57 Ketchen, Ralph. *James Madison, A Biography.* New York: Macmillan, 1971, pg. 597.

Pg. 59 Cappon, Lester. *The Adams Jefferson Letters.* Vol. 2. Chapel Hill, N. C. 1959. pg 507-508.

Chapter 5–James Monroe

Ammon, Harry. *James Monroe: The Quest for National Identity.* New York: McGraw-Hill, 1971.

Cresson, William Penn. *James Monroe,* Chapel Hill: University of North Carolina Press, 1946.

Marble, Harriet Clement. *James Monroe; Patriot and President.* New York: Putnam, 1970.

May, Earnest R.. *The Making of the Monroe Doctrine,* Cambridge, MA, Belknap Press of Harvard University Press, 1975.

Chapter 6–Andrew Jackson

Cole, Donald B. *The Presidency of Andrew Jackson,* Lawrence, KS: University Press of Kansas, 1993.

Remini, Robert V.. *The Revolutionary Age of Jackson,* New York: Harper & Row, 1976.

—. *The Life of Andrew Jackson.* New York: Harper and Row, 1988.

Schlessinger, Arthur M. Jr. *The Age of Jackson*, Boston: Little, Brown and Co., 1945.

Sellers, Charles. *The Market Revolution, Jacksonian America, 1815-1846*, New York, Oxford University Press, 1991.

Watson, Harry L. *Liberty & Power; the politics of Jacksonian America*, New York: Hill & Way, 1990.

—. *The Jackson Era*, Arlington Heights, IL: H. Davidson, 1989.

Chapter 7–Abraham Lincoln

Lincoln, Abraham. *Speeches and Writings,* 2 Vols. Don E. Fehrenbacher, notes, etc., New York: The Library of America, 1989.

McPherson, James. *Abraham Lincoln and the Second American Revolution.* New York: Oxford University Press, 1991.

Neely, Mark E. Jr. *The Fate of Liberty Abraham Lincoln and Civil Liberties*, New York: Oxford University Press, 1991.

—. *The Last Best Hope of Earth. Abraham Lincoln and the Promise of America.* Cambridge, MA: Harvard University Press, 1993.

Oates, Stephen B. *With Malice Toward None, The Life of Abraham Lincoln*, New York: Harper & Row, 1977.

Peterson, Merrill D. *"This Grand Pertinacity" Abraham Lincoln and the Declaration of Independence.* Fourteenth Annual R. Gerald McMurty Lecture, Fort Wayne, IN, 1991.

Phillips, Donald T. *Lincoln on Leadership, Executive Strategies for Tough Times*, New York: Warner Books, 1992.

Wills, Gary. *Lincoln at Gettysburg, The Words That Remade America*, New York: Simon & Schuster, 1992.

Notes

Pg. 99. Lincoln, Abraham. *Speeches and Writings 1832-1858,* New York: Library of America, 1989. pg. 32.

Pg. 100 Ibid 426.

Pg. 111 Ibid 687.

Chapter 8–Ulysses S. Grant

Grant, Ulysses S. *Memoirs and Selected Letters: Personal Memoirs of U. S.,* New York: Library of America, 1990.

—. *Personal Memoirs of U. S. Grant* in 2 Vols, New York: Charles L. Webster & Co., 1885.

Hesseltine, William B. *Ulysses S. Grant, Politician*, New York: Dodd, Mead & Co., 1935.

McFeely, William S. *Grant A Biography*, New York, W. W. Norton & Co., 1981.

Chapter 9–Grover Cleveland
Merrill, Horace Samuel. *Bourbon Leader: Grover Cleveland and the Democratic Party*, Boston: Litle Brown, 1957.
Nevins, Allan. *Grover Cleveland; A Study in Courage*, New York: Dodd, Mead & Co., 1932.
Tugwell, Rexford G. *Grover Cleveland*, New York: Macmillan, 1968.
Welch, Richard E. Jr. *The Presidencies of Grover Cleveland*, Lawrence, KS, University Press of Kansas, 1988.

Chapter 10–Theodore Roosevelt
Gould, Lewis L. *The Presidency of Theodore Roosevelt*, Lawrence, KS, University Press of Kansas, 1991.
Grantham, Davey H. *Theodore Roosevelt*, Englewood Cliffs, NJ: Prentice Hall, 1971.
Harbaugh, William H. *The Life and Times of Theodore Roosevelt*, New Revised Edition, London, Oxford University Press, 1975.
Lorant, Stefen. *The Life and Times of Theodore Roosevelt*, Garden City, NJ: Doubleday, 1959.
Miller, Nathan. *Theodore Roosevelt: A Life*, New York: Morroe, 1992.
Roosevelt, Theodore. *Theodore Roosevelt; an autobiography*, New York: Charles Scribner & Sons, 1929.
—. *The Words of Theodore Roosevelt*, Mount Vernon, NY: Peter Payser Press, 1970.
—. *Writings*. William H. Harbaugh, ed., The American Heritage Series, Indianapolis: Bobbs-Merrill.
—. *Addresses and Presidential Messages of Theodore Roosevelt*, New York: G. P. Putnam & Sons, 1922.
—. *American Ideals*, New York: Putnam, 1980.

Chapter 11–Woodrow Wilson
Bailey, Thomas A. *Woodrow Wilson and the Great Betrayal*, New York: Macmillan, 1945.
Clements, Kendrick A., *The Presidency of Woodrow Wilson*, Lawrence, KS: The University Press of Kansas, 1992.
George, Alexander L. and Juliette L. George. *Woodrow Wilson and Colonel House, A Personality Study*, New York: Dover, 1956.
Heckscher, August. *Woodrow Wilson*, New York: Scribner, 1991.
Smith, Gene. *When The Cheering Stopped, The Last Years of Woodrow Wilson*, New York: William Morrow & Co., 1964.
Wilson, Woodrow. *Woodrow Wilson, 1856-1924*; chronology, documents, bibliographic aids. Dobbs Ferry, NY: Oceana Publications, 1969.
—. *The Public Papers of Woodrow Wilson*, Edited by Ray Stannard Baker and William E. Dodd, New York: Harper & Row. 1925- 27-6 Vol.

Chapter 12–Calvin Coolidge

Coolidge, Calvin. *The Autobiography of Calvin Coolidge.* New York: Cosmopolitan Book Corp., 1929.

McCoy, Donald R. *Calvin Coolidge; The Quiet President.* New York: Macmillan, 1967.

Murray, Robert K. *The Politics of Normalcy: Governmental Theory and Practice in the Harding-Coolidge Era.* New York: Norton, 1973.

White, William Allen. *A Puritan In Babylon The Story of Calvin Coolidge,* Gloucester, MA: Peter Smith, 1938.

Chapter 13–Franklin D. Roosevelt

Freidel, Frank. *Franklin D. Roosevelt: A Rendezvous With Destiny.* Boston: Little Brown, 1990.

Morgan, Ted. *F. D. R. A Biography,* New York, Simon and Schuster, 1985.

Schlesinger, Arthur M. *The Age of Roosevelt.* Boston: Houghton Mifflin, 1988.

Sherwood, Robert E. *Roosevelt & Hopkins* 2 Vol. New York: Bantam Books, 1948.

Tugwell, Rexford G. *Roosevelt's Revolution:The First Year, a personal perspective.* New York:Macmillan, 1977.

—. *In Search of Roosevelt.* Cambrdge: Harvard University Press, 1992.

Ward, Geoffrey C. *A First-Class Temperament: The Emergence of Franklin Roosevelt.* New York: Harper and Row, 1989.

—. *Before the Trumpet, Young Franklin Roosevelt 1882-1905,* New York: Harper & Row, 1985.

Notes

I held a personal discussion in about 1950 concerning Franklin Roosevelt with Arthur E. Morgan, first Chairman of the Tennessee Valley Authority. He was fired by F. D. R.

Chapter 14–Harry Truman

Hersey, John. *Aspects of the Presidency,* New Haven: Ticknor & Fields, 1980.

Jenkins, Roy. *Truman,* New York: Harper & Row, 1986.

McCoy, Donald R., *The Presidency of Harry S. Truman*

Chapter 15–Dwight D. Eisenhower

Ambrose, Stephen E. *Eisenhower, The Inside Story*, New York: Harper, 1956.
—. *Eisenhower, Soldier and President*, New York: Touchstone, Simon and Schuster., 1990.
Eisenhower, Dwight D. *Peace with Justice, Selected Addresses of Dwight D. Eisenhower*, foreword by Grayson Kirk, New York: Columbia University Press, 1961.
—. *The Eisenhower Diaries*. ed. by Robert H. Ferrell. New York: W.W. Norton, 1981.
Greenstein, Fred I. *The Hidden-Hand Presidency, Eisenhower as Leader*, New York: Basic Books, 1982.
Hughes, Emmet John. *The Ordeal of Power, A Political Memoir of the Eisenhower Years*, New York: Dell, 1962.
Saulinier, Raymond J. *Constructive Years, The U. S. Economy Under Eisenhower*, Lanham, MD, University Press of America, 1991.

Chapter 16–Lyndon B. Johnson

Barrett, David M. *Uncertain Warriors: Lyndon Johnson and the Vietnam Advisors*, Lawrence, KS: University Press of Kansas, 1993.
Califano, Joseph A. *The Triumph and Tragedy of Lyndon Johnson: The White House Years*, New York: Simon & Schuster, 1991.
Caro, Robert A. *The Years of Lyndon Johnson, The Path to Power (V. 1) Means of Ascent (Vol. 2)*, New York: Knopf, 1982.
Goldman, Eric Frederick. *The Tragedy of Lyndon Johnson*, New York: Knopf, 1969.
Johnson, Lyndon Baines. *The Vantage Point Prespective of the Presidency 1963-1969*, New York, Holt, Rinehart and Winston, 1971.
Kearns, Doris. *Lyndon Johnson and the American Dream*, New York: Harper & Row, 1976.
Ready, George E. *Lyndon Johnson, A Memoir*, New York: Andrews & McNeel,1982.
White, Theodore Harold. *The Making of the Presidency*, New York: Atheneum,1965.

Chapter 17–Richard M. Nixon

Ambrose, Stephen E. *Nixon, The Education of a Politician 1913-1962*, New York: Simon & Schuster 1987.
—. *The Triumph of a Politician 1962-1972*, New York: Simon and Schuster, 1989.
—. *Rein and Recovery 1973-1990*, New York: Simon and Schuster, 1991.
Dash, Samuel. *Chief Counsel. Inside the Ervin Committee - The Untold Story of Watergate*, New York: Random House, 1976.
Hoff, Joan. *Nixon Reconsidered*, New York: Basic Books, 1994.
Kissinger, Henry. *White House Years*, Boston: Little Brown & Co., 1979.
Klein, Herbert G. *Making It Perfectly Clear*, Garden City, NY: Doubleday & Co., Inc., 1980.

Kutler, Stanley I. *The Wars of Watergate, The Last Crisis of Richard Nixon*, Alfred A. Knopf, 1990.

Mazo, Earl. *Richard Nixon, A Political and Personal Portrait*, New York: Harper & Brothers, 1959.

Nixon, Richard M.*The Memoirs of Richard Nixon*, New York: Grosset & Dunlap, 1978.

——. *In The Arena, A Memoir of Victory, Defeat and Renewal*, New York: Simon & Schuster, 1990.

——, *Six Crises*, New York: Simon and Schuster, 1990.

White, Theodore H. *Breach of Faith, The Fall of Richard Nixon*, New York: Atheneum, 1995.

Chapter 18–Ronald Reagan

Boskin, Michael J. *Reagan and the Economy*, San Francisco; Institute for Contemporary Studies, 1987.

Cannon, Lou. *President Reagan: The Role of a Lifetime.* New York: Simon & Schuster, 1991.

Draper, Theodore. *A Very Thin Line, The Iran-Contra Affair*, New York: Hill & Wang, 1991.

Muir, William K. *The Bully Pulpit: The Presidential Leadership of Ronald Reagan*, San Francisco: ICS Press, 1992.

Noonan, Peggy. *What I Saw At The Revolution, A Political LIfe in the Reagan Era*, New York: Random House, 1990.

Reagan, Ronald. *An American Life*, New York: Simon & Schuster, 1990.

Reeves, Richard. *The Reagan Detour: Conservative Revolutionary*, New York: Simon & Schuster, 1985.

Stockman, David Alan. *The Triumph of Politics; How the Reagan Revolution Failed*, New York: Harper & Row, 1986.

Wills, Gary. *Reagan's America Innocents At Home*, Garden City, NY: Doubleday, 1987.

★ INDEX ★

★ Order And Website Information ★

If your local bookstore is unable to obtain a copy of *Trial and Triumph* or if you have any questions or comments, please contact:

Presidential Press
444 East Main Street, Suite 203
Fort Wayne, Indiana 46802-1910
Phone: (800) 247-6553
Fax: (219) 422-9301

Presidential Press Web Address:
http://www.bookzone.com/
in the history, government and politics aisles, or just type "presidential" in the bookshop search engine.

Be sure to give your opinion on the presidential candidates and the potential problems for a Clinton second term in our site's forum.
Log on today!